Well-kr
what you

MW01074682

For many years, people have written about the importance of making an astral temple while almost ignoring the physical temple where magic is worked. Author William G. Gray, known for such works as *The Ladder of Lights, Magical Ritual Methods,* and *Seasonal Occult Rituals,* resolves this imbalance by looking, in-depth, at the way a Western magical temple should look and work.

Nothing is left out. Everything from what to wear to how to act is covered. Gray describes not only the outward appearance and function of the various temple trappings but also the importance of their symbolism, from both a metaphysical-occult and a psychological point of view. **Temple Magic** is the most comprehensive book of its type since Crowley's *Book 4,* and goes into far greater detail.

There are many magical groups in the world today, but the ones who will use this book are not the authoritarian orders. The people who will want **Temple Magic** are the individuals who are setting up their own temples for private use, and the groups of people who get together—without dues, autocratic structures or leaders—to practice magic.

This book deals with the problems and details you are likely to encounter in Western esoteric ceremonialism. Gray feels that it is a sequel to *Magical Ritual Methods.* It is truly an older man's legacy for the guidance of his successors, written in the hope that they will avoid the errors he made.

About the Author

William G. Gray received much of his early training in the Western Inner Tradition from an associate of Papus. This individual was a Qabbalistic Rosicrucian, and Gray believes that his writings were profoundly influenced by this person's teachings. Later, Gray became a member of the Society of the Inner Light.

His writing career commenced when he completed two projects that Dion Fortune left unfinished at her death. One manuscript became *The Talking Tree*, and the other, *The Magical Mass* (which later became *The Sangreal Sacrament*). However, Israel Regardie's enthusiastic response to the manuscript published as *The Ladder of Lights* provided the impetus for Gray's works to reach the public.

Since that time, Gray has written several books on Western esoteric ceremonialism, devoting particular attention to what he calls the Sangreal concept.

To Write to the Author

We cannot guarantee that every letter written to the author can be answered, but all will be forwarded. Both the author and the publisher appreciate hearing from readers, learning of your enjoyment and benefit from this book. Llewellyn also publishes a bi-monthly news magazine with news and reviews of practical esoteric studies and articles helpful to the student, and some readers' questions and comments to the author may be answered through this magazine's columns if permission to do is included in the original letter. The author sometimes participates in seminars and workshops, and dates and places are announced in *The Llewellyn New Times*. To write to the author, or to ask a question, write to:

William G. Gray
c/o THE LLEWELLYN NEW TIMES
P.O. Box 64383-274, St. Paul, MN 55164-0383, U.S.A.
Please enclose a self-addressed, stamped envelope for reply, or $1.00 to cover costs.

ABOUT LLEWELLYN'S HIGH MAGICK SERIES

Practical Magick is performed with the aid of ordinary, everyday implements, is concerned with the things of the Earth and the harmony of Nature, and is considered to be the magick of the common people. *High Magick*, on the other hand, has long been considered the prerogative of the affluent and the learned. Some aspects of it certainly call for items expensive to procure and for knowledge of ancient languages and tongues, though that is not true of all High Magick. There was a time when, to practice High Magick, it was necessary to apprentice oneself to a Master Magician, or *Mage*, and to spend many years studying and, later, practicing. Throughout the Middle Ages there were many high dignitaries of the Church who engaged in the practice of High Magick. They were the ones with both the wealth and the learning.

High Magick is the transformation of the Self to the Higher Self. Some aspects of it also consist of rites designed to conjure spirits, or entities, capable of doing one's bidding. Motive is the driving force of these magicks and is critical for success.

In recent years there has been a change from the traditional thoughts regarding High Magick. The average inteligence today is vastly superior to that of four or five centuries ago. Minds attuned to computers are finding a fascination with the mechanics of High Magical conjurations (this is especially true of the mechanics of Enochian Magick).

The Llewellyn High Magick Series has taken the place of the Mage, the Master Magician who would teach the apprentice. "Magick" is simply making happen what one desires to happen—as Aleister Crowley put it: "The art, or science, of causing change to occur in conformity with will." The Llewellyn High Magick Series shows how to effect that change and details the steps necessary to cause it.

Magick is a tool. High Magick is a potent tool. Learn to use it. Learn to put it to work to improve your life. This series will help you do just that.

Other Books by William G. Gray

The Ladder of Lights
Magical Ritual Methods
Inner Traditions of Magic
Seasonal Occult Rituals
The Tree of Evil
The Rollright Ritual
An Outlook on Our Inner Western Way
A Self Made by Magic
The Talking Tree
Western Inner Workings
The Sangreal Sacrament
Concepts of Qabalah
Sangreal Ceremonies and Rituals

Forthcoming

Sangreal Tarot (tentative)
Deliver Us from Evil
Bloodmother (tentative)

Llewellyn's High Magick Series

TEMPLE MAGIC

Building the Personal Temple: Gateway to Inner Worlds

William G. Gray

1988
Llewellyn Publications
St. Paul, Minnesota, 55164-0383, U.S.A.

International Standard Book Number: 0-87542-274-8
Library of Congress Catalog Number: 88-45184

First Edition, 1988
First Printing, 1988
Second Printing, 1988

Library of Congress Cataloging-in-Publication Data

Gray, William G.
   Temple magic.

   (Llewellyn's high magick series)
   1. Magic. 2. Occultism. 3. Ritual. I. Title.
II. Series.
BF1621.G7 1988   133.4'3   88-45184
ISBN 0-87542-274-8

Cover Painting: Martin Cannon

Produced by Llewellyn Publications
Typography and Art property of Chester-Kent, Inc.

Published by
LLEWELLYN PUBLICATIONS
A Division of Chester-Kent, Inc.
P.O. Box 64383
St. Paul, MN 55164-0383, U.S.A.

Printed in the United States of America

To Carr P. Collins

---

*whose insistence inspired me to
write this book. He is its
original instigator. May God
rest and refresh his soul.*

Contents

Preface

Some years ago I wrote a book entitled *Magical Ritual Methods* that is still very much in use yet now needs updating. I wrote it because at the time no such thing existed; members of esoteric associations had to learn how to work rituals the hard way, since no senior member seemed either able or willing to explain things in detail or satisfactorily. I wished with all my heart that there had been some kind of "*ABC* of Ritual Procedures" to guide my wandering way, but since there wasn't, I determined to remedy this deficiency once I had gained sufficient experience to do so. After all, every other art had its explanatory manuals and beginners books so why shouldn't ritualism have its equivalent? As an ex-soldier, I could appreciate the value of drill books and classified basic exercises out of which the most complicated maneuvers could subsequently be constructed. Why shouldn't this apply to other fields of action than merely to military behavior? It not only could but did, and so *Magical Ritual Methods* was the eventual result.

Sooner or later it seemed obvious to me that although books for beginners were useful in themselves, they had a strictly limited value and there was a definite need for extensions of them to help those who might be fairly called "going-on-ers." That is to say, whoever had passed the preliminary stages of ritual practice and sought further development along the psychodramatic path of ceremonial magic. This present book is the outcome of the observations and the years of experience that enabled it to be written.

Nevertheless *Temple Magic* is not intended to be a hard-and-fast, or in any sense immutable and unalterable, working way of Wesotericism. The book should rather be regarded as a reliable system of operating our general occult ceremonialism in a way that will lead to improved and extended expressions of this via the individual experience of each practitioner. Otherwise a sensible and reasonably reliable do-it-yourself system of developing your own spiritual potentials through this ancient path of access to our common cosmic state of attainment. It is my earnest hope that future writers will produce much more advanced and explicit works, making mine seem childish by contrast. By that time I hope to be guided by those myself in another incarnation. May I offer those authors-to-be many sincere thanks in advance.

William G. Gray
Spring 1988

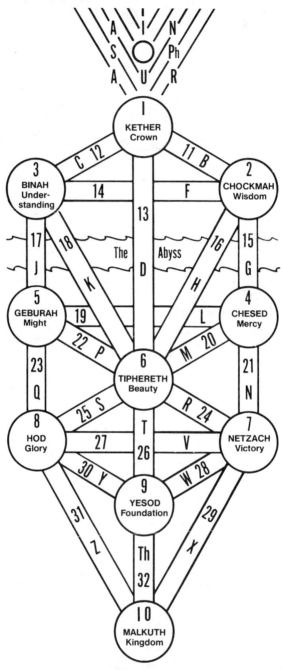

The Tree of Life

Chapter 1

TALKING OF TEMPLES

There are quite a large number of books written about esoteric Temples and many scripts of ceremonies or procedures concerning what to say or do in them, but little or nothing about the whys and hows or reasons for those behaviors and attitudes. In other words, little helpful guidance about how to arrange one's Inner Self so as to get the best results for the effort expended. This is rather regrettable, since it constitutes a very common weakness among most Western esoteric groupings (or "Wesoterics" for short).

The usual experience faced by most candidates for inclusion in such circles is to be told what to wear and how to wear it, given a copy of the ceremonies to study with perhaps some verbal explanation of the text, some of the working philosophy involved, after which they are expected to make like the others together with fellow participants. In other words, very inadequate training and preparation for the work in hand.

It is really quite extraordinary how many people with no previous experience of ceremonial Temple workings and thinkings are expected to jump in at the deep end and acquire proficiency by a sort of occult osmosis, or instinctive absorption of the ability from those who are probably not much in advance of the candidates. This is just as unreasonable as asking anyone to dress for a part and then expecting the person to perform it properly. Like dressing up as a surgeon and forthwith carrying out a life-and-death operation. No one would be insane enough (one hopes) to suggest such a thing, and yet there are plenty of people who presume that if they wear the right robes and say the prescribed words, magical miracles will automatically occur.

This is a complete cart-before-the-horse fallacy. The actual operative energy is consciousness itself, and all the appurtenances and arrangements of ceremonial procedures in any Temple are purely consciousness conditioners that assist the process of arousing, assembling, and concentrating human awareness to a point from which it can most effectively be applied for the purpose of the entire operation. Theoretically it is possible to do this without the physical presence of a Temple provided its mental equivalents are applied in the correct order and the needed energy is actually available. That, however, calls for abilities far beyond the range of average humans, and unless they can connect themselves to a supply source of spiritual energy, there will be little or no result worth considering.

This is precisely what all Temple procedures, whether religious, esoteric, or anything else, are chiefly concerned with. Humans have come up against the problem of their limitations and their need of extending these limitations by gaining the necessary knowledge and experience, or else by invoking the aid of some spiritual agency that is considered capable of such consciousness. In other words, calling in a specialist as one might invoke a plumber to correct a leaking pipe or a surgeon to rectify its equivalent in a human body. Both of these specialists would require recompense for their work in terms of money, whereas spiritual operative specialists require their just dues in terms of service from their human debtors.

That entire question was summed up long ago when humans were faced with the alternatives of devoting their spiritual abilities to either good, personified by God, or evil, personified by the Devil. Being free to choose either course, they might serve the Devil in return for material favors during earthly life at the cost of their immortal souls; or God, for the price of self-sacrifice on earth and the reward of spiritual bliss forever afterwards in heaven. God worked through the agency of angels, and his Satanic Opposite through demons.

Although few these days are very likely to believe in such a literal interpretation of the balance of life between its moral extremeties, the principles behind this simplistic concept are as perfectly valid in modern times as in medieval. First it amounts to an admission of human inadequacy with an implication that such a deficiency needs correcting by the action of a suprahuman agency. Then it suggests that the required energy may be drawn from a common source polarized for the dual purposes of either construction or destruction. As we know, energy is energy and may be used for whatever purpose it is put to. The entire issue depends on whether we want to use the energies of living consciousness for beneficial or malicious purposes. Things are still as simple as that.

To begin with, let us assume that such inner energies are going to be employed for beneficial reasons, and put into practice according to Wesoteric principles. Where and how is this to be accomplished? The natural answer is in the appropriate place and manner, which is in the environment of a Temple by means of whatever ceremony may be considered most suitable. How many people stop to think about what a Temple is in itself and why it might be necessary to select such a special site for making workable relationships with superphysical energies and entities? It might be well to consider these questions a little.

The word *Temple* in itself only means a specially cleared space for making observations. In ancient times the most rational place for this would be a hilltop. This was a good vantage point for defense, gave a clear view of the surrounding country, and afforded the best opportunity for observation of any celestial phenomena. It was definitely the most suitable location for humans wanting to make relationships with the physical world around them and the heavens above. Somewhere that would combine the circumstances of their external ambience with those of their internal awareness. There were also a number of side issues converging on the same point.

A hilltop takes time, trouble, and effort to ascend. The immediate need of those reaching such a height is rest, which has the effect of placing the consciousness in at least a momentarily receptive state. Then it is more easily reachable by whatever "inner awareness" may be focused on or around that particular spot. We are often apt to ignore or underestimate the factor of Omnipresent Awareness, which pervades all space equally, yet concentrates wherever there may be sensitive receptors of its innumerable frequencies. There is nothing really more remarkable in this than in modern radios tuning in to whatever comes within their wavebands. The basic principles are very similar, although the methodologies are so different. There has to be an energy output or transmission converted to terms of intelligent conscious reception by some agency in harmony with the fundamental frequency of mutual communication.

It is the exact nature and characteristics of natural physical surroundings that supply the harmonizing factors enabling sensitive humans to translate any metaphysical message they hold into terms a mortal may comprehend. Consciousness of the place experienced by such sensitives is sufficient to call up in them a corresponding awareness of the spiritual implications involved, and the better they are able to tune in, the clearer and more meaningful will be the import of whatever there may be to convey.

This spiritual specialness of a particular place may be due to any combination of factors. The shape or composition of stones for example, sounds of wind or water, soil chemicals, scents, atmospheric conditions, tree types or vegetation, seasonal tides, and times of day or night. All those physical constituents have to interrelate properly so that the total result produces a harmonious spiritual keynote. That in its turn has to produce a suitably responsive reply from humans in the vicinity. In fact, all natural surroundings have their own especial inner meanings to impart, but discovering which were most suitable for particular spiritual purposes of humankind was a matter that occupied many minds and souls for many millennia.

The gradual evolution of Temples as special sites for making special relationships with what may be called Overpowers, or divine conditions of consciousness, is an interesting process of human development. Orientation played a large part of this procedure. Because humans instinctively felt that their essential being derived from the stars, they believed their ideal condition must be somewhere "up there" and that their best hopes should therefore be directed toward the heavens. Light was good and dark was bad so their instinct was to turn sunwards. Since fearsome flames and fatal earthquakes came from somewhere beneath their feet, an opposite condition of horror and hellfire became equated with some kind of anti-God underneath the earth, whereby the happiness of humanity might be ruined and blasted beyond recovery. There is no doubt that our earliest attempts at theology were mainly influenced by our natural surroundings.

As the Bible suggests, it all began with polarizing human awareness into a distinction between what we considered good and evil. From that time forth we altered our evolutionary fate irrevocably, because every major decision made by humans came down on one side or the other until we learned how to juggle them around to suit our convenience. Yet our inherited instincts still incline us to associate up with good, down with bad, forward with progression and backward with regression, right with right and left with wrong. Such are the meridians of our moral codes of conduct, and we are unlikely to get them permanently out of our systems for a very long time yet. Simplistic as they are, those remain the general principles behind our most modern Wesoteric Temples.

Next came the problem of what adaptions or alterations humans might make to the scene for its improvement and amplification of purpose. Sooner or later it dawned on someone that the best contribution humans could bring would be the most precious thing they knew about—fire. It gave them superiority over every other animal on earth, and they were just learning how to handle it without too much fear, though they were still awed by its power and potentials. To them it seemed something given by a god. So they brought fire to their sacred sites and ringed it with stones to control it. Eventually such stones became an altar of Fire, built of unhewn rocks. Primitive Africans still build such altars today except that they sacrifice minor pieces of money on them in our times.

It is customary with modern esoteric altars, which are mostly made of wood, to place at their bases several small natural stones taken from sacred sites, and there is still fire on or above them in the shape of a sanctuary lamp. Descriptions of old-time "altars of incense" can be read in the Scriptures, wherefrom the ascending smoke arose heavenwards in a hopeful similitude to prayers and supplications arising in the direction of Divinity. Such altars were always made from loosely assembled stones, and other sacrificial altars were descendants from the old cooking fires where carcasses were once roasted whole for the entire tribe to feed from. Eventually the whole area was surrounded by a built-up perimeter that ultimately became the walls of a Temple sheltering the complete congregation. From such simple beginnings all the rest became matters of evolutionary elaboration. Our Temples may have become increasingly ornate or sophisticated, but their primal origins should never be forgotten, otherwise much of what happens in them, and the human responses therewith, will become meaningless and mechanistic instead of remaining mystic and marvelous.

Nevertheless, the purpose of Temples today should be to provide us with an artificial environment that will stimulate and strengthen spiritual abilities and create favorable conditions for communication with inner intelligences, not to remind us of a primitive past. Most of all they should be based on a pattern of principles that can be copied as a self-arrangement so that this pattern becomes an actual integral of the psyche. In other words, a Temple should become an environmental symbol of an ideal human individual. Any Temple that does not do this is of little or no value esoterically. Thus the idea is not unlike that of placing people in healthy and harmonious environments with a hope that this might encourage them to reflect those environments eventually in their own characters.

This means that everything contained in a Temple should be practical symbols for the self-construction and maintenance of a human soul. That of course includes personal attire and any decorations. Not only must every single item have its own special meaning and implications, but these are to be clearly comprehended by everyone using them. It is not enough to have such usage *explained* to anyone—the symbology must be actually *experienced* by those employing the Temple for spiritual advancement. That is to say, all the sensory impressions of Temple symbology should be translated in terms of responsional output, i.e., the sight or feel of a sword should evoke a sense of being keen and sharp-witted to a point, a rod or staff ought to cause a corresponding awareness of uprightness, and so with all other symbols. Unless and until this becomes possible, no practical use can be made of any Temple.

The science of creating an artificial environment that will successfully create the right kind of inner spiritual attitude is exemplified by the Japanese Zen gardens, which are specifically designed to promote the required response almost to a hairbreadth. So far as we are concerned, the difficulty is that they are designed entirely for an Oriental mind and soul, which are already aligned with matching ideology. Nevertheless the underlying principle of designing external environments that will induce specific spiritual states of self-attunement should certainly be applicable to every sort of requirement.

It was mainly our Western weather that induced us to transfer our old open-air methods of worship to more sheltered situations. Even so, attempts were made to reproduce original conditions by representative symbology. Early Temples were circular, and the Greek designs in particular were suggestive of stone circles wherein the rough, upright stones had evolved into graceful pillars roofed over for protection against rain, though not wind. In place of groves of sacred trees, collections of pillars surrounded the built-up site, and these were frequently carved to represent palm trees or other decorative foliage. Those pillars have now become mere porch pillars on the exterior or the two pillars before the sanctuary, but they derive from the ancient perimeter markers of a sacred site and should be treated as such. So too with the floral decorations still in use with us, which speak of outdoor conditions in earlier times.

In fact, the whole purpose of modern Temple symbology should be for providing practical links with our deepest inherited instincts and genetic roots extending back to our earliest existence on earth—and beyond that. Those, by projectional counterbalance, connect with our equivalent future, thereby putting a great deal of point into our present. Unless people become consciously aware of why everything to do with a Temple is what it is, where it is, and what happens with it, none of it will serve any useful purpose at all and might as well not be present at all. So the first instruction to any aspiring candidate in the Holy Mysteries could very well be *know thy temple.*

Esoteric environments can vary anywhere between the stark barrenness of a Zen garden or a Friends meeting-house and the most ornate interior of a Byzantine basilica or a Brahmin temple. Let us disregard creeds or denominations for the moment, and look for the common fundamental of arranging a locality with the intention of creating something that will help humans contact the higher type of unembodied awareness they call God or however they believe in that energy. We get an overall impression that some humans seem to need a profusion of symbology for that purpose, whereas others appear to require the barest minimum of any such external aids. Moreover, the indications are that the more independent and ascetically inclined individuals become, the less they demand suggestive symbolism in solid physical forms. This seems to happen because they have become capable of supplying their own symbolism on inner levels, but they still have to do this in patterns that would have been supplied by solid symbology in the first place, so all they really gain is economic independence.

The one type of symbology that no class of esotericist can dispense with is *fellow humans*. Though few might consider each other as parts of Temple symbology, that is exactly what they not only are but should make every possible effort to become. People are actually the most important symbols of all, because they are *living* symbols of the Power they are approaching and should be mediating that Power among themselves so all may share its influence. It may be that every single one of them has a different part to play or some specific function to fulfill in their mutual psychodrama, but if they do not cooperate properly and circulate the energy currents as they should, nothing effective can ever come of their association. There should be NO "audience observers" at any esoteric ceremonial. ALL should be fully active participants even if they do not move a muscle the whole time. All present should concert their concentrated consciousness as required for the purpose of the practice being performed. Every inner ability and attention should be focused on whatever is being directed from spiritual dimensions. If anyone is unable or unwilling to do this, then none of them ought to be present at all because that person is doing nothing except hindering the entire action.

There is only one way that members of a congregation of any creed, cult, or belief whatever ought to behave: as if each were an individual part of a machine made for some specific purpose that was being fulfilled because of their concerted actions. Alternately, they could consider themselves as separate instruments of an orchestra being conducted by its leader and producing a magnificent symphony. That would be more of an ideal condition than a common one, since it would imply that each individual member knew exactly what he/she was supposed to do and just when to do it. In the case of a single operative, such a soul has to supply the requirements of all instrumental needs, which is a much more demanding procedure yet probably a more precise and perfect one. To see that point more clearly it is necessary to compare the difference between a musical piece performed by a single, expert player on one instrument, and the same piece rendered by a whole orchestra out of time, tune, and practice. One has perfectly clear meaning but no volume to speak of, and therefore the range of distance is limited, while the other has a great deal of volume, which extends the range and probably causes a lot of annoyance to hearers considerably further away. On the other hand, if a single instrumentalist is a novice or is unskilled, it would obviously be best to practice in solitude until such time as he/she can harmonize reasonably with others.

Bearing in mind that the function of Temples is the facilitation of direct relationship between Divinity and humanity, let us consider the major factors involved in such an achievement. First there is Divinity, or God (however the Life Spirit may be called), presented as the Greater Cosmos, or *Macroprosopus*, and man, considered as the Lesser Cosmos, or *Microprosopus*, which is the "in his own image and likeness" of the Creation myth. The symbology of the Temple is supposed to represent the Containing Cosmos, which is reflected by the ceremonial clothing worn by the humans within it, and whatever is thought, said, or done stands for the relationship between the two parties. Thus the design of the Temple should signify the way we see Divinity, our own appearance should present the way we would like Divinity to view us, and our behavior, because of those two factors combined, ought to show how we want to relate them together as an experience of existence.

Those principles should be valid for any kind of religious or esoteric practice of whatever persuasion. They governed the conduct of medieval magicians, who clothed themselves properly for the ritual, traced ground designs in a circle around themselves to represent a protective perimeter,

wrote their ideology in symbolic form around it as a decla-
ration of their beliefs and intentions, and then presented
themselves through verbal and ceremonial formulae to
whichever aspect of Deity they meant to approach, and
asked for favors. The same could be said for Christians, who
constructed their Temples in the form of a cross, dressed in
formal attire and said or sung their supplications to God,
whose attention they hoped they were attracting by their
unusual behavior. Again, the identical principles would
apply to primitive Pagans, who chose some spot that was
sacred to them, disrobed entirely, then copulated cheer-
fully while inviting the God in themselves to enjoy the
experience. Behind all these totally different methodologies
lie the fundamentals of a *mutually mediative meeting between
macro- and microcosms.* Each in the Temple of its own
choice.

Now we have to consider those methodologies. They
are fairly limited and vary between the extreme starkness of
silent, undemonstrative gatherings dressed in the most
sober styles, and the most uproarious congregations of hys-
terical humans screaming their God-ideas amid stroboscopic
surroundings while they whirl and contort their bodies in
desperate efforts to detect Divinity by making such a fuss
that it can hardly help detecting them. We shall hope to aim
somewhere in the middle of these and reach a balanced
point of view concerning procedures and practices, which
are necessarily limited by our conscious capabilities. On
the surface of things there is relatively little that can be done
with dignity or decency in Temples of a Western nature.
What there is can be classed as behaviors of the body, mind,
or soul supervised by a controlling Spirit. This can be dealt
with as follows.

1. BODY. All bodily behaviors dedicated to establishing contacts with Deity. These will include the ingestion of

physical substances symbolic of such an end or those calculated to promote the process by psychedelic means. Every kind of stress technique, which will include processional marches, walks, or dances, plus postures and assumptions of God-forms. Exposure of bodies to the elements by being buried in earth, suspended in water, whirled through the air, or passed briefly through fire. All different kinds of breathing, including the physical side of singing or chanting. Motion or stability combined as alternations or continuations of conduct. Exclusion or intensification of specific senses, such as amplification of sound or silencing it. Increase or diminution of physical illumination. Anything altering sensual pain or pleasure. There is not very much that can be done with a body except vary the degree of its possible experiences or subject it to some new ones, after which acclimatization will cause a rapid fall-off in reactions. This reaction loss is a major reason why bodily experiences have to be calculated very carefully indeed when formulating ceremonial procedures. Something that at first produces a pronounced effect is liable to lose a great deal of its impact subsequently.

2. MIND. Here we have stimuli of a purely mental and intellectual nature. Applied ideology conveyed mostly through language and the spoken or written word. Mainly effective in the case of cultured or educated people, who are able to react to verbalized meanings because they have been conditioned to do so. A very great deal of this quotient depends on the ability of the utterer to have exactly the right type of intonation calculated to evoke exactly the required response from hearers. For instance, a harsh Bronx accent is scarcely likely to arouse sympathetic feelings in a cultured Virginian congregation. Also, the presentation of mental ideology must necessarily be acceptable to recipients. On the other hand, there could be situations where irritation and resentment might be exactly the reactions called for, and then the aforementioned circumstances would be entirely appropriate. Then too, the rate of presentation comes into the picture, and all the rules of elocution and dramatization apply here, including costume and gesture. Every possible adjunct to the proper presentation of ideology via the mind and intellect has to be fully considered and placed correctly in the context of whatever procedure is being followed, whether a solitary ceremonialist or a full congregation is involved.

3. SOUL. In this area responses must be obtained from purely emotional levels. Love, hate, and every condition of sentient consciousness between those extremeties must be evoked and utilized. It should be known precisely what is likely to arouse each sentiment in various classifications of awareness that depend mostly on characteristics. For instance, the presentation of an Indian picture of Ganesh, the elephant-headed god, is most unlikely to arouse confident or sympathetic feelings among European viewers. Individual cultures are paramount in deciding the right stimuli to use here. Swastikas could be contraindicated amongst Jewish people, or a cross amongst Muslims. Very abstract symbology is seldom much use for connecting with soul sensations. Physical symbolism such as perfumes, colors, and suitable sounds is much more likely here. Whatever carries a real gut reaction with it. For example, the color red combined with a strong smell of blood and the sound of metallic clashing can only suggest ideas of injury to a normal Western audience, and therefore will evoke corresponding feelings of fear, alertness, or concern among those subjected to such an experience. Different people react differently within every specific situation pattern, so only a general average can be calculated for any group working. As an instance, the presentation of some helpless child or animal being tortured would evoke horror, anger, and revulsion from normal people, but only a sense of gratification and approval from genuine sadists. Classification of attendant humans is always advisable.

4. SPIRIT. This is the animating principle of each human individual, which derives directly from Divinity, Deity, or whatever the Life Spirit may be named. It is alive in us to experience itself through all we think or do as conscious creatures. In other words, it is our self-share of Being becoming *as it will* because of our behavior. Individually it is our immortal identity, and collectively it amounts to the spiritual consciousness behind and within our distinctive species of humanity. Sometimes it is termed the Sangreal. So far as any type or classification of Temple is concerned, that is a nexus affording an opportunity for the human principles of body, mind, and soul to interact with each other so that Spirit may be served. This could be so in the case of all living experience, but when and where a Temple becomes involved there is an intentional commitment of relationship between the principles, which makes that factor of very special importance. We walk around, which is a physical activity of body without intentions of linking mind or soul. We read the day's newspapers, which is an affair of mind that does not specially call for body and soul to align themselves therewith. We encounter some tragedy that puts the soul into a state of stress beyond control by the mind or the bearing abilities of body, which both become casualties of consciousness. It is only when all three principles harmonize with each other that Spirit is able to experience them as a unity, and consequently make mutual and valuable relationships among them all. In a way, this is not unlike a three-legged stool on which the legs kept constantly changing length and strength so that it could not be sat on properly, and thus failed its function. Or a telescope with three lenses that continually altered their optical qualities and foci so that no one could see through it correctly. A Temple or its equivalent must be a spiritual situation wherein the three principles of body, mind, and soul are held together in at least approximate focus so that Spirit may make functional relationships with those humans concerned for the mutual satisfaction of all entities involved.

So for one century after another until it became genetically integral to us, we have been developing the idea of choosing special places and doing special things in order to "feel" right with the Spirit, which kept us alive in this world and would hopefully continue to do so after our bodily death. After many millennia of evolution, it began to dawn on us that we could create those conditions of consciousness in and around ourselves by our own enterprises and abilities. Eventually, increasing numbers of humans became independent of Temples as they learned how to build these for themselves as pure constructions of consciousness instead of using physical materials. Since it was companionable and pleasant to share inner experiences, however, and as we are usually a sociable species of being, earthly edifices continued to be erected for the convenience of those who wished to extend ancient esoteric customs into contemporary circumstances.

Perhaps the odd thing is that in the whole history of human Temple usage, so very little has been recorded in the way of objective evidence to suggest the actuality or authenticity of supernatural powers or presences. Isolated instances or hints and rumors of peculiar or unusual happenings have been told times without number right through the centuries down to the present day, but absolutely nothing of an indubitable and incontrovertible nature where, for example, it might be stated categorically, "If you think, say, and do so and so, then you may confidently expect an unusual manifestation of this and that description to happen as a result." In other words, there is no known certainty or even reliable probability concerning resultants of energy outputs for given energy inputs in the case of human conduct concerned with Temple activities. Ever since we began our earliest esoteric practices, we have been persisting in what might be described as a haze of holy hope or a fascinating fog of faith. Everything is only conditionally clear or provisionally plain, depending on so very many postulations.

The undeniable fact of the matter is that after so many millennia of so few supportive experiences, a relatively large proportion of humanity still believe in the reality of a spiritual structure behind the manifest universe. They continue to take for granted conditions of consciousness and actual existence quite apart from any physically provable or demonstrable evidence. However inferential the basis of beliefs may be, humans continue to congregate for the practice of cultural behavior related to their spiritual suppositions. So much is incontestible. The decisive question is, could human beings have continued so long and at such a considerable cost to themselves if there were no truth or value in following any form of faith?

The answer to this of course is a most definite *no* and the demonstrable evidence of human belief per se is observable at all points of our civilized existence. Our forms and objectives of belief may have altered immeasureably during the centuries, and will no doubt continue altering for the remainder of our time on earth, but the fundamental fact that we are believing beasts and aspiring animals has taken us to this present point of progression on our cosmic climb up the Ladder of Life. We could not have got where we are without the drive that continues to inspire and push us in the direction of what we once believed must be Divinity. So much is quite certain. Granted, we have diversified and reclassified this major motivation in every imaginable way, perhaps learning a little more at each step along every path. Maybe our terminology changes with every generation, but no matter how we dress it up with every variety of verbal camouflage, we can never escape from the fact of our original ideology being based on a life-enduring quest for the Divine both in ourselves and behind the whole of manifestation. That of course was, and still is, nurtured by the principles of Temple practice.

Where else would modern surgeons have acquired their skills except from the genetic progression of an instinct to lay hands on diseased people and correct their distressing conditions? Where would artists have obtained their abilities except from an inherited impulse to pictorially portray ideals that could evoke calculated responses from other humans? All developed human capabilities can be traced back to beginnings in our own blood, and their subsequent encouragement through what were once Temple techniques, however primitive. Furthermore, those techniques translated into modern terms or superseded by superior ones have considerable significance for us in contemporary values. They are not part of a dead-and-gone tradition but integrals of an ever-expanding Intelligence expressing itself on this earth through conscious creatures of all kinds, culminating in human beings.

It would seem fair to say that because we behaved as we did in our far past, we have become as we are now and will become in the distant future. Moreover, the influence of Temple behavior is traceable throughout the entire process, and therefore there is no reason for terminating it in principle, however its practices may be changed or presented. We should have advanced sufficiently at this era to realize that fundamentals are constants, while formalities are their varient changeables over a very wide spectrum of consciousness. The Energy and its categories, which were formerly called

God and different aspects of it, might now be thought of as a universal life force or any other abstraction, but whatever it might be, it remains the same as it always was. All that has altered is our awareness and attitudes. We shall change because we are evolving, while it seems static because it evolves at such a slow rate compared with ours as to appear eternal.

We have followed our God-concepts from the highly localized and personified presentations of the past to the depersonalized abstractions of our contemporary conceptions. Who knows when these abstractions are likely to continue this cyclic change and so to speak recondense themselves into closely focalized relationships with an awareness of a most intimate nature because that awareness will be our own intimacy with nature itself? What will happen when we are able to extend consciousness far beyond our mortal bodies and share such awareness not only with other humans but with animals, plants, and even minerals? Such are only questions of time and development extended to maybe the nth degree. The so-called mystical marriage, or "union with God," has always been considered the absolute apex of possible human progress, and that is what it would mean: constant companionship with Cosmos itself. The closest possible relationship with Infinite Identity. Not in the least an attenuation into an indefinable abstraction but to the contrary a concentration of consciousness to a point of perception that penetrates every part of existence. Living throughout Life as a Whole instead of being confined to minute mortal particles of it as individual human creatures.

It is for the achievement of our present possible degree of development toward such an ideal spiritual status that Temples of any description become either useful or necessary. As ordinary humans we can only expect to do as much in a single lifetime as comes within the competence of our genetic capabilities, and few enough get anywhere close to those limits, which does not excuse deliberate evasions of effort. Thus a principal function of any Temple is to provide environmental conditions that favor spiritual strivings at self-development toward a state of human perfection. Even the slightest advance in the direction of that aim is helpful to humanity as a whole and in particular. All advancements commence with intentions, and if any Temple is able to inspire humans with an intention or inclination to improve themselves in the slightest, it will have made a most significant contribution to Cosmos. Schools and universities have frequently been called "temples of learning," and such is surely their most apt and honorable title.

The acid test is whether or not Temple practices actually assist humans to become better beings in themselves or not. Do they really reach down to root levels and favor the growth of good potentials simultaneously with inhibiting that of bad ones? Such is the effect they should have, and if they do not, then something is wrong somewhere. Either the methodology is unsuitable for the souls concerned, or they are unable to respond to it appropriately. In either case there is incompatibility, for above all else, both methodology and the humans in question must have an affinity with each other. It is useless and counterproductive to force unsuitable souls and systems together. About the best that might be hoped for would be some spiritual system that was so broad, bland, and middle of the road that it would bring a minimum amount of benefit to the maximum amount of people. Though there is plenty of room in this world for such systems, usually the ones of most significance are the highly special and selective systems that produced the maximum effects in the minimum of humanity. Therefore it is imperative that souls and systems be properly matched for effective Temple practice.

With any of the public religions there is normally such

a wide choice in this world that virtually every class and variety of human temperament can be catered to, and it only needs individual selection for deciding which, if any, to follow. When it comes to the far more exclusive types of esoteric Temples, however, matters become increasingly difficult. Since the principal appeal is to a small minority of humans, and availability is reduced to a minimum, plus the fact that membership is usually conditional upon very definite and demanding characteristics, esoteric Temples mostly consist of only a few highly specialized types of humans.

Whereas most Christian churches are open to anyone willing to contribute money toward their funds, esoteric establishments are closed shops to all except the few who not only are committed to their basic beliefs but also are willing and able to participate in whatever practices they advocate or adopt. Most of them have some probationary training or indoctrination that neophytes must undergo prior to coming into contact with the "inner circle" of initiated members who actually run all the regular sessions of activities connected with each type of Temple. Many of them again have subclassifications of "degrees" that are supposed to determine the spiritual status of individual members, though this is seldom so much of an actuality as a presumption. All in all, the evidence goes to show that the wider and more open the membership of any spiritual system becomes, the slower and less specialized its effectiveness is apt to be. That may not be a bad thing at all, in view of human capabilities, but it does define the difference between actualities and give some guidelines in choosing a life course.

For instance, estimation of individual capabilities in relation to the demands of any spiritual system is highly important, and self-selection is seldom accurate within desirable degrees. That is why every applicant for membership of an esoteric Temple should be carefully tested for suitability by its controlling committee. This is no more than might be expected in the case of normal employment and no reasonable person would expect to obtain any kind of responsible job without such an interview. Besides, it would be grossly unfair to hire anyone for work he/she is incapable of doing, for the sake of future fellow employees alone. Why then should any human being be admitted to the company of others who are specializing in spiritual activities of specific kinds without sufficient screening to discover incompatibilities? That would be fair to neither party.

Temples, however, are essentially central organizations of human activity, and as such are similar in principle to most other types of occupation, including ordinary business enterprises. Consider the resemblances. Both are collections of humans with a common interest in some mutual purpose of association for presumed benefits shareable by all concerned. Both have physical premises convenient for the promotion and promulgation of their intended end effect, and these are furnished with every possible facility for achieving such an objective. This must include human teams specially trained and conditioned to obtain satisfactory results by any means, preferably ethical ones. Lastly both teams must be fully aware of their actions, their responsibility toward each other, and their common idea. Plus of course normal moral obligations to fellow humans outside their special spheres of interest.

Therefore sound business acumen is a useful quality to possess where the organization and running of earthly Temples is concerned. There are so many needs that only practical and down-to-earth people can possibly fulfill. Purely spiritual souls are only too apt to neglect or overlook the necessary nuts and bolts of normal human association. Things like rent, lighting and heating, or even the simplest requirements of any ordinary gathering. Someone has to arrange for all such items to converge into a coordinated whole, and this takes what might be termed average business ability. Those who are thinking about the spread of early Christianity and wondering what made this possible might give less credit to the preaching power of Apostles and spare some thoughts for the people that picked up their expenses, freely offered them hospitality, arranged their itineraries, and otherwise gave them all the support without which not a single mission could have been accomplished.

With the primitive Church it was bishops (or inspectors) whose job it was to travel around making sure the various congregations more or less agreed with doctrines taught as common beliefs. Later, however, the office of cardinal was instituted to ensure that the Church had sufficient funds and political power to make its influence felt throughout the world. Cardinals were not originally priests but wealthy and powerful men who were also patrons of the arts and valued contributors to culture and socioeconomic expansion. They ranked above bishops and still control the Roman section of the Church, although full ordination is now obligatory. While it is undesirable in esoteric circles to put many individuals in such positions of power, this does illustrate the necessity for having humans with sound business sense when operating any kind of esoteric enterprise.

The majority of esoteric Temples nowadays are factually very small groups of people collecting around a central nuclear personage having the charisma needed to cause such an effect. Though this can and often does produce some quite remarkable results, these groups frequently collapse on the death, disgrace, desertion, or other disinvolvement removing the founder-focus. No spiritual affair poised on the pivot of a human personality alone can persist for very long after its dissolution. Only the very strongest spiritual links can continue holding humans together much longer than a normal lifetime, which is why those based on ethnic or familial ties or some kind of blood-belief have lasted longest. Christianity can be classed as such because of its association with a "Blood-salvation," however much mythologized or distorted in significance. A lot of the old Pagan esotericism was, and still is, confined to family or clan traditions, and there were legends attached to specific blood-lines supposed to stem from some very superior source in the days of antiquity. However it might be wrapped up, there had to be a central nuclear power attracting people together and holding them in common relationship. In the case of human beings this power often consists of sex, money, race, class, or mutual survival motivation. Either they are compelled together by external circumstances because of some common threat (such as a war on their species), or they are attracted together by an inner central energy much as the sun holds its planets in orbit. Sometimes there might be a combination of both factors, but the nuclear principle applies in all cases.

What holds any single human being together as a functioning body, mind, and soul comprising what we think of as an individual intelligence? There may be a multiplicity of entirely different forces coordinating to produce the phenomenon, but the centralizing focal factor is the active intention of being itself, or what is sometimes called the "will to live." If that will becomes weakened beyond a certain point, say by age, disease, despair, or any other reason, then the individual just dies, and bereft of its nuclear energy the conglomeration of atoms and units that constituted the person soon begins disassociating into decomposition and decay. True, they will all be recycled and eventually reappear in other combinations, but they can no longer remain in relation with each other once the uniting Spirit leaves them. The same holds true of esoterics, and in order to keep them together it is essential to maintain their mutual "will to live as one." That is only possible if their nuclear pivotal point is a purely spiritual one that they all love enough to stay with.

In olden Temples the central figure was usually the priest or priestess, who personified the God by dressing and acting in an appropriate style, which led to a lot of complications and errors when his/her personality intruded, and when the person put his/her own interpretations into every pronouncement. In some Temples an artificial image of the God-concept acted as a focus, or it could be a plain natural stone of singular shape and appearance. The priest or priestess was then considered as a principal server of the Concept. This failed when people did not distinguish between the Idea and its symbolic image, hence the horror of idolatry in later times. Nevertheless the Hebrews constructed their Temples with a holy of holies, or sanctuary where their God was believed to concentrate invisibly around the ark of the covenant. Later synagogues reduced this to a cupboard in which was kept the Scrolls of the Law, and that Law was God himself. This is fundamentally the same as the Christian church making use of a tabernacle or small safe in which is stored the sacred vessels and the Sacrament, which is believed to be the actual body and blood of Christ. Subsequent Protestant sectarians came to see their God as being an invisible presence among themselves that made itself evident mainly through the preaching of its word from the Scriptures, which were no longer kept locked up, but were freely available to literate members as a printed book prominently displayed and circulated. Eventually this extended to minority groups that believed their God only manifested in and through themselves. All these examples are based on the same Temple formation formula of a universal Spirit manifesting among humanity because of their mutual attraction for and to each other and so providing a physical focus for that purpose in human congregations.

Temples of every religion are based on those principles. One might say with perfect truth that the religion of communism has its central shrine in the tomb of Lenin and its scriptural laws in the *Manifesto* and *Das Kapital*. Its once prayerful church services with their wonderful choral effects have turned into workers committee meetings and singing the "Internationale," but the underlying behavior is still there. Translate the fundamental behavior of human beings into terms of any level whatever and they will be parallels of each other all the way. In the case of esoteric Temples, the usual question arising is, what sort of nuclear grouping should be adopted in order to achieve maximum mutual adherence? Or, what factor will cause any given collection of humans to remain in harmonious and beneficial relationship with each other for the longest possible period? First it must be spiritual, second it must supply satisfaction, and third it must be self-fulfilling. It might be added that such a nucleus should act as an energy exchanger between those gathered around it so that all may interrelate themselves with each other through its means. It has to act as the sun around which individual people process like planets, each with its own orbit and particular purpose yet together serving the same system as parts of a whole universe.

As a rule, such a central nucleus is expressed as a positive spiritual ideal attracting negative electrons around itself, which are actually the needs of human beings seeking fulfillment. A simple case of the + in one compensating for the − in the other. Since humans have both plus and minus in themselves, if these can be brought into careful contact with each other through the medium of their central symbol this should help to harmonize mutually into a much better relationship. In other words, if someone with the character deficiencies of a quick temper and a hasty judgement was brought into contact with an individual possessing great patience, calm, and deliberation through a spiritual medium they both valued highly, then the hasty one should tone down and become a lot more cautious, while the other would speed up and become more decisive. Such is an ideal instance of the faults of one person being converted into the virtues of another. It is totally dependent on the right kind of mutual relational means being employed, and that is why it is so essential that the full membership of an esoteric Temple be adequately assessed for character balance before admission. Someday perhaps a "character compatibility" computer will be devised for this purpose, somewhat on the lines of those used by marriage bureaus for finding ideal partners. Whether this would ever supersede the astrological method of matching used quite successfully for so many centuries is very problematical.

The selection and choice of a central nuclear symbol to represent the especial type of Spirit sought for in any particular Temple is more than important. It is vital. For example, the Masonic Square and Compasses depicting the relationship of man with God through one's profession or work in this world is a very widely understood one. It clearly calls for men who are careful and conscientious craftsmen to work with as much skill and attention for good relationships between God and man as if they were constructing some earthly edifice demanding both dedication and precision. This implies brotherhood and loyalty among them all if such a spiritual structure is ever to be achieved. Their watchword is "Work." Usually by this is understood the Great Work, or magnum opus. Through their symbology of Craft tools and procedures they remind themselves of every quality and process of character development they should work for in order to become better builders of a Temple fit for God to dwell in, i.e., themselves, and to improve the world they live in. All the required ethical and cultural values for making at least greatly improved versions of the men of the species. Such is the inspiration that should animate initiates of the Masonic Craft.

In the case of the Rosy Cross symbolism, its immediate implication is the quaternion for the cosmic quest and the

Rose for spiritual secrecy. The secret quest that humans must make in search of their own souls and Spirit. Since the rose is the special flower of Venus, the deity of sexual and sensual love, the hint here is that this major drive of human life may be centralized to power the pursuit of Perfection, yet such an intimate relationship is something to keep secret rather than reveal to those who would probably malign or misuse it. The correct cross employed with this God-idea should be the cosmic or solar wheel type to indicate the interlinkage of time, space, and events, plus every variation of our Creation. When the long or Christian type of cross is used, this specifically signifies the Christian valency of its meaning and that there is a sub-rosa side of the faith, which should be mystically interpreted by those initiated in such circles. This is represented by the petals of the rose and their numerical attributions. It emphasizes in particular that Love in its deepest and truest sense is indeed the power that makes the world go round, because the representative red rose can be considered as the pivot of the crossed or quartered circle of our globe. The red of the rose signifies the Blessed Blood behind our being, although it is sometimes shown with alternating petals of white for semen and red for blood to illustrate the productive elements of our existence. From a Christian standpoint the symbol could sum up its Founder's main injunction to "love ye one another."

Should it be the Tree of Life symbol that is used to sum up and centralize esoteric ideology, this should have an especial significance for those with mathematical minds, who tend to see everything in terms of exact values and precise layouts of logical reasoning and step-by-step approaches. There is a very special spiritual meaning behind every point of the Tree plan, though its overall attractions are intellectual rather than emotional. Its amazing multiplicity of meanings is intensely stimulating for the provocation of thought and speculation along every angle of inner approach to the Eternal Enigma. Its singular combinations of Spheres and Paths cover Cosmos from top to bottom with a virtually endless line of enquiry. It affords scope for many lifetimes of investigative probings and procedures in search of an ultimate answer—if such exists. One great advantage of the Tree is that it can never be dull for those dedicated to discovering hidden truths in cosmic conundrums. Whoever looks at life as a constant challenge to human ingenuity will find a perpetual puzzle confronting him/her in the Tree plan. No sooner does one solution seem certain than another problem instantly arises out of that solution. Scholars have been engaged with the Tree's queries for several centuries and still have not produced a definitive result of their labors. Those that centralize themselves around this symbol have chosen a lifelong thought track to follow.

They that accept the Sangreal as a central concept, with its primal symbology of a Light behind the Blood, are dedicating themselves to the discovery of Divinity within their own beings and those of their companions by every means at the disposal of Wesoterics. That is to say, souls born within the Western Inner Tradition are seeking spiritual development through beliefs and behaviors that reach them by their own bloodlines rather than those of alien yet equally effective spiritual systems. Their particular symbol combines the major sacred signs of Western mysticism. Again the quaternion of the quest surrounded by the connecting cord of truth. All the adjuncts of the Holy Hunt. The Cross itself is the Shield, the tip of a Rod or Staff indicates both a bow and an arrow-shaft, the Lance-head could also be a Sword or arrow-point, and lastly the Cup or Grail contains the Blessed Blood, which may be dispensed to those who have earned it. The drops of that Blood descending into the Cup form the patterns of the Tree of Life, while the design of the Cup has a square base representing humanity, and a circular bowl for God. The Cord has thirty-two twists for the

Paths of the Tree. In fact, all the essential elements of our esoteric ancestry and faith of the future are expressed in the Sangreal sign. Its attractive appeal should be especially for those who could be called "traditionalistic innovators," or souls who believe that while ancient customs should be respected and preserved in spirit, they can only continue to live and survive if they are being constantly adapted to contemporary conditions. The Grail motto is "I seek to serve," and the implications of this simple saying are truly of the deepest profundity.

These four examples are by no means the only centralizations of Wesotericism, but they are good typifications of them. They clearly indicate that the best thing to do, if one is genuinely seeking a philosophy to follow or a Temple to work with in this world, is to find out which central nuclear symbol seems to attract one most, then proceed from that point. Any affair that does not appear to have such a central concept is better avoided altogether, or else entered in the hope of finding or creating one. It is well to remember that whatever is based on a purely human personality cannot outlive that person very long unless a spiritual substitute is found and placed in the nuclear position as soon as possible. Christians need not point to the instance of their Leader as the sole exception, because they have personalized the power he preached as a formalized image of all the spiritual ideals he stood for while inhabiting a human body on earth. Thus they have not built their central concept on the actual personality of Jesus so much as on the Spirit that motivated his mission. Esoteric endeavors intending to last as long as Christianity would be well advised to follow a similar course.

So to sum up this section of study, the instinct in human beings to establish Temples wherein to deal with their ideas of Divinity is as old as humanity itself, and the only serious question is one of finding something suitable for the type of soul concerned. This should not be too difficult if we accept that a genuine Temple is not a physical building at all but a clearance in one's own consciousness that makes it possible to realize an intimate relationship between oneself and a spiritual state of being. The externalities of physical locations are only aids for creating such a condition. Nevertheless there are some basic rules of behavior and codes of conduct to observe in order to obtain the most satisfactory results from the Temple process of pushing human beings even a fraction closer to their eventual peak of perfection. Therefore let us turn our attention to the reasons for these from a Wesoteric viewpoint.

Chapter 2

SURROUNDING SYMBOLOGY

Human beings normally exist in distinct and definable areas of life. First they exist within themselves as a consciousness confined to individuals; next, within the circle of their blood-related families and close friends; containing that circle is the extent of their ethnic or national existence, and outside that again is the wholeness of humanity itself. Though all those categories can be subdivided into classifications of the most minute description, they will serve as the fourfold combination of a conscious conglomerate. Qabbalists might note a linkage within the four Letters of the Name. An individual is the Yod, the family Heh, the ethnic group Vau, and the combination of humanity the final Heh. Others might compare the development with the expansion of a wave spreading outward from the center of a circular pool. In the logical course of progression this awareness should extend beyond our world altogether until it reaches the end of our universe, but for the moment we will regard the given boundaries of being only.

When it comes to making relationships with what is acceptable as Divinity, that process was once possible according to customs applicable within the divisions named. First there was a purely personal one, then a private familial contact, followed by a public tribal or national type of gathering, and lastly a comprehensive collection of typifications. Four quite different classifications of Temples to serve multitudes of humans. The first is the secret and individual Temple of a single human soul; the second, the private and restricted Temple of familiar and friendly gatherings; the third, the public denominational meetings available to those of like mind, and the fourth is mainly theoretical and inclusive of all human approaches to the Absolute. Although the edges of these areas are by no means so sharp and distinct as they were formerly, they still stand for demarcation lines between spiritual sectors of people on this planet. The general recognition rules seem to be that the closer they are confined to intimate circles, the more esoteric beliefs and behavior become. The divisionary differences depend entirely on arbitrary factors like nomenclature, procedures, methodology, and pure technicalities. Behind these they all have a common concern of establishing conscious contact with higher than human orders of intelligence.

Again and again people have supposed how wonderful it might be if everyone on earth believed exactly the same things and behaved in precisely the same way in common conformity with each other. Factually of course that would be disastrous and utterly prohibitive of progress along any lines of useful development. What is deplorable is that our natural differences should result in antagonism instead of compensatory cooperation. It is only when humans realize the necessity for variation and specialized fulfillment of function amongst themselves that we will be likely to find progressive peace and harmony prevailing on earth.

Although there is a kind of instinctive recognition of this fact awakening in human nature, it has not yet reached a degree of development that would be strongly sufficient enough to solve our spiritual problems on this planet for the remainder of our sojourn here. This cannot happen until it evidences through our genetics as a dominant characteristic of human behavior, and that will take many generations to come. In the meantime no more may be done than urge this improvement of intelligence into incarnation by every spiritual energy available to willing workers, and that calls for Temple operations on an unprecedented scale.

The plain facts of this matter are that specific fundamental arrangements of human awareness that have mainly derived from inherited or instinctual traces of Temple training along ancestral lines still influence our lives in present times, and consequently have a calculable effect on our coming future. Habits and thinking patterns that originated with very old Temple procedures of earlier generations project into contemporary consciousness and reappear as mental, moral, or even physical forms of behavior. Their seminal influence on our lives contributes very greatly to the thought currents we circulate amongst ourselves, which will eventually change the course of our civilization for better or worse. We may not be objectively aware of this in the least, and it is very unlikely that many people would consciously recognize the extent to which our lives are affected by this factor. On the surface we might have altered all our inherited instincts of esoteric values into scientific, sociological, or political terminologies, but the basics of these values were encountered a very long time ago when we were first learning how to concert our consciousness and focus it on aims far beyond our very limited capabilities. The cradle of this propensity was the Temple as a principle of human evolutionary development.

It may be fashionable nowadays to deride or belittle

the so-called superstitions of our far-off ancestors, reject their religious suppositions altogether, and presume that we have reached our present position entirely by our own efforts, unaided by anything except human intelligence. Such could be very unwise indeed. Modern humans should never underestimate the debt we owe to Temple practice of the past, which encouraged the efforts we have made in coordinating our consciousness. If we had never imagined there might be a superior state of being than ours and tried to reach anywhere close to it through Temple environments, we would still be crawling around caves. The initial idea that there could be a power, person, or something in the nature of an entitled energy that we might approach for practical assistance with our living problems was the beginning of our betterment. Once that possibility occurred to us, the rest followed as a sequence of evolutionary events.

What we frequently fail to understand today is the state of the psychic atmosphere of the world then as contrasted with what it is now in relation to human receptivity. Amazing changes have taken place during the millennia we have endured this earth. Consciousness itself is ambient. Literally it is all around us like an ocean or atmosphere that we absorb or receive much as a radio receiver absorbs electromagnetic energy and translates it into audible sounds. The implications of this are almost incalculable. In our early days on earth the "awareness atmosphere" would have emanated largely from plant and animal life plus a cosmic background of consciousness originating from very remote sources. The interaction of these resulted in a force field in which early humans began to master their minds and sensed that they had souls as well as bodies. Because they received such spiritual signals directly, they were in much closer contact with Divinity than most moderns. Since that time, however, humans have created such a cacophony of consciousness in the vicinity of this planet that it has become increasingly difficult, and often impossible, to distinguish anything of a divine character about impressions received by inner sensoria. Multimillions of human minds are continually confusing, and often deliberately altering, the ambience of awareness around the earth, while suffering souls are exuding emotional stresses everywhere, so it is scarcely surprising we cannot see much, if any, clearly spiritual structure behind our earthly environments.

Through sheer necessity and experience we may have learned how to safeguard ourselves from spiritual suffering by creating a sort of psychic shell around our sensitive inner selves, but that naturally has an isolating effect that cuts us off from communication with the finer frequencies of spiritual living. Nowadays we hear a lot about environmental pollution and its hazards to human health, but we are insufficiently concerned with its inner equivalent, the psychic pollution in which we are forced to live by common circumstances. Future generations may become wiser than we are and give a great deal of serious attention to the problem, but it could be as well to anticipate their actions by some present perceptions of the problem. Common sense alone tells us that permanent living in a grimy atmosphere makes everything unpleasantly dirty so that we need frequent bathing and washing of clothes. Exactly that equivalent is true about living in contaminated consciousness. When faced with highly dangerous atmospheres charged with chemical or radioactive contaminants, humans dare not enter them unprotected by special clothing, which may even have its own container of air that is safe to breathe. Again there are psychic circumstances that necessitate comparable protective precautions. Whatever is possible in physical terms is duplicated by psychical counterparts. The laws of life have many levels, whereon everything repeats itself in appropriate terms.

In esoteric language, "building a Temple" means creating a clearance of consciousness with a minimum of contamination so that purely spiritual energies can be contacted therein as fully and freely as possible. This process can be considered as a fourfold one. Firstly as a self-structure, secondly a familial one, thirdly as denominational, and fourthly as a hoped-for esoteric ecumenical agreement among all sections of humanity. This movement must start with the individual and expand outward instead of being controlled from an external consortium and forced inward to exact conformity from all unwilling individuals. In other words, individual souls must prepare and condition themselves to work with groups that only seek extension in order to include others for the ultimate universal cause of companionship with Cosmos.

To some extent this could be compared with an underwater swimmer coming to the surface for periodic gulps of air in order to survive. Working as we do in an earthly atmosphere of psychic pollutants, we need to surface in spirit, so to speak, for a soulful of refreshment from time to time so as to survive without suffocation. Alternately we need to construct and live in a "survival suit" capable of connecting us with higher than human levels of life. Such suits are symbolized by the special ceremonial clothing assumed for esoteric activities or meditative exercises. Somehow the right ambience has to be reached before any intake or release of functional force becomes possible. The synthetic simulation of this ambience by physical symbolism is intended to assist the imaginative awareness, which actually accomplishes the arrangements of required self-states. That is to say, whatever may be said or done with externals must be internally reproduced by coincidental consciousness, or nothing of a psychic nature will have happened. It is quite useless to say words and manipulate material objects unless the maximum energies of intention and comprehension are accompanying the process. The acquisition and accomplishment of such an art is an absolutely primal part of Temple practice.

Fundamentally this art depends on what is known theatrically as the "suspension of disbelief and audience involvement," which is a basic necessity of our sentient nature. This peculiar capability is what makes us "alive" and active participants in the cosmos, whereas the diminution or lack of it results in disinterest, low vitality, and general ineffectuality. In modern parlance we are either turned on or off. The point at issue here is that such a process should be a controllable one and capable of being regulated to fine degrees by whatever may be thought, said, or done inside our Temples. Not only there of course, because the experience is a normal one of reaction with the circumstances of life according to whatever stimulus they may present. It becomes a question of presenting and applying such stimuli in the specialized conditions of a Temple, which are specifically designed to evoke the maximum self-states of those present for that purpose.

Let us look back a few years to the days of really powerful preachers. The average congregation had little enough to rouse or raise their spirits during their daily lives. They suffered from a lack of interesting stimulation, or what might be called spiritual malnutrition. The Sunday sermon was then a main means of supplying such stimulation. Whether the uttered words were true or not was neither here nor there. If the preacher could capture the interest and full attention of the audience, arousing feelings and emotions to a high pitch of action, that was the result the audience wanted. They luxuriated in the weekly experience while they underwent a sort of internal catharsis that left them feeling clean and satisfied to a delightful degree. Their general summing up was that they felt a lot better and improved because of what they had just undergone.

Few of them may have suspected, let alone realized,

that they had been enjoying the spiritual equivalent of a sexual experience, yet that is precisely what it was. The expert style of a skilled orator could supply all the needed elements: the wooing words, the suggestive and stimulating ones, the arousing and passionate phrases, the agonizing and intensified moans, the climacteric cries and ejaculatory exclamations, then the sudden silence followed by soothing and gentle assurances like a lover's lullaby at the very end. If the preacher was a good-looking man and used the right gestures of embracing, arousing, and pushing home his points, every woman present felt that she had been subjected to something that her husband or lover had never accomplished with a few indifferent thrusts and grunts. The subject matter of the sermon was entirely secondary to its style and the sequence of its stimuli. First interest, then arouse, intensify, climax, and finally soothe to satisfaction. It is scarcely surprising that one celebrated order of preachers is named the Passionists. The secret of successful preaching is euphemized sex tacitly recognized on both sides of the words. If churches and chapels were the only places this might be encountered, then they would indeed be filled to capacity.

That scarcely applies at all today, since preaching styles have altered altogether and so many substitutes are readily available. TV has mostly supplanted the theater's function of former times, although it will never fulfill a person's deep need for direct and intimate involvement in the direction of Divinity together with other human beings seeking the same advancement. People of that caliber realize very well the difference between a synthetic experience and a real one. Only participation in a "live" Temple can convert the one into the other: the real process is controlled with will according to intention. Thus it becomes a definite discipline in its own right, deserving every consideration from serious students of spiritual procedures. It is all a question of training.

Just as parade grounds and maneuver areas are specific places for training and producing soldiers, so are Temples constructed as suitable places for conditioning the consciousness of humans along spiritual lines that will both encourage and assist the development of inner characteristics most likely to result in enlightenment on every level. In both cases intensive effort is called for during repeated exercises of basic practice, which develops into specialized achievements of ability within the designated field of action. It is impossible to produce an effective soldier without field experience, or an effective esotericist apart from Temple experience, even if the Temple is limited to the physical body of the practitioner. Meditation therein is only movement of mind and soul working from a motionless body serving as a Temple environment for all the action within it.

Training for ceremonial procedures in conventional Temples of our Western Inner Tradition has been considerably dealt with in *Magical Ritual Methods* (Helios 1969, reprinted Weiser 1980), but there are many points that would bear expanding, clarifying, and reopening along other lines, besides some auxiliary information that may be of considerable help to those seeking esoteric expression through Temples of some sort. This work therefore is not so much seeking to supersede its predecessor as to augment it advantageously and enlarge on previous inadequacies while perhaps introducing fresh information.

Despite every advice to the contrary from experienced people, newcomers to the active areas of esotericism still seem to suppose that if they get enough gear together, wear the correct costumes, and persuade a few friends to share their amateur activities while they call themselves something exotic as a collective, wonderful things will surely happen. The best they are likely to get out of all this is a few evenings of entertainment spent to better social advantage than is the case with TV, and the worst is either disillusionment plus boredom, or perhaps a few bad frights due to the breakdown of unstable characters among them. If they come out of the whole experience with more good than bad to their credit, they will be either lucky or privileged. Temples can be either traumatic or transcendental experiences.

Somehow it never seems to strike ambitious amateurs that the best thing to do wold be to commence on a modest basis and work up the commonplace techniques of Temple procedures instead of leaping in at the luxury end and demanding direct manifestations of Deity itself, with all the trimmings. Failing that, a few assorted archangels might satisfy them, or they could be consoled by a common poltergeist provided *something* startling happens. It seldom dawns on them that if any kind of Temple could help them develop their inner qualities and characters to a significant degree, that would be the most remarkable fulfillment of its true function and a manifestation of Divinity *in themselves*. Only those who can clearly see this paramount point and who are prepared to work for it patiently and consistently are likely to get any real good out of their esoteric Temples.

Since there has to be a starting position somewhere, let us commence by discussing the general design of an average Wesoteric Temple. It is commonly constructed to represent the spiritual structure of the Greater Creation, or Macrocosmos, in which we live and move. This should be familiar to those who may never have entered one physically. Though it may be and probably is square or four sided, it is always considered to be circular and quaternate in nature to correspond with the quadruplicity of classification into which we divide our consciousness of ambient creation. This gives us a definable approach along which to relate anything containable in Cosmos that is attributable to any particular quarter. This is commonly called a frame of reference.

In other words, a convenient structure of consciousness that indicates where, when, how, and why to establish contact with any of the contents of Cosmos. Something like a "Directory of Divinity" showing the most direct connection between an enquirer and whatever item he/she is seeking in the containing Cosmic Consciousness.

The efficiency of this arrangement depends on the quality and accuracy of such a classification in the minds and souls of seekers. There obviously has to be some standard acceptable to enquirers, and this standard should be as familiar to every working Wesoteric as the letters of our alphabet and the way we combine them to make meaningful words. Though this may be so, the categories will be given again here for the sake of clarity and to show how they are arranged according to the seven divisions of space. (See Table 1 on page 44.)

With the aid of such concepts classified in a quaternary system, an entire cosmos of consciousness can be constructed, and in fact a genuine Wesoteric Temple *is* such a state of consciousness rather than a physical room and its ornaments, which represent that state. This distinction must be realized at the very commencement of training or the entire meaning of Temples will be missed altogether. Unless this particular point is hammered home until it becomes not only feasible but factual, no one will get any good from the most elaborate Temple ever assembled by the hands of humans. Again and again references are encountered that mention the Temple "not made with hands nor the sound of a hammer," and most readers seem to miss the point fairly widely.

Most Wesoteric Temples are far from being elaborate in physical terms. Their material symbology is liable to be sparse. Their quadrate proportions are often suggested by the walls, which are colored to match the seasons and have an appropriate symbol displayed on each, while the ceiling

TABLE 1

The Seven Divisions of Space

Direction	East	South	West	North	Up	Center	Down
Element	Air	Fire	Water	Earth	The Absolute	Human Life	Other Life
Symbol	Sword	Rod	Cup	Shield	Crown	Star	Cube
Season	Spring	Summer	Autumn	Winter			
Time	Dawn	Noon	Dusk	Night	Future	Present	Past
Tarot	Swords	Wands	Cups	Coins	Trumps	People	Pips
Vowel	E	I	O	A	W	U	Y
Principle	Life	Light	Love	Law	Plus	Neutral	Minus
Arch-angel	Raphael	Michael	Gabriel	Auriel	Metatron	Suvuviel	Sandalaphon
Color	Blue	Yellow	Red	Indigo	Ultraviolet	Visible	Infrared
Letters of Name	Yod	Vau	Heh	Heh	Aleph	Mem	Tau

and floor are suitably designed to show the heavens and the lower world. The central point is mostly marked by an altar with a lamp on it, although there is a modern tendency to place the altar in the Western quarter as a sanctuary, with a standard behind its displaying the aegis or emblem under which that particular Temple is offering its services. In this case the center is signified in some other way, such as by an upright Staff or crystal sphere. Apart from useful items like seating arrangements, side tables, lecterns and so forth, such are the average spatial outlines of a Western Temple. The temporal dimensions of course are regulated by the frequency of workings in it, and the eventual factor is governed by the type of service performed and the membership present. A really well balanced operative Temple should combine these three constituents of its cosmos as evenly and effectively as possible.

Like all cosmic phenomena a Temple is composed of time, space, and event components. It is, after all, a location in space wherein events occur at specific times, and if these components are to balance each other properly, then they must fit within their framework as perfectly as possible. That is to say, once a suitable place has been found, the right people have to find the right performance before everything will come together and form the right presentation. Place, people, and performance. Which should come first is as difficult to determine as is the most important leg of a three-legged stool. The only certainty is that they must either combine in a single individual or be forthcoming from those who can work the wonder together.

Many people are more concerned with making a physical Temple than they are with making themselves ready for one, which is not unlike setting up a technical workshop without the slightest skill, knowledge of how to proceed, or any experience with tools and equipment. Few people would be so stupid, and yet they will buy all sorts of expensive artifacts from "occult suppliers" in the vague hope that these objects will work all kind of wonders by themselves. Such hopes have about as much chance of fulfillment as those of a primitive Pagan who hangs a micrometer round his/her neck in the supposition that this would bring him/her a lot of luck and money. The interesting thing is that the strange fascination that "occult equipment" seems to arouse in certain souls shows their instinctive and possibly hereditary recognition of its symbolic significance. They will probably be most attracted to whatever symbol indicates their main deficiency of character because that is what they hope to compensate for by its possession or usage. For instance, someone whose chief spiritual disability is lack of love will be particularly fascinated by cups; and an indecisive and weak-willed person, by rods and swords. Such predilections clearly indicate a deep inner awareness of which activities would bring the most benefits to that particular soul. Mostly, however, there is more or less a general need for spiritual growth and character change in accordance with the symbology of any esoteric system.

This in itself is a good thing. It means that there is at least a tacit acknowledgment of dissatisfaction with one's own self-state, coupled with an unspoken appeal to a superior spiritual Life Power for help in a self-correction program. A human soul is admitting its imperfections and seeking some improvement in itself toward what might be thought of as Divinity. The beginning of all betterment. Up till recently in history, this would have been interpreted as a salutary admission of sin and guilt needing God's merciful forgiveness for wickedness worked against his grace and goodness. Though few esotericists would now accept the "sin against God" angle, most would agree that the sin, if any, was chiefly against the self for failing to make the best of inherited potentials and for neglecting to take advantage of opportunities. At all events, an unusual concern for, or pronounced involvement with, what is really the trivia of Temple paraphernalia usually indicates an inner state of disquiet on account of a disturbing need for spiritual satisfaction. This is certainly more preferable than seeking dubious chemical compensation with drugs, or self-assurances from aggression and antisocial behavior. Temple activities may be a lot slower to produce obvious results, but they are infinitely safer.

Looking back with hindsight, many may wonder why they did not stop to think everything over very carefully at the commencement of their involvement with esotericism and why they did not begin with the simple self-arrangements they had to learn in the end anyway and ultimately came to depend on for the rest of an incarnation. They could have saved so much time and money for more profitable activities, to say nothing of all the mental and spiritual energy wasted on unsystematic and pointless procedures. Before anything can be properly learned or studied, it should be discovered how and why to do so. We have to learn not only why to learn but also how to do so. Learning is an ability of consciousness just as living is an ability of the human body, and both have to be done by an intentional effort of whoever exists through their combination. First we have to adapt to this world by control and development of the body and all its functions; then the same process has to be repeated with the mind and soul. They are all interrelated, and if they were correctly geared to the same system, some remarkable people would probably be produced, but as it happens they seldom are.

We learn to use our bodies by trial and error with their functions and some assistance from adult humans. If we intend to specialize with them later on, we shall have to rely on specialists who have systematized physical training and know how to share the process. The same is true with minds; our awareness has to cope with concepts assembled from past experience and adapted to contemporary usage. Here we rely on professional teachers' presenting us with information we are supposed to accept without much questioning, plus some supplementary information reaching us from all sides, which we are supposed to sort out for ourselves, though we are seldom shown any dependable system of doing so. This is called education, the ability to lead our learning faculties out of ourselves into a semblance of order and at the command of consciousness. When it comes to spiritual teaching, however, human experience is relatively chaotic.

Here we are confronted with an incredible mass of mixed consciousness from all angles and levels of life, through which we have to pick our paths as carefully as we can. The thoughts we have to deal with come from every different time, place, and event that humanity has ever passed through, and probably from the future as well. This is not unlike being faced with crossing an expanse of quicksand by stepping on stones that are based on firm ground. Other stones are everywhere, but some may sink slowly and others rapidly or almost instantaneously. A slowly sinking stone gives a chance to find a firmer one, while a faster-sinking one affords proportionately less opportunity. In the end a struggling soul is left floundering erratically among them, sometimes nearly sinking altogether but occasionally perching precariously on one firm rock, frightened of moving away from it, yet realizing that a remorseless tide is slowly moving in to drown all those who have not crossed in time to save themselves from the advancing flood.

This analogy is not a bad one, because it further shows that successful followers of paths between such straits may have either marked the firm stones they found for the benefit of future pilgrims or provided a map of which stones were reliable and which were not. Firm stones, for instance, might only be reached by treading over temporary ones, some at a reasonable pace while others might only be traversed at considerable speed by swift and light people. The problem here is a classification of stones, since they have a nasty habit of shifting around between tides. This creates a great deal of uncertainty as to their properties and casts serious doubts on the reliability of many charts. Some of the old ones are still accurate essentially, though the dependable stones they indicate are so far apart that progression from one to the next is impossible for humans except by taking the perilous pathways between them. The Qabbalistic chart of the Tree of Life, for instance, shows ten absolutely firm stages from humanity to God, but the Paths or channels between them are full of problems and pitfalls.

The so-called great religions of this world are presented to their followers along such lines. They are founded on basic truths, but how to get from one to the next across the gaps separating them is frequently a matter of guesswork and experience that puzzles many mortals, especially those who have difficulty in dealing with more than one truth at a time or who are incapable of seeing any connection between them at all. It is when they approach the immediate problem of how to proceed from their present standstone to a proximal one that their difficulties are greatest. It is often a more complicated problem to move inches than miles, yet unless there are clear ideas covering the whole route, no one is likely to get anywhere worth arriving at. To say "To get from New York to India you have to go somewhat south across the Atlantic Ocean and then carry on over Africa and a few other places until you come to the next continent" might be true but is not in the least helpful. Only a complete itinerary with full details of all flights, stopovers, and details of costs would be of any value, and preferably it would include alternative routes, places of interest on the way, rates of exchange, and other such useful information. The equivalent of this in spiritual terms is frequently lacking or inadequate in many systems open to public membership.

Not that esoteric affairs are necessarily any better or more advantageous, but they usually go into much greater detail and specialize considerably more as well. They are not concerned with the mass-production methods more suitable for the average aggregate of humans, but they concentrate on individual evolvement and unusual characteristics developed for spiritual service to whichever concept of Divinity they are dedicated. Although such systems usually work through Temples for their congregational gatherings, all members are supposed to be trained in how to become such a Temple in themselves so that their entire lives become a constant celebration of the various services they carry out symbolically in psychodramatic form. In other words, all their Temple procedures are or should be actual patterns of life connected with the real spiritual powers and principles that underlie and activate our existence as people of some particular purpose. By setting these patterns up in our minds through practicing them in Temples, we alter ourselves accordingly and also make a significant impression on the currents of Cosmic Consciousness circulating through our own beings. A reciprocal response in the two-way direction of humano-Divine relationships.

Every human alive exists in a self-state, which might be termed a psychic force field much like the magnetic field in and around a magnet, yet a magnet is not alive in our sense of the word. A self-state is a condition of energy derived from a single Life Source and distributed through a great number of channels. It is every individual's relationship with *LIFE* and *life*, to signify the difference between major and minor conditions. That is to say, it is what we *are* at any given instant, and hence of primal importance to everyone on earth since it is the "I AM WHAT I AM" of us all. It is, however, very easily altered by so many different things, some impacting from outer sources and others from inner ones, so the average self-state is a balance between both. Keeping it more or less balanced is as much of an art as was keeping an early aircraft on an even course. A minor misfortune might be enough to cause a bad nose dive, or an overdose of optimism might send the craft into a dangerous sidespin. There are many parallels between manual control of a light aircraft and steering a self-state with safety. One day we might discover the spiritual equivalent of an autopilot, and then we may fly without fear through inner dimensions of spiritual space.

At present the nearest thing to an autopilot we have are the combined control symbols of a Wesoteric Temple. Apart from anything else, they represent the major qualities of a self-state that can be called to consciousness or "invoked" by humans with sufficient conditioned command over themselves. Like any other skill, that ability can be acquired by straightforward training and application, and it only requires enough determination coupled with an intelligently designed program in order to make this possible. The principles are simple enough.

Through psychodramatic exercises, the trainee is conditioned to associate each of the symbols with a definite quality of a human self-state. This association is vitally necessary to a balanced and harmonious condition of being. Their mutual relationships are taken into account and combined to form a favorable total. Eventually this originally imaginative procedure becomes a usable psychic reality amenable to the command of whoever intends it. This is no more than a perfectly normal process of conditioning deliberately applied to obtain specific spiritual results. Temples of every denomination apply it to their congregations, frequently in a haphazard and generalized way. The esoteric way is simply a carefully calculated one intended to obtain positive results from particular types of people in the most reasonable period of time-space-event circumstances.

Let us consider what the average Wesoteric Temple is expected to do for those human members who attend regular services in its precincts. We will presume it provides them with a background philosophy of ethics and a code of conduct that they are asked to agree with in at least broad principles. If it is a Christian church they are given a focal figure in the person of Jesus as a savior and exemplar, a paternalistic deity, and a power called the Holy Spirit. A triune concept of energy expressed as a sentient superbeing. Having set up this "faith framework," acquiescent members are called on to congregate at set times for Christian conditioning.

This normally involves being dressed in neat and presentable clothing, obtaining the correct service books, and taking their individual places in church on their best behavior. The place will be furnished according to their denomination, which allows for very considerable variation, but generally finds them facing some kind of Christian symbol, such as a cross, on or above an altar. Somewhere between that point and the congregation is likely to be a very prominent pulpit, or preaching place, from which the priest, pastor, or minister is supposed to expound scriptural or doctrinal matters. There will also be a convenient place for musicians or vocalists who will lead and back up the congregational efforts at sonic harmony.

The average pattern of Christian worship has only three elements to it. Praying, preaching, and singing. All are purely verbal procedures and depend for success on comprehension of, and reaction with, the meanings of the words. There may also be some visual stimulus from the environment itself, depending on the denomination, but the greatest proportion of conditioning comes from word appeal augmented by music and rhythm. It is seldom that these factors are assembled with great precision as to detail, and a conventional Christian mostly has to select whatever may be wanted and make the best of it.

In the case of esoteric Temples the same factors are present, though in highly specialized forms employed in accordance with whatever spiritual system the much smaller congregations may be following. As a rule, two main Christian features are absent altogether: preaching and paying. Normally the former is confined to lectures or discussions quite apart from Temple practice, and the latter comes as contributions collected however seems most practical outside the Temple itself. In many Temples there is a custom that money must not enter in any form, which presumably applies to credit cards and checkbooks. Thus all Temple procedures will concentrate entirely on the mystical methodology of the humans in question. Most of these humans regard this as a considerable advantage over the conventional Christian intrusions of collecting money during a service and listening to the personal opinions of a professional preacher paid for his oratorical abilities.

The main reasons why an esoteric minority preferred to separate themselves from what they regarded as "orthodox oppression" from ruling religions were an enforced ideology they did not agree with, and a blatantly profiteering and corrupt priesthood. Most independent mystics regarded it as normally wrong to practice either compulsion or coercion on their fellow beings, and there is no doubt that official churches of all creeds were doing both with increasing impunity. Esoterics objected to having their minds and souls compulsorily controlled and their money confiscated by authoritarians claiming exclusive rights to spiritual salvation and sole ownership of secrets guaranteed to gain special favors from God. So they opted out and supported their private Temples, wherein they sought Divinity by every different way they had discovered. The irony of all this was that in cases where the grouping grew large enough to exert considerable power over a biggish membership body, most of them became guilty of exactly the same spiritual tyranny practiced by the churches they had abandoned. We may be reminded of a very significant cartoon depicting a Puritan landing in North America, with a loaded musket in hand, and exclaiming: "Thank God, free from religious persecution in Europe at last! Now where's those filthy heathen Indians?"

Like Christians, Wesoterics constructed patterns of consciousness for themselves in their Temples, but in conformity with an arrangement of spiritual principles symbolized by the Temple itself combined with their ceremonial clothing. This was worked out as follows. Above their heads the Crown and their headgear represented the acme of reason and respect for the Sovereign Spirit. Below their feet the floor and their footwear signified the spiritual standpoint on which their faith was based. The star on their breasts and the flame of the altar stood for the inspiring illumination of their ideology. The Sword of the East called up their qualities of keenness, flexibility, and good temper, plus every ability of attack called for to combat antagonists. The Rod-Staff of the South showed their qualities of uprightness and directness, plus the need to probe every point with care before relying on it for support. The Cup of the West contained their qualities of love and companionship for each other and the cause they served, while the Shield of the North showed how they should defend each other, to the death if need be, with care and caution. Lastly, the cord they wore around their waists reminded them of how to tie all this ideology around themselves in a centralized Middle Way manner.

None of this will work by itself, and although symbol conditioning is possible by attending sufficient services in a Temple, it is best to practice it at home until it becomes second nature. This can actually be done by drawing them on paper and meditating about them, but it makes a much more pleasing exercise if one uses a miniature set of symbols that can be easily handled. It is essential that the full significance of each symbol be completely comprehended before beginning any exercise with them, which has been dealt with in detail in other works but it will not hurt to recapitulate the information here for the sake of completeness.

1. THE CROWN. Assumption of this symbol signifies reaching an arrival at the apex or maximum meaning of anything. There has to be a peak point that is the very most a human can attain in some particular direction at any period. The summit of striving so to speak. Such a point will naturally vary with every different being alive, yet the principle would be the same. It will vary with the same individual over different time-space-event circumstances, and the top ability for one soul might be bottom ability for another. So the Crown symbol is to be understood as the maximum that a human may reach at any given instant.

In esoteric work this is generally taken to mean the closest that its wearer is able to approach God or imagine the Ideal Identity. That is why the symbol adopted by pious Jews is a prayer cap, or yarmulke, since with it they invoke their Deity as Faithful King, whose symbol is the Crown. Its assumption does not mean that its wearer has a very wonderful grasp of God, but signifies that he is at least striving to reach his own highest concept of a directing deity. Every symbol should be a visible sign of the invisible energy being expended to reach what it represents.

There has always been a human instinct that God, or whatever, is somehow up there in the heavens, and this undoubtedly stems from our genetic memories of the Star Home from which we originally came and toward which we have been subconsciously directing ourselves ever since.

Small wonder that celestial phenomena have been objects of worship from time immemorial, and people still seek relations with them via astrology and related symbology such as lucky birthstones. As our heads are the part of our bodies normally nearest the heavens and are the house of our brains, which govern our bodily beings, the head ornament of a crowning cap signifies the rulership of righteousness, which should control our conduct as creatures of Cosmos.

Our highest human ability is self-government, and without it we amount to very little. Madhouses and asylums are full of people who cannot govern themselves to any satisfactory social degree. Self-government has many forms, and we may be proficient at one yet lacking in others. For instance, some people might be very good at governing their musculature and physical functions while being notably deficient in moral or social control. Again, the highest form of human government is a spiritual one which exerts its influence on all lesser forms, summing them up into a single consortium of consciousness subject to a crowning control. Just as all the differently functional nerves of the body should come under the single command of the human self they are supposed to serve, so must those who seek to serve the Supreme Spirit come under its control in an appropriate fashion, and this is symbolized by the Crown of consciousness. Whoever assumes it in any Temple practice should imply thereby:

> I am putting this on my head not to make me look important but to demonstrate by a practical action that I am willing to rule myself as I believe you require. If I am right, then assist me, and if I am wrong, correct me. In either case, guide me. I realize that self-rulership is a responsibility I must accept and a burden I must bear with honor if I ever intend to become any higher than a

human being. Spirit of Life and Light, crown my consciousness with the illumination of Understanding Wisdom.

Any such thoughts are appropriate when directing them to the top of a Temple, where the Crown of Light symbol should be located, or to one's own head when assuming its representative in the form of a headdress. These are usually skullcaps ornamented as seems best for the system being served. They should never be carelessly crammed on without a single thought being spared concerning their significance, nor for that matter should any other wearable or portable symbol be employed until at least a minimum of thinking has energized it. This may take a little time at first, but with a bit of practice, will only occupy a moment of time yet be deep enough to be effective.

The correct procedure in this case is to take the physical cap between both hands so that its edges are folded inwards, which is suggestive of a female sex organ. Maybe this hints at the wonders and mystery of life emerging from the eternal womb of nature. Opening the cap out to view its empty interior might suggest the contents of a brain with no worthwhile thoughts in it. Placing it firmly on the head with both hands and adjusting it could call to mind all the responsibility it represents, plus a feeling that only special thoughts should occupy the mind while wearing it. Remove the cap and start thinking trivialities, then replace it and alter the thinking entirely to sacred subjects. Repeat this until it becomes a procedural pattern. Should unsuitable thoughts occur while the cap is being worn, remove it at once; then after altering the thinking, replace the cap firmly. The idea is to associate the physical item with spiritual thinking alone. Eventually the exercise should be tried with no cap at all, but just the fingers and palms of both hands smoothing back the hair from the forehead and resting on the crown of the head. Lastly it may be tried with one hand only.

2. THE CUBE. Theoretically this is the stone on which one stands because it is the firmest foundation of one's faith, based on rock-solid principles instead of shaky ground or shifting sands. No house is any stronger than its foundation, and here is signified the most trustworthy of spiritual standpoints available to an individual. In practice the symbol of the cube signifies the floor of the Temple and the sandals or slippers on one's feet. (The sandals should have square toes and buckles.) Factually it is the feeling of firmness between one's feet and the floor, which is sometimes patterned with black and white squares. Each square is big enough for one person to stand on and is conventionally assumed to be the top of a solid cube. Each cube is assumed to be composed of six solid pyramids with their points meeting in the center. Masonically these cubes are considered to be ashlars, or building blocks, each representing a human being. Some (the black ones) are regarded as rough or presenting the condition of an ordinary man, and others as being "finished" or smooth, with polished sides so that they will fit together without need of mortar. This is said to show how humans ought to assemble themselves together as the most splendid of all Temples, bonded by brotherly love alone. Getting himself into this sort of shape is supposed to be the work allotted to every Mason. Hence the saying "There's a divinity that shapes our ends, rough-hew them how we will."

The esoteric association to be made with the Cube symbol is with one's basic faith foundation at rock bottom. There is a tendency nowadays to deny such a possibility altogether and claim that if nothing spiritual can be proved to the satisfaction of a scientific enquirer, then all beliefs must necessarily be false and so we should believe in nothing. To believe firmly enough in a nil-space, nil-time, and nil-event universe would actually be the same as believing in Infinite Entity, and in fact to demand proof in terms that are utterly unreasonable is unscientific in itself. If the evidence of Creation itself is insufficient for assuming that some kind of Superconsciousness is responsible, then where is the sense of being asked to believe that humans are the highest form of existing intelligence and the only ones of their species in an entire galaxy? Are there humans conceited enough to believe this seriously? Strange to say—yes there are.

The forms of anyone's faith may certainly be fallible, but what really matters are the fundamentals behind and underneath one's formalized and expressed ideology. Should such a "rock bottom" seem uncertain, the thing to do is accept a temporary set of workable beliefs with the proviso "These will serve me until I have reason to alter them into improved ideology." In other words, set up what scientists term a "working hypothesis," or a collection of concepts that appear to cover the area of investigation satisfactorily. Here we come back to the analogy of the firm and sinking stones. Provided we can find one that will bear our spiritual weight for a prolonged period, that will serve as a spiritual support until we have good reason for changing our standpoint. Nothing on this earth is eternal and the earth, like ourselves, has a limited life. Nevertheless quite a number of standpoints have lasted for many centuries or maybe millennia, so there should be no shortage of choices when one is seeking relatively firm footholds in spiritual dimensions.

The type of associated exercise to practice at this point would be to plant the feet very firmly on the floor, visualize one's chosen basics of belief very clearly, and think something on the lines of Luther's famous words "Here stand I, I cannot do otherwise." Go on to enlarge to: "This is what I firmly believe at present, and only the very best reasons could make me change that. It supplies my faith in life and gives me grounds for basing myself on what I feel is spiritually solid enough to last my lifetime. As my feet have to support my body, so does my belief support my soul. May I always find some good grounds wherever I may wander through the ways of living and serving the Supreme Spirit."

A symbolic Cube should have one's creed engraved or imprinted on it, because any firm creed should be composed of whatever concepts form a fundamental life faith. A creed is a spiritual standpoint that is represented by the Cube, and many esoteric concerns have their creeds condensed into neat composite symbology such as the Masonic Square and Compasses, or the Cosmic Cross and Rose. They could also be combined as buckles on the shoes, or otherwise linked with basic behavior. Again, the creed could be recited while treading any pattern on the floor, doing dance steps, or just tapping the feet on the floor while thinking things out. Anything that associates footholds with faith and firmness.

It would also be possible to have one white and one black slipper appropriately embellished, and work out some complicated footwork on the Temple floor arranged as the "checkerboard of nights and days" on which the dance of destiny may be done. Before attempting this, however, it is best to persist with much simpler practices until the concepts of finding an acceptable creed while wearing the footgear, in which many paths may be plodded, are welded into one unit of consciousness. It is always possible to elaborate *after* essential basics have been properly assimilated. Perhaps it might help to think of ceremonial footwear as "Path plodders" or maybe "searchers and faithfinders." Right and left footcovers might even be given different names, such as "Stride" and "Glide," to signify the methodology of progression. All sorts of procedures are possible with whatever is worn on the feet provided that it enhances or emphasizes the main ideology.

While we are considering the lower extremities it may be well to mention that seasonal color changes may be necessary. Light green socks are appropriate for spring, dark green for summer, russet for autumn, and dark brown or black for winter. Also, trouser legs should never be seen beneath the lower edges of the robe. They must be kept well turned up, and if need be, secured with elastic bands. Few things look worse than ill-chosen socks on celebrants or participants in any ceremony. For private practice of course, sock color is immaterial, though correct procedures are always advisable for their own sake.

In olden times it was generally considered that the left or sinister foot was the unlucky one, and people had to be very careful in placing their right feet forward first when starting any journey, and especially in crossing a threshold. The fact that one had to stop and think "I mean to go the right way in this direction" would have its own effect on forthcoming progress. As an intention enforcer, this small practice of placing the feet in what was considered a favorable position would certainly have made a useful contribution to the harmony of the proceedings. Movements of the physical feet tied up with movements of faith as well. A faith was always *followed*, implying that feet would bring the body and soul wherever the light of that faith led. Such was symbolized by the central balancing Star between our earthly and heavenly extremities, which we shall see symbolically as the lamp and Lamen.

3. THE STAR. This, the most significant symbol, calls for the least explanation, since its ideology is really beyond much human description. Essentially it signifies the central "Light Within," which motivates humanity in as many ways as there are humans to hold it. Its physical symbols are the lamp of the altar and the Lamen on the breast of whoever serves it, which could be a whole congregation. This breastplate is frequently in the form of a pentacle or "Star of Man," with the upright point representing a flame, the body of the pentacle/Star representing the lamp beneath, and the two lower points signifying supporting feet. The altar lamp is seldom in the shape of a hexagram or "Star of God," although it should be so considered however it is formed.

As a rule, the Lamens worn by ceremonialists in esoteric Temples take the shape of whatever symbol represents the spiritual system they are serving. Thus a Christian would have a crucifix or plain cross, a Rosicrucian the Rose Cross, and so forth. Though all are differently designed, each typifies the Inner Light as experienced by their wearers, and this is the associative idea to aim for by every exercise imaginable. Thoughts should be along these lines:

> This emblem signifies my spiritual origin and hoped-for end in Eternity. If humanity came from the stars in the first place and must eventually return thence when this planet is no longer possible for us, then let this symbol stand for my inner instinct that enlightens me on this quest and guides me Godward. I know that if I follow this faculty faithfully enough, it will lead me to the ultimate aim I seek, for it cannot do otherwise. This little light bears in itself the sign of my salvation and I must keep in sight at all times, however dim it may seem to me. If I lose track of it I may lose myself at the same time, for it represents the Divine Spark that is really *me*. A God-glow as it were. Sometimes it may seem bright, and at other times feeble, but so long as it shines at all, it will ensure my spiritual safety. It is literally the Light of my Life, and the most important item of my identity. It and I are *one*.

The physical action of association may be made by hanging the Lamen on its chain around the neck and lighting a small candle or lamp, preferably one with a red glass to signify the Light behind the Blood. The Lamen could factually be a lapel badge or a brooch with a stick-pin, and small lamps with colored glasses are easily obtained. The important thing is that it should be a living flame and not any sort of electric illumination, which would be a totally wrong symbology. While lighting the flame one might think something like: "If the big bang theory is true, everything in existence is really made out of Light, and that includes *me*. I could say that I am constructed out of solidified Light and that all my thinking is an illumination of intelligence. Therefore I am lighting this lamp to represent the Living Spirit, of which I am a very minor miniature myself. *Let There Be Light!*"

It makes a nice gesture if the match is struck on a stone that came from some sacred site, although the ancient flint and steel combination is technically observed by the use of a modern lighter. It could be well to remember that just as light and fire began our civilization, so is light about our oldest symbol of Divinity or Superhumanity, and is something very special to think about. It represents the best of our intelligence, the finest of our culture, and the purest potentials of all we are or ever will be. We liken light to God and good, whereas darkness signifies the Devil and sin. The Star symbolizes the Light in Darkness, and is therefore a sign of salvation. Christians could think of the fabled star of Bethlehem leading the Magi to the Light of the World.

We forget too frequently that stars are suns and have the right to be considered as such. In that light we have to see them as central energies of other solar systems, power sources for people. Without them we could not live at all, and without the central Source of Life in every embodied soul, none of us could exist. Whatever that may be, we might as well call it *God*, however we misuse the word. The Star symbols hanging on our breasts represent evidence that at least we openly acknowledge such a presence in ourselves, however much we dare not claim to understand it. Now we must consider the inner environments with which we must relate ourselves and that radiant central Energy.

4. THE SWORD. This is really our attentive engagement with all the problems, dangers, and difficulties we have to face and fight in this world. This can be almost constant, calling for every faculty of keenness and alertness at our command. Like a Sword, we have to be sharp, flexible, pointed, and ready to defend ourselves in all directions. The physical Sword symbol is simply a signal for us to evoke those necessary qualities in ourselves.

We might also remember that the Sword is synonymous with the Arrow, which is calculated to keep danger at a distance if it can be dealt with that way. Arrows represent the flight of thoughts, and to this day we use arrows to direct attention or indicate something in particular. Nowadays they may be marks on paper, but in principle they are still arrows. Arrows at a distance and swords for close combat—both combine and connect all ideas of keeping hostile influences at bay by making ourselves into difficulties they would prefer not to tangle with. All creatures of any kind have the natural right of self-defense when their existence is threatened, and the Sword or Arrow symbols show our right of self-defense by spiritual means if we feel our lives are endangered on that level.

In older times humans fought with and killed each other in defense of what they believed were their spiritual liberties, which really amounted to their own opinions of religious ideology involved with commercial and political advantages. So-called religious wars were invariably motivated by human greeds and material gains concealed beneath cloaks of holy hypocrisy. Nevertheless, when humans feel that their souls are being seriously threatened or oppressed by other humans for whatever reason, it is amazing what lengths they will go to in defense of their Deity-concepts. They seldom, if ever, see that their best beliefs are threatened most of all by themselves and that their spiritual Swords would be put to better use if employed to control their own worst natures. Therefore thoughts connected with these symbolic weapons should reflect the following:

> This Sword signifies the control I need to keep over my own ill-conduct and the sharp supervision I would expect my spiritual superiors to maintain over me. I know that we humans have a negligent nature and can seldom keep fully awake and alert to all the perils we encounter on our paths through life. Let me hope that the Sword of God will prick me to full wakefulness at moments of danger and inspire me how to deal with it inside myself. If I can be confident that I can fully trust a finer Sword than mine to fight for me in preservation of the principles I seek to serve with honor, then I shall strive with all my strength of soul until the end of everything. If I can see the mark at which to aim the arrows of my noblest intentions, then I will fire them frequently in that direction in the hope of hitting what may help me most. Now let this symbol of a Sword suffice to stir me spiritually so that I shall look for truth and keep on questing for it everywhere.

All this and similar thinking should be accompanied by handling a physical Sword symbol, which could factually be a common paperknife. Its point may be felt with a fingertip or motions made with it that have some special significance for the holder. Every effort must be made to associate the symbol of a Sword with abilities of spiritual self-defense from all sensible standpoints. On no account, however, should harming other humans vindictively or needlessly be visualized. As for example, injuring others whose religious or cultural opinions differ from one's own. The principal place to look for opposition is inside oneself. The Sword symbol could be thought of in terms of a scalpel searching for diseased tissue or malignant growths to excise from one's soul so that healthier and happier conditions will prevail. That is one of the most advisable ways to think of the Sword symbol.

The use of a Sword causes pain that may bring distress, but its use can also save as well as take lives. If, say, a foot is caught in a deadly trap and only the severance of an ankle will ensure timely release, that deed must be done as swiftly as possible. An actual example is the case of an Australian farmer who was bitten on a finger by a lethal snake. Since he was chopping wood at the time, it was almost less than a second before he had chopped the finger off at its root before killing the serpent with the same axe. He lived to tell the tale. Surgeons are saving countless lives around the world everyday with their Sword-scalpels, and if it might hurt somewhat to dig a bit of harm out of ourselves with their equivalents on a spiritual scale, so much the better in the long run. There is such a thing as helpful hurting, and that should always be kept in mind during associative exercises with the Sword symbol.

The archangel-ideas in connection with the symbols are helpful here because their invocation helps to conceptualize the characteristics of whichever symbol is in question. It may be difficult to see Raphael, who is a reputed healer, as a being with a Sword until we discover that he specializes in healing *wounds* that are normally made with sharp edges. If all cutting implements are to be classed under a Sword heading, what about scythes, which help harvest grain, or knives, which cut up our food, or saws and chisels, which work with wood? Our Sword symbol applies to any such physical category and all mental or spiritual equivalents also. This has to be carefully considered during esoteric exercises while playing around with a paperknife and trying to translate its inner meanings comprehensible by higher than human types of consciousness. That makes good value to be obtained from such a small item often found in a desk tray. Near it might be lying the next symbol.

5. THE ROD. Perhaps in the shape of a cylindrical ruler or a pointer of any sort. This symbol has so many meanings, yet signifies basically our best qualities of straightness and right rulership so commonly associated with honest and upright humans worthy of anyone's complete confidence and trust. We usually associate Rods with rulers to this day, and they were once borne by kings and commanders to show their office and order respect for it from less important mortals. It means that we are being entrusted with the command of our own faculties, and how well or badly we do this will determine our fate as humans.

Rods can be correctors of conduct if applied the right way, with sufficient severity to sting but with no intent of actual injury. They can probe paths ahead to give timely warning of weakness or hidden dangers. As sticks or staffs they offer us support, while as pointers they signify investigative intelligence. As tool handles they provide a means of bringing our skills to bear on whatever we want to shape for our use. There are thousands of different applications of the Rod principle to consider. Maybe it might mean the mythical lever long enough to lift the world, or the trunk of the World Tree itself. It was certainly the fabled baculus with which Prometheus brought fire from heaven after Zeus put humanity into cold storage. No wonder the symbol is regarded as the root of all magical powers. It has good reason to be.

Nor should we forget that the Rod represents a rigid phallus, which is the normal means of human fertility. Without such an ability humans would be unable to reproduce themselves unless artificial insemination were constantly employed. A flaccid phallus was a very frighening thing in olden times, for which the worst type of witchcraft was usually blamed and innocent victims killed in consequence. It was also one of the worst insults to imput impotence to any male who valued his reputation among men. The word *virility*, which we use to signify sexual potency, derives from the Latin *vir*, "a man," because of his erectile member. Strictly speaking, a boy becomes a man at his first erection and ejaculation, just as a girl becomes a woman at her first menstruation. The Rod is a symbol of man erect in more senses than one.

Co-equal with physical fecundity, the Rod should signify such an ability on inner levels of life also. Mental and spiritual factors ought to "be fruitful and multiply" as well. Ideas and qualities can increase and grow up quite as much as children. The Rod symbol relates with all these variations of itself, everyone of which should be sought by everyone trying to make the best use of Temple facilities. Thoughts should be along these lines:

> This Rod represents everything in and around me with enough energy to arouse my capabilities of creative consciousness. It rules and regulates my conduct, measures the reach of my mind, stands for my most spiritual faculties, and it means my kingship, pointing to the Royal Blood I bear from my most ancient ancestry. When I hold it in my hands it indicates my royal responsibilities and tells me that I must command myself before I dare decree what other humans should attempt.

A long time ago, primitive humans helped themselves to stay upright by means of staffs and thus
began the magic of humanity's evolution. The
Rod was the first instrument that helped us to
control the fatal element of Fire; since that time
we have progressed until our present point of
peril: we have fixed a form of Fire that can destroy
us in a flash. This symbol of a Rod means all I ever
may accomplish by applied intelligence and
educated inspiration. It points to every letter of
each law there is to learn in life. It guides my
glance to wherever I should look for some enlightenment. It may chastise me if I need correc-
tion, but it will not bruise or brutalize me. I respect
its sexual implications as a sign of life and our gift
of generation so that the human race may live on
earth until we shall evolve elsewhere as better
beings altogether. Let the symbolism of a Rod
mean all of this to me and much, much more as I
have any hope of comprehending what it points
at.

While thoughts like that are passing through the mind,
bodily fingers and hands ought to be occupied with whatever
form the physical representation of a Rod may take. That
symbol could be a pen capable of writing such thoughts
down on paper, or a brush to paint them with. Perhaps it
might be a simple pointer like a thin rod with a tiny right
hand having an extended forefinger at the end of it. Such
pointers were once used for following the scriptural writings
letter by letter on the sacred Scrolls lying on reading desks
in synagogues. This practice avoided anyone's contaminating the parchment with greasy fingers. The miniature hands
were mostly of ivory or silver, and they had the effect of
enhancing respect for what was regarded as the Word of
God. Some are still in use today.

No folktale would be complete without mention of magic wands or Rods, and no modern magician of the stage variety would dare be entirely without one if she/he expected to keep credibility with children. Yet who can deny the sexual symbology of placing one end of a Rod into an apparently empty hat, giving a quick stir, and then pulling all sorts of objects out of it immediately afterwards. That is about the most blatantly Freudian phenomenon of all effects, though it is seldom seen in that light by adult audiences, who should instinctively recognize the symbology. It should be seen by now that both Sword and Rod are distinctly masculine symbols, while the next two, the Cup and Shield, are feminine. The Rod is the complementary partner for the Cup, as the Sword is for the Shield. Also, the masculine symbols are chiefly concerned with the intellect and action, while the feminine ones stand for emotive and protective instincts. In correct combination with each other, they make a complete circle of creative consciousness around the human race. After sufficient familiarity has been gained with the Rod, one's attention may be turned to the first feminine symbol.

6. THE CUP. Here we should see immediately the principle of a container. The womb in women, receptivity in men, and a capacity for loving care in all creatures. The Cup symbolizes the Sangreal, or vessel of every virtue possible for humans. It specially indicates whoever bears the Blessed Blood, which all souls relating themselves with Cosmos can share in kinship with creation. The Cup represents the nearest condition to an ideal heaven that we are likely to find on this earth. It signifies a spiritual state of sheer love far beyond anything we could imagine with our minds, and we might only experience a trace of it with our souls extended to their fullest capacity. Few mortals could endure that state very long without breaking apart. Excruciating pain can kill in its extremity, and so can the pressure of maximum bliss, which cannot be borne by unaccustomed mortals. The Cup symbolizes the greatest bliss that may be endured by humans in spiritual safety, but it must be considered as enlargeable to any extent that human capacity is capable of reaching. Perhaps we might also think of it as containing the Elixir of Life, with the statutory warning "It is dangerous to exceed the stated dose."

The Cup signifies our capability of love in terms of liquidity just as its complementary symbol, the Rod, measures the reach of our intellect in terms of length and reach. The Shield of course indicates breadth and area of coverage, while the Sword or Arrow marks the exact point of position where all the action and attention are concentrated within a collection of consciousness. Nothing but the Cup, however, conveys the sense of companionship and conviviality that makes life really worthwhile as a spiritual experience. We associate Cups with cheerfulness whether they contain a welcome wine or just a friendly cup of tea. We also associate them with some success, especially in sports or athletic events, wherein they are modern descendants of the ancient cauldrons that were once won for outstanding conduct in competitive games of all kinds.

In fact, the physical symbol that may be handled for conditioning the consciousness of a ceremonialist may be a miniature of such cups, which are sold by most sports shops, or it may be a metal eggcup or similar item. Whatever conveys the concept of a special Cup standing for everything believed to be fine, friendly, and all we are fondest of in life. Perhaps a small vessel given by a much-loved companion. Those are the associations to be thought of while looking at it, holding it in the hands, or maybe sipping something pleasant from it. Especially the idea of sharing whatever is best in ourselves with other souls who will be glad of this. The old adage "A sorrow shared is a sorrow halved, but a joy shared is a joy doubled." Memories of past pleasures should be recalled, and expectations of future happiness hoped and prayed for. Somehow the Cup must be made a symbol for spiritual splendors past, present, and to come. Thinking patterns ought to run along these lines:

Human existence may be a strange mixture of sorrow and joy both drunk from the same Cup of experience, but it has to be drained to the very dregs as I drink, in common with everyone I share it with. At least I am not alone, and this is the Cup of companionship with those others I would most willingly share it with. I need love more than anything life has to offer, and without it I would be empty, desolate, and altogether abandoned. This is the Cup that brings the blessing of Blood brotherhood, which saves me from a solitary, sad, and miserable state of isolation in my own identity alone. While I can keep contact with the concept I shall never feel neglected or forsaken by the Power of Providence. It is true that the Cup can be a bitter one upon occasion, but it always brings experience that will enlighten me and bring me good in some eventual way. I may not like this, but I have to learn whatever lessons it is sent to teach me in a spiritual shape for the improvement of my soul and the enlargement of my spirit. Most of all I value the inestimable blessing of the Blood relationship this symbol shows that I should have with God and mortals, sharing the communion of a common spiritual consciousness among us all. This is the most precious thing that I possess in my whole life upon this planet. It is all that makes life bearable as an embodied being. Apart from this, what hope is there for our humanity together? This Cup alone is everything that offers any confidence in life or holds out hopes of betterment beyond our bodies into spiritual states of an Elysian existence. I am therefore holding the most precious, valuable, prized, and vital symbol of eventual perfection. May it bless me always.

The Cup concept may indeed be our best hope in this world for any future human happiness, and it may also be our last hope in that direction of finding anything divine in ourselves. Usually many people have something they hold on to with a kind of desperation as a sort of "last hope" talisman that might bring them good luck in life-or-death situations. It was incredible what wartime airmen and soldiers would carry in their pockets as mascots. In Wesotericism the symbol of the Cup bears such a significance for those who honor it as a sign of the Blessed Blood among them. The Cup may be plenty of other things as well, such as the Cornucopia, the Magic Cauldron, or whatever offers some especial potion to partake of, but it is essentially a container of liquid, and always holds somthing very potent in it. Sometimes the liquid is a healing brew, sometimes it is a very bitter draught that has to be swallowed to effect an intended alteration to its consumer, but it is the *capacity* of a cup that is essentially important. All are expected to measure themselves spiritually by comparison with its capacity. We speak of souls as being "deep" or "shallow," as if they had liquid meaning, and we talk about our "last drop of blood" as an absolute ultimate. Without the implication of a cup those comments would mean nothing at all.

Possibly the Cup is most familiar to us as the Grail or Greal, that wonderful mystic container or vessel of uncertain appearance but of surpassing spiritual sweetness and ineffable joy. All stories connected with the Grail apply to the Cup symbol, and any of these stories may be thought of while the little physical cup is being handled. Like a chalice, the Cup is always held with both hands except momentarily. This is really a precaution against dropping it, but it makes for more meaningful gestures. The thing never to do is invert the Cup completely. It may be poured or libated, but not turned upside down entirely. That reverses its meaning altogether and signifies trouble.

All these thoughts and actions are to be combined and woven into a meaningful pattern of maximum significance for its maker. What really matters is the effect on the humans concerned. Since people are impressed or influenced by such a diversity of things, it is best if each individual relates the symbols to terms of special significance to him/her if possible. For instance, a very sexually oriented man might see the Rod as his penis, the Cup as his partner's vagina, the Sword as their teeth, and the Shield as their skin. Though there are much better meanings than those, they would serve if nothing else would do. This may sound Freudian, but could be workable until improved ideology put something more spiritual in its place. After considering the Cup most carefully from all possible angles, we must turn our attention to the next symbol.

7. THE SHIELD. This symbol is sometimes called the Platter, Disc, Coin, or Pentacle. In principle it is simply a flat plate or frequently round surface, often polished, ornamented with a design and mostly made of metal, though sometimes wood is used. This symbol varies greatly in size, from a convenient coin to a full body-sized shield. At one time it completely covered the body since it was borne around to protect its possessor from hostile actions. Since humans did not have any shells of their own they had to get some from somewhere else, and it is conceivable that very primitive Shields were gigantic shells from large tortoises or turtles.

The fundamental ideology of this symbol is protection

and preservation by means of shelter. It was something to place between oneself and an aggressor or, for that matter, to hold in front of someone whose life was valued very highly, such as a king. It also served useful functions like bearing anything around between two people sharing the same burden. The saying "Bear ye one another's burdens" applies very much here. In theory a Shield applies to anything with a protective purpose. We talk about a *heat shield* or, in sports, a *gumshield*. A connected word is *screen*, and there are millions of those for every kind of reason all around the world.

For instance, a common blanket could be classed as a Shield quite accurately, because it protects from cold and draughts. So might a raincoat or a diving suit, which excludes water and dampness. There are endless physical examples of Shields everywhere, and we should not have got far in this world without them. How long would an unshielded baby last in the frozen North? Or a stark naked astronaut in space? Most of us would have perished without our artificial "skins"; we are such fragile folk without our clothes.

The sort of spiritual Shield we should find in our Temples, however, is a great deal more subtle. It is constructed by and of consciousness alone, and in one way represents every misfortune and accident that has been averted from all people present. The "slings and arrows of outrageous fortune" either dodged or stopped by the "hand of God" or prevented by the intervention of fate. Perhaps one may never be certain what it is, but the protective effect is as if a merciful Providence were indeed watching over helpless humans caringly. Millions of people would have multimillions of strange tales to tell of incidents that could come into such a category.

Again and again we find references to this protective Power or singular spiritual influence that seems to save some humans from harm while others are perishing all around them. It could be interesting to calculate the circumstances and how often any particular person has been rescued from ruin during a long lifetime, often by the most narrow margin, and then work out the odds against those rescues. Of course the opposite possibility of a single fatal accident in unlikely circumstances must also be taken into account, but on the whole the balance would be in favor of the fortunate. Whatever saves them is certainly symbolized by the Shield. So while this symbol, which can physically be any sort of a small coin, medal, or similar artifact, is being handled the general thought pattern could be something like the following:

> This is the sign and symbol of the Protective Power in life that shields me from potential spiritual dangers and averts those that attack me with injurious intentions. It will not save me if I approach dangers deliberately and in defiance of all care or caution. Nevertheless I can expect the Shield of God to cover me with confidence if I invoke it with a humble heart and hopes held high. Since we are Blood kin to Divinity itself, it is only natural that the Divine protects its special people, yet it does so with discrimination and discernment, while it always counsels caution. No good God is going to sanction idiotic acts and insane impulses. Common sense is always asked for and expected if a special Shield is granted to a mortal man or woman. We dare not demand the privilege of such protection as an entitlement because of birth or any manmade merit. Also, it imposes its own obligation. Whosoever is shielded, so are they supposed to shield all those in turn whom they can cover. Whosoever shields the seed when it is weak shall be supported by the tree when it is strong. In this world we have to

lend each other strength and succor as we need them. If we prove unwilling to do that, how can we reasonably hope that the Higher Power will shield us in an hour of need? Therefore let us pledge protection for those people who invoke our aid, especially our bretheren of the Blood and our companions in the cosmic cause.

The Shield, however, is not only a protection but also a burden. Sometimes when we scream extra loudly for screening we might catch a little echo that says something like, "Yes, I can protect you, but can you carry the necessary weight of armor?" In other words, to what degree would we be able to bear the spiritual equivalent of weight. All physical qualities have their counterparts on higher levels of life, and weight is no exception. In the old days armored knights had shield bearers whose job it was to carry this heavy weight around so that the soldiers' strength was saved for actual combat. A knightly warrior's life possibly depended more on the skill of his shield bearer than on his own dexterity. An echo of that today is the carrier transport of heavy tanks to the battle zone. Men still fatigue more easily than machines.

No Shield symbol should ever be looked at lightly or carelessly, with its protection just taken for granted automatically. It must never be expected to supplant any need for practical physical precautions. People may quite well be bodily killed while being simultaneously re-created otherwise. Cosmos does not view death in the drastic light that we do. To the Superior Intelligence, safeguarding means preserving the spiritual essence however most practical. This might mean scrapping the husk in order to save the part it once protected. After all, if a glass phial full of valuable perfume were accidentally cracked, we would try and rescue as much of the liquid as we could in any convenient container rather than attempt to save the worthless glass fragments.

Lastly, Shields were made to look at since they had familial and other identification devices painted on them for the information of the observer. There were mainly two things all were interested in discovering. One was the bloodline of the bearer, as well as the family motto, and the other was the bearer's personal motto, which he had chosen for himself. From an esoteric angle these devices would show what sort of man he was. For example, they might clearly indicate, to anyone accustomed to reading symbols, that the man was an Anglican Christian and also a Freemason and that he had been to a good school and university. One would therefore expect a reasonably high standard of behavior from such an individual provided the symbology was true. It would be more or less like having a certificate of health, education, social status, business and club cards plus letters of reference on public view all the time.

The point is, why not? Why shouldn't we admit what we are to each other? If a Shield is a convenient method of presenting our souls for free inspection by Blood-bonded brethren, then we should value and respect it very highly. Apart from this facility, a Temple Shield should be representative of the Temple as an operative group of people, and the group's peculiarities should be portrayed in heraldic or hieroglyphic style. Perhaps a sort of spiritual shorthand might be the idea to convey. At all events there should certainly be a community Shield, preferably on the North wall of the Temple, and every member ought to have his/her own miniature version for display when called for. It amounts to an esoteric identity card, and in these days it could be a rubber stamp.

There are almost endless combinations of consciousness to work and play with on the last four major symbols alone—one can make patterns and project all sorts of designs and arrangements out of them. It is even possible to invent games and quite a few formulae from their relationships. To a great extent they could be thought of as the basic language for a computer and built into a communications code of totally new spiritual significance. The more they are maneuvered with outside the Temple, the more meaning may be gained from them *inside* it. After we have finished turning our Shields into personal seals, checkbooks, insurance certificates, and passports (to say nothing of diplomas, degrees, and dog licenses), we might as well meet the last of this family of special symbols.

8. THE CORD. It is more or less instinctive for male humans to carry some string or cord around with them. For many thousands of years cord of some kind has helped humanity in countless cases. We constantly use cord in one form or another for binding things up, and knots had a magic of their own that still fascinates people today. In a Temple the Cord symbol represents the mysterious element of truth that binds all the different items of existence together and makes meaning of them all as a continuum of consciousness. Unless this can be done effectively, nothing would mean anything or bring much benefit anywhere. Losing a sense of continuity is a most distressing symptom of psychiatric abberation. The sick person literally cannot connect any two things together so as to make sense out of them, and therefore is hopelessly lost and probably weeping with frustration or else sunk in bewildered apathy, waiting for anything to happen that might break such a horrible spell.

In a sense the Cord is an awareness of time and meaning. We take it so much for granted, as a rule, that we scarcely appreciate its significance, but if we do not have a fair degree of this awareness we would be intellectually quite blind. It is as important as that. The physical symbol of the Cord is normally worn around each waist and around the horns of the altar. In that placement it signifies the umbilical cord connecting us both individually and collectively with the Mother of all Meaning and our spiritual Source of Life. It was also once the means of binding voluntary victims to the altar of sacrifice, but now it denotes self-dedication and devotion to Deity. As a miniature it may be a thin scarlet cord of maybe a foot long, which is manipulated while one is thinking about its spiritual significance. Perhaps it may be twisted around different fingers while meditating on set subjects, like a rosary.

With a Cord to complete the circle of consciousness, and the few small symbols lying on a table or desk to think about, it is amazing what inner vistas can be opened up to an experimenter's imagination. The various symbols should be seen as components of consciousness, each linked with the rest by the most wonderful web of awareness tautened like invisible cords between them and holding everything together as a whole. Imagine the whole of existence connected item by item by cords of pure consciousness. Perhaps a better simile is a space-wide telephone network where the actual cords are satellite channels. It is tempting to wonder what made esoteric Temple members choose a Cord for a communications symbol in the first place. Perhaps it was as simple as their having a very long line with a human pulling at each end of it to send a silent message from one to the other. That is a very old way of communicating between hunters—but it worked.

If a physical cord can connect bodies together, why should not a spiritual one link lives and souls? It is the *idea* that is operative in a Temple. The entire structure is constructed from ideas and concepts, and this means that Temple members must always bear in mind that physical symbols do nothing of themselves at all except represent their counterparts of spiritual consciousness that accomplish the real work. This does not devalue the physical symbols in the least, but only places them in proper proportion to their inner actualities. A major difficulty is that few people are ever told what to do with their inner symbols in a 1-2-3-4 fashion. Most are left to find this out for themselves from their experience of handling the concepts and moving them around with mind and soul. That may be a time-honored way of working, but it is also a time-wasting one, and with the spiritual problems of our modern world we may not have much time to spare before they solve themselves with unthinkable results.

In olden times, members of esoteric congregations were not allowed to take part in corporate work, then termed *theurgy*, or "God work," until they had served an apprenticeship under a tutor and finally "passed the pylons." These pylons were literally doorposts that marked the person's metaphorical readiness for group work: when the average soul had studied and practiced by him- or herself up to a point of preparedness for working with others that satisfied his/her tutor. Such was a normal practice with all the so-called mystery religions and esoteric spiritual systems. The Christian churches eventually allowed it to fall into disuse and are now very lax indeed concerning membership training, and in general are accepting increasingly low standards of spiritual aptitude. Only a relatively few esoteric concerns are still insisting on adequate initial training, though many of those are apt to be overly rigid and intolerant, confusing intellectuality with genuine spiritual qualities.

For those responsible souls who prefer to take their training in their own hands under direct guidance from whatever spiritual supervision they can contact by their own efforts, the best beginning would be to acclimatize themselves to the simple basic symbology in the manner suggested. The most complicated and elaborate ceremonies of any esoteric Temple in this world are only extensions of the same basics. The mechanical performance of them does absolutely nothing of itself. All the energy releases that accomplish anything whatever are activated by conditioned consciousness intentionally applied by the trained minds of those present.

Increasing numbers of Wesoterics prefer to remain independent of organized and authoritarian "occult" associations, though of course this is only possible on purely material levels. There may be no formal membership in anything tangible, no dues paid, no signed certificates in handsome frames hung anywhere, and nothing to show the connection between individuals and their inner loyalties whatsoever. None of those would be spiritual realities anyway. They are only physical tokens symbolizing their spiritual counterparts. Anyone achieving a spiritual status of his/her own accord with the natural assistance of inner and invisible companions has earned that status and the right to exist in it. Genuine initiation always has to be earned by experience of life and the right reactions with it. Ceremonial initiation is only a psychodramatic acknowledgment of this by others, or else an expression of pious hopes that such will be possible if the candidate follows a laid-out course of action.

Therefore it must remain a purely personal decision whether or not to "join a Temple" and work bodily with other souls on physical as well as spiritual levels. Many very well worthwhile Wesoterics appear to work best on their own, though that can only apply on material levels since spiritually we are all connected with each other, whatever our personal preferences may be. Assuming that anyone does so wish to limit his/her activities within definite circles of consciousness, that could certainly be arranged by designing the Temple accordingly. This means that the type, range, and other requirements can be deliberately determined by the overall setup of the Temple to be used. Again, this is not so much a matter of physical environment and expensive equipment as of inward mental and spiritual attitude adoption. Let us have a look at this particular problem.

Chapter 3

THE TUNING OF TEMPLES

Both the internal and external designs of churches and Temples are supposed to induce specific conditions of consciousness in their congregations. The external appearance should straightaway suggest the general purpose and distinction from all other types of human behavior, while the internal impact ought to arouse the strongest sense of immediate intention behind any particular attendance. This is to say, churches and Temples should most clearly proclaim, through every way possible for observing mortals to experience, not only what they are for but also why they exist and how they function. Valid Temples and churches ought to be self-explanatory, displaying suggestive symbolism appealing directly to the psyche of an average user.

For example, a Christian church, by its cruciform shape and central spire pointing heavenwards, says silently "This is where Christian thought and prayer are directed toward Divinity." The summoning bell is intended to act as an attuning device for fixing a common frequency to resonate with as a "homing signal" guiding worshippers along their way. Little entry rituals, like using holy water to bless oneself before entering a Christian church, the washing of feet prior to entering a mosque, the removal of headgear by male Christians and the assumption of it by Jews, are all adjuncts meant to help people get into a suitable state of mind before entering the place physically. Once inside, the ambience itself should augment the semiprepared spiritual state of the entrant. No matter how familiar this may be in fact, every entrance ought to be made as if it were for a very special occasion. Not only should one enter a Temple physically, but the Temple in turn should enter the soul of the entrant and there create its own conditions by the stimulus of its symbolism. In the old days this was known as "assuming the God," or characterizing the type of consciousness attributed to the Deity or God-aspect to whom the Temple or its immediate service was dedicated. One did not so much go inside a Temple as put it on, like a suit of clothing, or *assume* it.

In earlier times it was not uncommon for Temples to have specific functions and be furnished and decorated accordingly throughout their interiors. A Temple of Venus, for instance, would have her statue in the adytum, and all its pictures would be of an erotic nature. Incense and music would match with sweet smells and seductive sounds. Colors would blend greens of every type with copper ornaments and vessels. Personal accommodation would very likely be of the most comfortable kind, with the softest and springiest seating. Every possible artifact and appurtenance had to harmonize with the specific frequency used to contact the God-aspect being appealed to or invoked for its own specialized purposes. Although the theoretical benefits of this mood-inducing methodology are obvious, its practical difficulties in terms of expense, distribution, and other associated factors should also be plain enough. Then again, if there were a largish congregation all with different and divergent purposes, the conflict of consciousness with a single-purpose decor would tend to invalidate whatever workings were being attempted. Therefore we need either an all-purpose Temple or one that can be tuned to any particular intention with a minimum of effort. Preferably one combining both facilities.

Tuning a Temple to a required keynote means setting all its sensory and spiritual stimuli in accordance with whatever is being worked for. In the old days this was done by classifying everything under some planetary heading and utilizing only the things and themes considered proper to that planet. If we are to adopt a modern extension of that system, it would be reasonable to suppose that our frame of reference would most naturally be the Tree of Life, with its ten options of approach to the Absolute in which each option has a whole gamut of properties connected with its particular type of consciousness. It would afterwards be easy to decide which Tree Sphere in particular pertains closest to the approach being attempted, and then to select from the list of its attributes whatever seems most appropriate for tuning the Temple accordingly.

This will only work for those who are familiar with and acclimatized to the Tree framework, who have conditioned themselves therewith by meditations and exercises covering all the Paths and Spheres. The general principles of this, however, are common to every spiritual system. The basics involved are the association of each distinctive self-state with some definite color, sound, smell, shape, and particular environmental arrangement until they all become mutually connected to an extent where they will also be interevocative. That is to say, an experience of one will automatically call up the other. For example, if people have trained and conditioned themselves to link a state of sadness and sorrow with a Sphere Three attribution of dark grey, mournful music and sorrowful scents, together with a heavy and lugubrious atmosphere of appropriate accessories such as weeping willows and cypresses, it should be known how to rig a Temple so as to match the most melancholy of human moods. Conversely it would equally be realized how to counter it by arranging a Sphere Six rig of bright yellow hangings, cheerful music, flowers to match, brass or gilt ornaments, and all other appropriate trimmings.

Those able to gear themselves to the ten all-covering Spheres of the Tree will have a ready-made means of tuning their Temples to any kind of ceremony that reasonable human beings could ask for. Although there is fundamentally but a single Self-state, it is capable of varying through a very considerable range of experience, and each section of that can be considered as a self-state in its own right. Let us take for granted that a human being is able to live from the highest sort of heaven to the lowest kind of hell, and between those opposite ends of experience there is an unbroken condition of consciousness that could be called a "state scale." Beyond each end of that of course, consciousness for the human concerned ceases altogether. At any given instant, that human's awareness may be focused at any point of the scale, depending on circumstances. That exact position is the self-state of the soul at that precise moment. Thus we can mark out a calibrated linkage from top to bottom of life as we know it, and if we make it a decimal scale it will be easily connectable with the well-known Tree of Life. Although this should be sufficiently comprehended by the majority of Wesoterics, a quick recapitulation in regard to the ten self-states those Spheres stand for will not be amiss for purposes of reference. We shall start with the zero end of the scale.

0. THE NIL-STATE. This Sphere is unimaginable by

any capability of human consciousness. A "beyond all belief" state past the supremacy of all spiritual heights possible for the most advanced human being.

1. THE CROWN OR SUMMIT. The absolute limit possible for human consciousness pushed to an ultimate condition. Certainly not available to an average mortal except symbolically in simulated states. These would apply if sheer love and devotion to Divinity were raised to an absolute maximum and applied with full force and power of pressure. It should be taken that this at best might be a momentary experience or the briefest flicker of a needle representing the self-state applicable to any soul.

2. WISDOM. This Sphere, being the topmost of the right-hand Pillar, indicates a maximum of human happiness because of complete self-confidence and an awareness of ability to deal with whatever life may present. There is nothing of unwarranted assumption in this attitude, because it is based on knowledge and experience, plus the firmest faith that the Supreme Spirit of all wisdom will cooperate fully with human endeavors extended to this point.

3. UNDERSTANDING. This Sphere, which is at the top of the left-hand Pillar, indicates a maximum of human sorrow due to comprehension of what lies behind life and the conditions of Cosmos. By and large, the Left Pillar associates with sadness as the Right one signifies joy. So here we have a self-state that has experienced and understood the extreme conditions that cause humans to interpret them as misery and grief of the most profound kind. It is here that we recognize the necessity for death and the sorrow of birth. This is the self-state regarded by Buddhists as being vitally necessary before the "Great Liberation" into the non-state of Nirvana, from whence there was no more need to be anything or anyone evermore. It has to be carefully understood that at this position there is no malevolent motivation whatsoever. Nothing except sheer sadness and anguish caused by the need for specific cosmic effects that involve humans because of their existence alone.

4. MERCY. Back to the Pillar of Joy again. Here is a happy and bountiful self-state due to what were once called the "benefits of Providence." Abundant health, freedom from worldly worries about money and irritating conditions. Bonhomie and blessings everywhere. The generosity of God converted to the magnanimity of humans. Perhaps a rare state in this world, and it would not be entirely good for us to try and live in it permanently, because that would cause euphoria, but an entitled sojourn in this self-state is welcome for as long as it lasts, which is usually brief as lifetimes go.

5. MIGHT. A self-state in which there are plenty of worries and adversities to make life difficult. Here one is very conscious of disappointment and possibly disaster following one's footsteps. There may be a feeling that fate is threatening all sorts of unpleasant happenings, and in the past, one might have supposed the Devil himself was doing his damnedest. There could be a certain amount of self-guilt and a suspicion that an offended God might be demanding retribution for past sins. A disturbed self-state that is a mixture of fear and anger at all the oppositions encountered, coupled with a demand for the fighting energy to cope with them.

6. BEAUTY AND HARMONY. Another very rare self-state, this one consists of poise, balance, and a sense of harmonious happiness due to exact equilibrium between all forces focused on the sensorium. This is a lot closer to our normal world than is self-state one, though still very remote from it, and is a condition of "heaven" reachable by imaginative humans. It is a "Middle Pillar" state of mind and soul where everything seems to be exactly as and where it should be and maybe was meant to be from the very beginning. We are seldom able to stay in this self-state very long, though quite long enough to remember it and look forward to a future return.

7. VICTORY. Though this is the happy side of the Tree, it is not without its worries. Here is not only a sense of success but all the struggles and anxieties leading up to the most trivial of triumphs. The self-state will be one of striving to achieve some definite aim in life. Not usually a very high aim at this level of the Tree, but anything to the good that will make life a bit better without hurting anyone else. No victory at the expense of other humans is even worthy of the name, and the best victory of all is over the worst in one's own nature.

8. GLORY (or Honor). This again is a mixed self-state, in which the predominant factor is concern about matters of principle and intelligence, such as scholastic status or ethical problems. Generally speaking, it is more a self-state of curiosity and enquiry rather than doubt and suspicion, though there is a hint of those also. On the whole this is a straightforward investigative condition of consciousness doing no more than seeking some sensible solutions to the multiple problems of life in a satisfactory and honorable style.

9. FOUNDATION (or Basics). Although this is on the Middle Pillar again, we have here about the most mixed-up self-state of the lot, from both a mental and spiritual viewpoint. Ideas and ideals become tangled with thoughts to an amazing extent, which was probably why the thorn bush

was an old emblem here. This is where humans start looking for their spiritual foundations and learning by trial and
error. Here is the dream state and the uncertainty of everything. A reflective and puzzling condition of consciousness
that points at problems yet suggests no certain solutions. At
the same time, it indicates almost everything that can be
actualized on higher levels, and affords a great deal of
inspiration leading in those directions. It is positively a
passing-through stage where we must marshal our thinking and make sound sense of it before we go any further.

10. THE KINGDOM (or Natural World). This world
and what we have made of it with our attempts at civilization. The self-state here could be a combination of any or all
previously described. Say just the average condition of
human consciousness ready to select any single state needed
at any instant. Most people seldom trouble with such selection, being content to drift around as the ambient currents
of consciousness move them. Therefore the appropriate
self-state of Sphere Ten could be described as the "norm" of
any given individual. Ground level as it were.

What we need to know about Temples is the most efficient way to tune or harmonize them with any required
self-state. If a Tree of Life framework were acceptable, it
would be theoretically possible to have an absolutely neutral background and a simple numeral displayed in a prominent position. A trained congregation would then adapt
their self-states according to whichever Sphere was indicated.
Not many humans have that expertise readily available,
however; so they have to depend on the more conventional
methods of sensual stimuli linked to specific self-states.
There should at least be some commonly agreed-on system
among Wesoteric workers for setting a Temple to easily
recognized keynotes suitable for whatever practice might

be prevailing within its walls. It is again submitted here that there can scarcely be a simpler system than that of the Tree, which is now so well known to the majority of Wesoterics.

In Temples where a model or diagram of the Tree is prominently displayed, it would be an easy matter to spotlight any of the Spheres or indicate a Sphere in some way that called special attention to its properties. Otherwise there are many alternative methods of matching the prevailing moods of Temples and people. For instance, if one sees a congregation in colorful clothes, with floral buttonholes for the males, it is safe to assume a wedding, or if they are all wearing very dark clothing and if black armbands abound, there would be no prizes for guessing a funeral. In the case of esoterics their activities would be indicated by their regalia. Here, colors of sashes, robes, jewels, or special ensignia all have to accord with the overall intention. Though members should be warned about correct costumes well in advance of a ceremony, and especially concerning permissible alternatives, they ought to know this anyway if they have been properly instructed. They should also be fully aware of every reason for the color, design, or maybe the material of each single symbol they are expected to wear, nor should any personal symbol that could conceivably clash with the proposed ceremony be worn in company. Finger rings or necklaces would be cases in point. No unauthorized ornamentation should ever be seen in well-ordered Temples, and some will not even permit it to be carried in pockets, believing that its mere presence during a ceremony contravenes the ancient prohibition of private possessions during a communal congregation.

In recent years many experiments have been made with the electronic tuning of esoteric tuning of esoteric Temples, but as yet there is insufficient evidence to show that this is really useful. A possible exception is the complete screening of a Temple with metal foil or mesh that covers walls, ceiling, and floor and is effectively earthed at several points. In other words, an efficient Faraday cage. This certainly excludes interference from any electrical source such as radio, TV, and high-frequency equipment, and even atmospheric electricity, which could be a good idea especially in urban areas where a concentration of these energies would be densest. A great deal more study is obviously needed in matters concerning connections between human consciousness and electromagnetic energy of all frequencies.

Other attempts have been made to tune Temples by converting their working interiors into large solenoids; in effect this causes a modern magical circle to become electrically charged, but again there is no reason for believing this gives any advantage over conventional Temples. Besides, since earlier Temples were working quite satisfactorily, their effectiveness surely shows that it was the construction of consciousness itself that really mattered. However, what might enhance or improve the qualities of belief in that awareness could be a useful thing to know and apply, and if people believed in the efficacy of their electrical equipment it probably *did* improve the atmosphere to that extent.

We have to remember that the first protective perimeters set up by humans to surround their special activities were physical constructions offering as much opposition to ill-intentioned invaders as could be built into them. Those hostile creatures were very solid beings of flesh and blood, whether human or animal. When people began to see antagonists as spirit beings, they realized that no material defenses could exclude those beings, and so they started to make spiritual perimeters on the same pattern as their previous protections. An old-time magician's circle was only a ground plan of what was once a solid stone wall. The complicated design of the Middle Ages having a square with a circle around it was no more than a two-dimensional projection of a strong tower surrounded by a deep moat. All the various sigils and God-names symbolized various powers considered likely to protect people against evil. They might just as well have written a plain prohibition such as "Demons of all classes are strictly forbidden to cross this line." Illiterate fiends were presumably scared away by the pictographs.

Eventually it became a question of beliefs and contra-conceptions. Belief battled with belief and concepts were contradicted by alternatives. In the end it worked out as a warfare of pure ideologies with Goodies versus Baddies, or angels against devils. As such it remains very much with us today except that we have replaced religion with politics as an excuse for continuing the conflict. All we have done is alter terminologies and extend areas. Otherwise the opposition between human ideologies remains exactly the same as ever. Our modern magic words are acronyms for political potencies like NATO and SEAC, while the God-names have become those of ideological innovators like Marx or Sartre. We still use words to condition our consciousness and symbols to tune our thoughts in keeping with specific themes. Maybe in times to come we shall discover more precise ways of tuning ourselves to whatever self-state we require by varying the field frequency of our living energies with electrochemical or similar means. Meanwhile there seems no reason why we should not continue with time-honored systems of Temple tuning.

After all, we shall only be applying the principles of purposefully motivated environmental control for religious and mystical reasons. Although the ideas of this have been known from almost the dawn of time, it is only relatively recently that they are being studied as an exact science. Basically the notion is that if any specific activity is being practiced, this is best carried out in an environment especially designed and contrived for the furtherance of that particular purpose alone. In other words, control the immediate environment so as to concentrate maximum consciousness on the activity alone, or custom-build a location for a single intention. Two examples that come to mind immediately are a kitchen and a lavatory. The first exists for the preparation of food and possibly the eating of it, and the second for disposal of it when bodies have absorbed the energies it afforded. These two locations might be labelled "Input" and "Output," and one would hope that the functions of both would remain confined to correct quarters since they are diametrically opposite. Civilized people should not prepare or cook food in lavatories nor excrete it in kitchens.

If an ordinary house can thus contain a number of compartments tuned to their own functions, why should not a Temple have its equivalents? This was in fact attempted by Christian cathedrals, abbeys, and ministers wherein there was sufficient space to create a considerable number of chapels and chantries for different purposes, some of which still operate in our times. First of course would be the principal nave and sanctuary, devoted to general worship; then the chapel of the Reserved Sacrament, where Jesus could be approached in person. Next came the Lady Chapel, where the feminine aspect of the Deity could be contacted under the guise of the Virgin Mary. Then followed a number of side chapels, each with its own patron saint dedicated to some particular cause: St. Cecilia for music, St. Luke for medicine, St. Hubert for hunting, and St. Anthony of Padua for eloquence and finding lost property, to name only a few of them. Every contingency that might apply to humans in difficulties was catered to. You knew exactly whom to ask for any spiritual service, just as a modern knows (or can find out) which government department to contact for any particular reason. Which procedure obtained better results would be a moot point.

In the case of esoteric Temples one could imagine a circular construction with divisions like the Zodiac, each division being dedicated to some tutelary archetypal figure or God-aspect that could be approached on a person-to-person basis for distinct reasons connected with individual needs. This would admittedly involve complicated and probably very costly designing. Therefore the general rule in most Wesoteric Temples is to recognize each quarter as being under the patronage of an archangelic archetype, each representing some special quality or aspect of Deity itself. These could be further subdivided into more and more specialized categories of esoteric energies until very fine degrees of difference might be determined. There seems to be little to gain by doing this, however, because the breadth of the archangelic concepts is quite sufficient to cover all reasonable requirements of human nature.

Thus for a rapid "rough tuning" of an average Wesoteric Temple, we could conceive its perimeter as being a continuum calculated in this fashion. Its Eastern quarter is assigned Archangel Raphael and is aligned with alert and energetic moods, travel, sudden changes, injuries, short-term activities, and unexpected events. The Southern quarter corresponds with Archangel Michael and with ideas of justice, decisions of right and wrong, all ethical questions, healing of diseases, spiritual support, defense against evils, and moral judgments. The Western quarter, with Archangel Gabriel or Jivrael, is concerned with love, compassion, consolation, and everything to do with companionship and fellow feeling. Lastly, the Northern quarter of Archangel Auriel the Enlightener is associated with deep deliberations, careful counseling, serious subjects, quiet meditation, and all else concerned with pondering on profound issues. At least Wesoterics should know which way to turn for specialized spiritual help.

So a Wesoteric Temple could be taken as a clock face with the hours representing the quarters, the minute hand

98 / Temple Magic

pointing out the precise degrees, and the second hand signifying the constant connection between them all, which is kept by Archangel Suvuviel of the Cord, who is continually on the move with his element of truth linking one item of Cosmos with the rest everywhere. All individuals willing to accept this idea should be able to align themselves with great precision by facing whichever point of the Temple's perimeter accords closest to their own self-states. The procedure would be to first diagnose the state of self at that instant, secondly harmonize this with the Tree Sphere nearest to it, then line up with the precise point of the Temple perimeter needed to deal with it as desired. However Wesoteric Temples may be shaped, they are always considered to be circular. Lodges, on the other hand, are square since they symbolize the work of humankind.

This would seem to argue a central altar as a focal point, whereas many altars are located at the Western point of the perimeter. There is no reason why they should not remain there provided the central axis is marked by a minor altar, which could be a shortish circular pillar on a base, say about three feet (or one meter) high, surmounted by a flat round top maybe six inches wide that should bear some special symbol or a plain crystal ball for a focus. At the selected spot on the perimeter could stand a ceremonial staff indicating the approach angle for the particular ceremony in progress. Thus the tuning of a Temple might be made as simply as possible once the meanings of all the angles were definitely determined. This would have to be done by conditioning consciousness, right around the clock as it were, until crystal clear ideas emerged concerned with the exact nature of self-state alteration to align with each change of angle. In this way an entire "compass of consciousness" could easily be worked out for the complete 360° of difference, covering all angles of approach to the single source of spiritual energy symbolized by the crystal in the center.

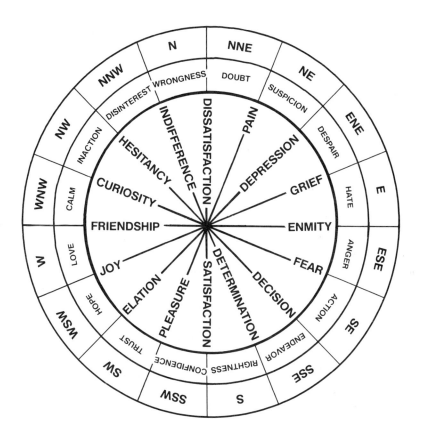

The Compass of Consciousness

This diagram shows how our moods and feelings align with the containing cycle of the compass around us, and which way to turn for the correct summoning of each indicated attitude or its opposite.

Surely this would be a great deal more practical and economical than changing the colors completely, together with the robes and all the symbology that was once expected in esoteric Temples. It could also be that the floor design was a literal circle marked in degrees so that there could be no doubt whatever concerning the placement of a pointer. The symbolic staff and center column, however, should have some physical presence. In fact, a modern mystic could set up a Temple anywhere by tracing a circle around him- or herself, aligning it with the quarters, and then pointing its purpose with a stick or staff stuck in the ground appropriately on its perimeter.

If this system is being used, something that has to be considered is whether any particular operation is "inworking" or "outworking." If the energy is being directed internally then the practitioner should work from the perimeter toward the center, but if it is intended to direct it outwardly so as to include a wider area of influence especially in this world, then the direction should be from the center to the perimeter point. If both directions are involved, then all incoming energy should be invoked or "drawn in" from the center, and expelled or projected toward the perimeter. A useful practice here is to turn toward the perimeter point and exhale, then face the center point and breathe in deeply with appropriate arm gestures. At the same time, imagine pure psychic energy flowing in or out of the self-system. This of course is only from the "Divine-human" direction. For the opposite or "human-Divine" direction, the intake of breath would be from the perimeter and the output toward the center. It is important to align awareness of direction-intent with each breathing so as to coordinate consciousness with intensive action.

Nothing, however, should ever obscure or worse still obliterate the fact that the only true Temple of Wesoteric practice is the Cosmos itself and our relationship with it. Every single individual is, or should be, a Temple serving the Holy Spirit by his/her own self-arrangement. Therefore a truly tuned Temple can only be one in which all the members have tuned themselves to as fine a pitch as possible and preferably to the same keynote. That is why every individual or collective attendance at a Temple should commence with an appropriate "summons sound." This is a sonic signal of any suitable kind that will accord with whatever will be immediately worked. It could be simply a number of knocks to signify the Sphere of the Tree most in keeping with the occasion, or a vocal call indicating the same. More elaborately it might be an entire musical piece played on an organ or any other suitable instrument. In the case of a single individual it could be an internally uttered keynote, inaudible to any except the utterer and the Spirit it was directed toward. Whatever the signal may be, it is an essential preliminary of all Wesoteric Temple practice.

We are familiar with the standard invocation "O Lord, hear my prayer" and its response "and let my cry come unto thee." The original Latin word for *cry* here was *clamor*, literally a noise to attract attention. We instinctively make such noises as *Hey! Hoi! Hi!* and perhaps *Yoo-Hoo!* (*Ieu Hu*) to alert other humans. All very ancient and primitive names for God. Just plain vowel sounds by themselves. The Great Name of God, IHVH (sometimes transliterated as YAHWEH), is only a double vowel sonic that Jews have brought into modernity as their famous *Oi Veh!* The Yiddish exclamation of distress is equivalent to the Gentile *My God!* That is typical of the clamor meant by the response in question. A noise of sufficient sincerity and intensity to attract the attention of the Spirit at which it was directed.

When very primitive people called upon their Gods, they did exactly what babies do when they want to attract their mothers' attention. They yelled. All normal human mothers can distinguish their babies' needs by the quality of the yells they utter. One type of yell means "Help." Another, "I want food," and another again, "I want changing," and so on. All basic human needs for safety, sustenance, and reassurance. Creature comforts. Every one of them is "I want." In adults it would be called the "gimme syndrome." Although the average human can usually see a bit further than applying this principle alone to prayer, the general reasons for prayers of any kind are wants or needs of contact with a higher type of consciousness than merely human. If that would satisfy by itself, no one would ever pray at all. It is the fundamental *need* to feel reassured by the attention of some Superbeing that prompts human prayers in the first place. So it is a perfectly natural thing to commence communication with such a being by an equivalent of the invocative cries we used with our mothers at the beginning of our evolution.

Just as there were different sorts of yells for letting our mothers know our wants, so there are different cries or clamors intended to do the same in the case of Divinity. These are undoubtedly the old Barbaric Names of Evocation, which later civilized people were warned never to change on any account. Many sophisticated priests became doubtful of phonetics that seemed to have no meaning in any cultured language, so they were inclined to remove them from inherited religious rituals. Yet some deep unexplained instinct convinced their critics that such apparently senseless sounds connected with our most profound levels of awareness at the absolute back of every human being. Therefore it would be idiotic to deny or ignore them altogether and they should be left alone, however silly or childish they might seem.

While there is a lot of controversy in our times concerning what those Barbaric Names really were, it is reasonable to suppose they would be very primitive and almost animal sounds coming from the very depths of sentient beings. In other words, plain baby talk. *Mm. Daa. Gaa.* (*Mum, Dad, God.*) Mostly vowel sounds with *ahs* and *oohs*. It would be mostly the tone or manner in which they were uttered that put any meaning into them. About the only survivor today is *Amen;* and the oriental *Om* and the druidic *Ahoon* have the same significance, All mean much the same as "Mother-Father-God," or just "Divine Parent."

It is the intensity and sincerity of any invocation that make for close contact with higher than human consciousness. We have many sublime orisons of outstanding literary excellence, couched in the most eloquent terms, yet these may mean no more to Divinity than maybe a pleasant background murmur from human sources when repeated by professional priests for the benefit of a paying congregation. A single scream from some agonized individual in dire need would make better contact with Deity than the ornate orison coming from a comfortably contented congregation. So would a silent scream heard only in the heart. Verbalization is only a civilized form of sound making that shapes sounds into intellectual patterns, but the basis of it all is the so-called primal scream intended to attract the maximum of attention from human or divine sources of aid.

The instinct in humans to approach Divinity for assistance with problems beyond their powers of solution or comprehension is only an extension of their early dependency on parental aid. After all, we needed parents so that we might get into the world as individuals. In infancy we needed their care and attention so we would survive until we could care for ourselves, and without that early care we would have no hope whatever. Our most natural concepts of God therefore are extensions of our own parents on a much greater scale in totally different dimensions. If we intend to acquire any sort of spiritual existence elsewhere than on earth, we shall need God to be both father and mother for us in that kind of life. There are endless instances of soldiers dying in conflict who call for their mothers as they expire. This is probably much more than temporary infantilism, being an instinctive cry to the Creator by its oldest title, *Mother*! An appeal for another life in place of that which has been taken. A desperate cry to the Eternal Womb that will most certainly be heard.

So the secret of the ancient Barbarous Names is not lost forever in the oblivion of human forgetfulness but is sealed into the genetic structure of our species, ready for release in the extremity of emergency together with other associated awareness. This could account for legends concerning "savior-heroes" supposed to be asleep in caves, awaiting calls of distress from their endangered peoples. These are factually our "extra-reserve abilities," which are called out of our hidden depths when extreme pressures are applied by circumstances. Even proclaimed atheists have been known to call on a Deity they have denied all their lives when the moment of death approaches. The rational, logical, thinking part of our awareness may deny Divinity as much as it likes, but the instinctive, intuitional, and basic level of human beliefs will deny such a denial. It knows quite well that life has a spiritual source of origin far beyond the reach of our ordinary consciousness, and that is where our "calls on Cosmos" come from.

Therefore a good deal of attention and thought should be given to the "summoning sonics" that should precede any formalized prayers or invocations. Not only are they important, but they enhance efficacy very considerably. This is why so many invocative prayers begin with the monosyllable *O*. It is not meant to be a mere honorific of whatever God-title may follow; it stands for a preparatory signal during which the invoker should tune him- or herself to a maximum awareness of the Name to come. That is why it was stipulated that all those special Names should be uttered very slowly in a long drawn-out manner. This allowed time for adjustment of the psyche to the concept expressed. Behind most of those old injunctions there was usually some perfectly sound, practical reason, which we frequently fail to observe nowadays.

Quite probably none of the foregoing remarks would meet with the approval of dedicated dowsers who believe that all sacred sites should be selected by one of their number with the aid of his/her approved equipment, whether rod, pendulum, or anything else. Given absolute freedom of choice, there seems no doubt that such gifted people could indeed find the most favorable spot for a Temple from a telluric viewpoint and give it a great advantage of a naturally tuned environment, but how often is such an opportunity likely to occur? Most Wesoteric Temples are converted rooms in private houses or apartments. In the relatively few cases of custom-built Temples they are understandably limited to land availability, especially in urban areas. So it is usually a case of "Take what you can get and be thankful." At the same time, it could be a good idea to have a good dowser check any proposed premises for possible adverse earth currents in the vicinity, and it would also be well to have any findings checked by another dowser, unbeknown to the first, in order to confirm or contradict the initial report.

Assuming there might be unfavorable telluric currents present, the conventional way of circumventing them is first to find the location and direction of flow, and secondly to interpose some symbol of a circle cross in its path. Since a Wesoteric Temple *is* a circle cross in itself, that should be normally sufficient to prevent the average contra-current from operating in its vicinity. It is interesting to note that earlier Christian churches had these "consecration crosses" cut into their walls and that they were blessed by a bishop at the building's inauguration. There were also five similar crosses cut into the top of an altar, which were sanctified by holy water, oil, and fire during the same rite. These crosses were said to represent the five wounds of Jesus Christ, but they actually derive from much older symbology.

In ancient times it was customary to sacrifice a human victim in the precincts of a Temple and then bury the body, or perhaps only the skull, under the foundation stone so as to placate any disturbed earth spirits. In reality this would have the effect of altering any adverse telluric currents by interposing the mechanism of a human consciousness (the brain) into their circuit. The physical decomposition of the body or skull would still leave its psychic pattern in the place, so therefore the victim had to be very carefully chosen. These "doorkeepers," as they came to be called, were often buried beneath the threshold so that all who entered legitimately would have to cross their dead bodies. Their discarnate task was to avert evilly inclined entrants as far as they could, and live mortals realized the psychic risk they ran if they entered with ill intentions. A doorkeeper might well have been a former warrior or champion whom they had known personally while he was alive, or whose formidable reputation had survived long after his physical death. To this day the saying "Over my dead body!" has links with that ancient practice.

Later on, sacrificial customs altered, requiring the use of animals and, after that, metallic talismans or other symbols. Even today we place coins and similar tokens under foundations and doorsteps. Our instincts do not die but only alter as we evolve. In the early Christian church, Eucharist was most frequently celebrated at tombs of defunct members so that the gathering might seem like a few friends commemorating their departed companion with a farewell drink. Afterwards it became the custom to include some relics in every altar, preferably of the patron saint, usually at the point where the priest puts the chalice and paten during Mass. To this day the Roman Catholic church supplies small portable "altar stones" for priests so that they can set up a service wherever one is required. These are rarely more than four to six inches square and have a minute relic that is a microscopic fragment of bone from some minor saint sealed into them. An affidavit as to authenticity is included with each stone.

While there would be nothing to prevent any Wesoteric Temple from following some comparable custom, it should be remembered that a corpse was considered a contaminating influence in sacred premises, and at every funeral it was left outside in a specially unconsecrated chapel while mourners prayed in the regular Temple. Orthodox Jews observed that old custom until modern times. Once, there were special "lych gates" at many country churches, which were a sort of thatched shelter where the coffin could be rested while the funeral party waited for the priest to arrive and take the service from there. There seem to be no inflexible rules about including fragments of former friends in Wesoteric Temples, but considering the prevalence of cremation nowadays, there should be little difficulty in finding space for a morsel of ash somewhere at the Northern quarter.

One important point to bear in mind when considering the tuning of Temples is that absolutely nothing should be visibly displayed which will not have some essential part to play in the proceedings. That is to say, there should be no items standing around that are not directly connected with the ceremony in progress. That would be something like a stage on which act 2 of a play went on while props and scenery needed only for acts 3 and 1 were pointlessly present. There is actually a considerable connection between the rules of good play production and effective Temple working, which should scarcely be surprising when one realizes the direct descent of commercial drama from original Temple worship. In fact, the relatively modern word *psychodrama* is very aptly chosen, because that is exactly what it is. A dramatic presentation for the involvement of the soul.

So every effort should be made to ensure that a Temple is properly tuned to the required keynote. First by the rough tuning of its alignments and general symbology, and second by the fine tuning of its specializing symbology, such as correct colors, incense, music, and other devices calculated to harmonize the place with whatever purpose is being worked for. Yet it should never be lost sight of that this is only an auxiliary action to help tune the souls of those present for such a specific reason. That is the real objective to be served.

There is one hazard to avoid with Temple tuning: becoming so fascinated with the relatively minor details of the art that sight is lost of the major aims behind the whole spiritual structure. Provided that these are regularly reviewed and revered, there need not be a serious danger of this, but purely technical trivia can be a real trap for the unwary. This could be as anomalous as a motor mechanic so engrossed in the fine points of his craft that he forgot motor cars were primarily for convenient transport of people. Or a priest so concerned with the physical observance of ceremonial symbolism that he ignored the spiritual meaning of it. That can also happen with congregations when they get so caught up with being correct in procedures that they lose track of the principles they are there to honor.

This does not mean that trying to tune a Temple is unimportant. It means that we have to see that procedure in its right light and for its proper value. If any Temple is going to be used at all, it should be tuned as perfectly as possible, but a furnished and functional physical Temple is more of a luxury than a necessity as far as genuine Wesotericism is concerned. It should always be considered a convenience for communal working rather than an absolute essential for individual working. Humans unable to make Temples of themselves would be very unlikely to benefit very much from the most magnificent Temple ever built by the hands of mortal people. The sole purpose of such a place should be to provide a pattern on which to construct one's own self-arrangement of consciousness in keeping with some special ideology of spiritual perfection. That is the next point we shall have to consider.

Chapter 4

CEREMONIAL CLOTHING

"Ceremonies are something you dress up specially for," said a young person who enjoyed them very particularly on that account. In her eyes this was an end in itself rather than a customary requirement for any other reason. Since time immemorial humans have given ceremonial clothing a very high place of importance, and on the top of the list would be any that was associated with purely spiritual motivations. Why should this be in particular?

The reasons are mainly psychological. Humans are the only animals that kill other life species for the sake of their fur, feathers, or armament in order to adorn or protect themselves with these. In relatively recent times we have manufactured textiles that have replaced the comparatively crude clothing of our very ancient ancestors and now have a very wide range of much better materials to choose from, yet despite that there still lingers an atavistic demand for the original skins and furs. There seems to have always been a genetically inherited fascination with clothing, which links with our very oldest instincts and has a peculiar magic of its own.

Possibly the primal motivation behind any sort of clothing at all was differentiation or distinction. That is to say, clothing served as a mark of authority, rank, or superiority over others of the tribe, who would recognize this visibly. Among a herd of humans, leaders would feel an over-powering need for something that would proclaim their power and position at a distance and enhance their im-portance. In our modern phrase—ego boost. At first this was probably something stuck in their hair, such as feathers, or carried in their hands, such as sticks, which later developed into ceremonial staffs and scepters. Later, hunters would drape whole skins of the animals they had killed around their own bodies first to proclaim their abilities publically, and then to protect themselves from adverse weather or disguise themselves for future hunting. It must have taken many millennia before the convention of clothing was es-tablished among humans, but it became so instinctual that it is not likely to diminish at this distant date.

Eventually it worked out that the style and type of clothing indicated the social status of its wearer, which is roughly true to this day despite every anomaly. The higher the status, the finer the quality and style adopted. Ultimately the clothing became equated with the actual function that specific humans were fulfilling at the time of wearing it, and that has more or less persisted to the present period. Cloth-ing for the job is a normal requirement of our culture. Therefore the provision of special clothing for the practice of any Wesoteric form of ceremony is no more than normal procedure for other activities. What is of particular interest is that every item has, or should have, special spiritual significance. Some of that may be obvious, but much has been obscured and calls for clarification in terms of our times. The first step to such a study is plainly to consider the naked human body without any adornment at all.

Complete nudity for ceremonial practice is the oldest possible style dating from our most primitive past and is still in use among Pagans, though far from being very widely popular. From time to time it has been practiced by specific Christian sects, notably the Adamites, who claimed that such was a true "Garden of Eden" condition (when humans' relationship with God was an ideal one) and should therefore be emulated. The argument in favor of nudity was that it reduced everyone to a common condition of defenseless-ness and equality, which is the best theoretical base for approaching the Power that presumably created those bodies as they are. Thus they were in a far more genuine state than if they were dressed up in their "pretend" clothes, which concealed the creatures beneath them. It was best, they thought, to approach God in the most natural way, and what could possibly be more natural than nudity?

The objection to nudity was that it exposed the sex organs, which excited others to thoughts of lust or disgust or, worse still, ridicule. Besides which it was scarcely possi-ble out-of-doors in Western countries except maybe in the summer on rare occasions. Then, nudity did not entirely abolish rank if the officers still wore beads, feathers, or any decoration to indicate their status. Probably the main moti-vation against nudity was purely aesthetic since so many bodies were the reverse of beautiful, with potbellies, sag-ging or pendulous breasts, or some malformation making them unattractive in the eyes of viewers. In other words, there was fear of being laughed at, or losing face, before fellow beings. The reply to that, as might be expected, was that people should have better and bigger minds than to look at such low levels, but the fact remained that a majority of ordinary folk felt uncomfortable or embarrassed by bodily exposure in common company, so nudity remains a minority practice confined to those able to cope with it adequately rather than a customary religious convention.

Traditionally the first garments ever worn by humans were aprons, or genital coverings reputedly made of fig leaves and later of leather. Decorated ones are still used by members of esoteric Lodges. The real reason for these in the first place was for practical protection; modesty had nothing whatever to do with them. Once humans had assumed a mainly upright manner of posture, the men felt that their genitals were particularly vulnerable, and that feeling is still a characteristic of male psychology. Just as a woman instinctively shields her breasts, so does a man try to shield his genitals. Both are bodily protrusions of great sensitivity and very liable to injury from hostile contacts, while both are directly connected with the principle of life itself. The males with life origins, and the females with nourishment and continuance of it. So the association of an apron with protection and preservation of life is a natural and normal outcome.

The earliest apron would only have been a piece of animal skin bound around the waist to keep it in place. Later this would typify into a visible indication of purpose. Perhaps some special skin or fur to indicate a high-ranking person, which all others would be forbidden to wear, and there would be several different variations for lesser classes. Thus social status would be clearly seen from the type of apron worn, and behavior would be modified by this factor. Later again, when making marks on artifacts became possible, aprons were embellished with significant designs to proclaim some recognizable meaning. So our modern Lodge aprons are of very great antiquity in principle.

When woven fabrics came into use they were soon adopted by the ruling classes because they were much more comfortable to wear next to the skin than leather, though they did not afford leather's protective properties.

Therefore leather was still worn externally for protection in occupations like riding, fighting, or manually working. For the latter activity the best design was an apron and tool bag combined, so at least the most valuable smaller tools might be kept in close custody on the person. The flap of this bag could be turned up in front of the body and pinned or buttoned to the chest for extra protection, and this type of apron is the one from which modern Masonic aprons descended. Another legacy is the slang word *tool* applied to male genitals, which were formerly covered by a worker's bag-apron containing the tools of his trade.

No one knows for certain how the primitive priests distinguished themselves from the laity by special markings on their aprons, but by recorded times most priests were wearing linen clothing, which was subsequently replaced by silk in the higher ranks. Of course aprons eventually became associated with menial occupations and so became demoted in consideration by society in general. The waist cord, which once bound them around the loins of a wearer, remains with us as a girdle, and the apron itself is still to be seen as part of a bishop's ensignia. It was once a riding apron worn when a bishop would visit all the parishes of his diocese on horseback. There was also a practical use for an apron known as a gremial; this type of apron was spread across the knees of a seated dignitary when robed, to prevent his hands from soiling the gorgeous embroidery.

Eventually what is known as the "work and service ethic" grew very strongly among Western humanity in particular. The idea of "serving God and fellow humans" became a major life guide of moral conduct. Esoteric and religious ceremonials became known as *services* or, particularly, *Divine Service* and these were linked with the ideology of serving humanity by supplying whatever abilities might be available. A fighting man for instance would offer his skills in the service of a collective community, and the armed services came into being. The Pope had taken as his proudest title the motto *Servitor Servientes*, or "Servant of the Servants," and the later motto of the Holy Grail was "I seek to serve." Even the Crown Prince of Britain had adopted *Ich Dien* (I Serve) as his personal motto, so the concept of service became a very noble one indeed.

In the end it became a custom to adopt modifications of the old work apron as honorable emblems for all who wished to serve their fellow mortals for the sake of a Divine Master. Monastic orders hung protective panels from their shoulders, which became known as scapulars for that reason, and fraternal orders among the laity accepted token waist aprons with embellishments to indicate status or specifications of office. Many were the customs and peculiarities that arose in connection with this practice. Some made their probationers wear the front flaps pinned up to their chests until they were fully initiated. Others tied aprons in front and others again at the rear. The strings might be in two different colors to distinguish between the right and left of life objectives, and of course the various symbols displayed on the front of the apron could be very widely varied. Much might be done with the humble apron as a sign of honorable voluntary service.

It was for this reason that the traditional material for ceremonial aprons was white lambskin. Apart from the Christian implications of sheep being likened to the faithful flock of the Divine Shepherd, and the "Lamb of God" description of Jesus, a lamb was the traditional animal sacrificed in the Temple by an average middle-class family on ceremonial occasions. Thus to wear a portion of lambskin signified: "I am offering myself to God as a sacrifice on behalf of my human family. Take me, Lord, and *do what thou wilt.*" In other words, the mere wearing of the lambskin apron was an unspoken yet fully recognized prayer of oblation in itself. This point should always be carefully considered by anyone assuming an apron prior to entering a Lodge or Temple. It specifically means the free offering of Self on the altar of service, and unless such is sincerely intended, it could be construed as a blasphemy against the Spirit the wearer is claiming to serve.

The commonplace function of an apron of course is to absorb stains from whatever would be unwelcome on the clothing or the person. To keep dirt where it may be easily washed off. In the case of a ceremonial apron, this would signify a "character shield" that could be cleansed from the figurative mud slung by other humans or just the common dirt that one picks up in the normal course of living. A symbolic reminder that we need the spiritual equivalent of an apron that will prevent the psychic soiling of our souls and keep such dirt where it should be, which is superficially on the surface of a garment that may be easily removed for cleansing. That is to say, something to prevent any pollution from actually penetrating our characters and making indelible stains on them. This is a highly important function of the symbolic apron and should be given the fullest consideration.

All the foregoing applies to the external pollution of an individual from outside sources, but there is also the much more intimate matter of pollution from him/her affecting others coming in close contact. In the case of a female, an apron over the genitals affords some protection to others from the once-feared menstrual blood, and in the case of a male, would do the same for any spontaneous spermous discharge. The symbology of this would seem to show that other people should be protected from unwelcome issues derived from individual depths. In other words, we should at least make an attempt to screen our immediate contacts from what may emerge from us that might harm them, as we might place our hands before our mouths when coughing or sneezing. Thus a symbolic apron is a way of saying: "I will place this protection between my pollutions and your purity. May nothing offensive from me contaminate you." The apron is the equivalent of a surgical mask or clothing.

Such a lot of significance from so small a garment. One wonders how often the average Mason meditates on the meaning of his apron and attempts to penetrate beyond its purely decorative appearance. Does he ever wonder why the symbol calls attention to his sexual area? Is it not saying that this "site of life" *is* the foundation stone on which he must build not the Temple of Solomon but the Temple of himself? The symbol it conceals, which consists of a literal penis and two testicles, can be construed as a triangle that outlines both the Square and Compasses together with the eternal eye of the omniscient Overseer.

By centering attention on the genitals, the apron also emphasizes the significance of genetics and their vital importance in the development of self. In these so-called democratic days it is regarded as somewhat reprehensible to stress any assumed superiority because of birth or breeding, but this is totally unrealistic. Good genetics *do* produce the best types of human beings despite whatever the most liberal environmentalists may pretend. All anyone can do is develop the genes he/she was born with, encouraging the best and trying to manage the worst by rearrangement. This is the task of a lifetime and the "work" tacitly acknowledged by the symbolic apron worn by a spiritual worker.

Inferentially, the genetic significance of an apron points to an inheritance of the Blessed Blood or Sangreal, from which the inherent Divinity in man is reputedly derived. As the Holy Grail and all the legends connected therewith, it became a major factor of Western esoteric mysticism and motivated a great part of our practices. If a symbolic apron indicated the best blood in humans by mere inference, it was very well worth wearing by the highest of society. Finally there is a reference in the New Testament to Jesus' assuming an apron for a specific task: "He riseth from supper and laid aside his garments and took a towel and girded himself. After that he poureth water into a basin and began to wash the disciples' feet and to wipe them with the towel wherewith he was girded" (John 13:4-5).

Christian Masons would like to think this was the origin of their ceremonial aprons, even though this would be obviously untrue. The chief interest of this incident is that Jesus had removed the rest of his clothing before assuming his temporary covering, and Jewish culture had a normal taboo against total nudity in company. There was also the curious custom of swearing their most sacred promises to each other while placing their hands above each other's genitals. Therefore, could this have been some private rite amongst themselves wherein the disciples swore something to Jesus on his genitals, and he acknowledged this by a traditional washing of their feet? We shall never be certain but the possibility has to be considered since it raises quite a few implications.

Maybe a final point to think about concerning aprons is their physical size. Theoretically the correct size for a ceremonial apron is an exact square with a triangular flap having a point reaching the center bottom precisely. So when it opens it forms a five-sided figure for humanity, and when closed, a four-sided one for Divinity. It also makes a triplicity for the Christian God and a quaternary for the Jewish one, emphasizing the Judaeo-Christian nature of conventional Western worship and its inherited tradition. It proclaims a belief in squaring up to problems in life, and the square deal that Westerners are said to value from each other. This last is supposed to derive from card playing, meaning that each player sitting at a square table would be dealt the next card off the pack with no cheating. Hence the saying "fair and square," which implied honesty and integrity, two qualities commanding great respect within Western humanity.

Then again, a square represents perfection in human-kind as a life species, just as a true circle stands for Divine perfection. Hence the linked Square and Compasses symbolize an ideal humano-divine relationship. Besides, who ever heard of a circular apron? We have to remember too that Hebrew is written in squarish characters and the Divine Name can be combined as a monogram to form a complete square with a dot (the Yod) in the center. Bisect a square from its corners and we get four triangles, which could represent the twelve signs of the Zodiac, or the letter Chi (*X*) in Greek, which is the initial of the title *Christos*. Then if we form a square out of four Gammas, we find the letter *G* identifies the old Earth Goddess (Ge), so we can tie in the four corners of the earth plus a few other items connected therewith, like *genia* (birth and origins of race), *gametes* and *gamete* (husband and wife), *gnosis* (knowledge), and many other Greek words of singular significance. If a square is made with Latin *L*'s, we have life, love, law, and learning. In fact, since there are so many meanings that can be associated with a ceremonial apron, it could well be regarded as a compendium of occult philosophy in itself.

Extending an apron to complete body coverage, we find that this is generally accomplished by two garments. The Inner Robe of Glory and the Outer Robe of Concealment. As might be guessed from their names, the upper and outer garment represents the intended bodily appearance of the wearer, while the inmost one stands for the soul state of that being. The Outer Robe is supposed to represent not only a physical body but a mental and spiritual one also, though in the condition he/she would wish others to see him/her from a purely objective angle. The Inner Robe symbolizes whatever self-state its wearer would wish to be seen from an entirely inner viewpoint, which is theoretically reachable only by Divinity. Thus the rough rule of the gar-

Temple Robes and Aprons

ments is that the inner one represents the person as he/she would like God to see him/her, and the outer one is what the person wants others to observe.

As Wesoterics should realize clearly enough, their practical work in this world is reconciling and relating the objective and obvious state of existence with the subjective and spiritual conditions of consciousness, thus establishing a reality value between both so that life achieves maximum meaning in each direction. They symbolize this by wearing these two robes of different appearance and coloring, which move together in harmony when worn simultaneously. This is a symbology of its own. Two distinct and contrasting garments with one factor in common—movement or a semblance of life. Opposites combining in a single effect producing an impression of energy and motion. In a way it is a simulated kind of creation, as for instance when God was said to have made man out of normally immobile earth. So do clothes seem to have a life of their own when worn by humans. Granted, this is only an illusory semblance but it is symbolic of our bodies when animated by our souls. We lay aside our bodies when we have finished with them as we remove our garments at the end of a day. So should we have a feeling of putting on a fresh type of life when we assume our ceremonial clothing. Such indeed is what we ought to do. Take on a temporary sort of body expressly for a spiritual purpose. In other words, the clothes are symbolic of the changes we must make in our own natures so as to become fit for service in and to a Divine Cause.

It may be noticed that these robes are arranged in the reverse way to conventional Christian methods, where a white surplice is usually worn on top of a black gown, this arrangement symbolizing purity of intention assumed above a dark human nature. Esoterically, however, the white garment would be the inner one and the dark, the outer one because external appearances hide the true brightness of the Light Within. There were also some very practical reasons involved, especially in the Middle Ages. The thick outer cloak and hood not only protected against bad weather but also hid the identity of its wearer, even making the sex uncertain, especially if the hood was a deep one. Anonymity was frequently a major safety factor among members of the Mysteries.

Additionally a heavy and comfortable cloak of blanket-like quality made meditation a lot easier in chilly climates. With the comfort of a silk undergarment in contact with the skin combined with the cocooning effect of a warm and protective wraparound cloak, a mystically minded wearer could summon up impressions of spiritual security and inner strength with relative ease. In earlier times people were unaware of the electrostatic properties of silk, and all they knew was that it made them feel good when worn as an undergarment. That was enough for them to know there must be something very special about silk, and so it was classified as being highly suitable for ceremonial purposes. Only the very wealthy could afford silk, however; others had to accept fine linen, which was quite costly.

Normally the Inner Robe of Glory is an absolutely plain body garment with longish sleeves fairly wide at the wrist so that they can be tucked up easily. Sometimes it buttons down the front, often with ten buttons for the ten Spheres of the Tree. Modern ones may have a velcro fastening and zippers are not uncommon. The essential idea is to have a garment that washes and cleans very easily. There is no reason why it should not be nylon or any other synthetic, and it must certainly be of ankle length. Traditionally the Inner Robe must not be ornamented in any way, and this prohibition includes the fabric itself, which must not have any design embroidered on it or woven into it. Nowadays that would apply to printed fabric as well. This is to symbolize the clean and clear condition of the soul that is being presented to the Deity for making what impression it wills upon that individual. Almost as if the wearer was a blank sheet of parchment offering itself and saying "Here I am, Lord; now write your Word on me."

In one sense the Inner Robe signifies nakedness since it is blank, presents a uniform surface, bears no mark of rank or distinction, and does not stand out in any way. It is no more than a covering, like the skin of any body. To some extent it represents the "wall" of an individual cell in a mass of protoplasm forming the body of a greater being. If each of us is a single cell in the "body" of God, the Inner Robe defines the distinction between ourselves and our prox- imal cell brethren, each clothed in a similar garment. Simultaneously it reduces us to a common condition of existence while enhancing all individuality therein. It should stimulate the thought: "As a unit of God I am like all the other countless millions of human beings, but *as me*, I am absolutely unique. Here I am, wearing the uniform of an incredibly vast army, and at the same time I have my own particular place in it, which no one else can fill. Outwardly we may all look alike, but inwardly we are all distinct from each other and God alone knows the difference. May this garment signify that Mystery to me."

It is highly important that all ceremonial clothing causes intelligent interest and contemplation concerning the pur- pose behind it. Every piece of it is worn for some specific reason and this should always be sought for on each occa- sion it is assumed. When robing for a ceremony no garment should be put on thoughtlessly. They are all symbols of *something*, and symbols exist to teach us whatever we have become incarnate to learn. So let us not miss the oppor- tunities offered by such simple symbols as ceremonial clothes, each item having its particular lesson incorporated in its nature and purpose. We might miss more in a moment than we could catch up with in a millenium. The very least to be done is to consider each article very carefully and think, "what does this thing mean, and why am I putting it on?"

The Inner Robe of Glory is not inevitably white, though it is always unadorned. It may be the color of the season or specific intention, or even the office held by the wearer. For instance, it might be light green for East, yellow for South, russet for West, and deep indigo for North. It could be blood red to signify the Sangreal. Any color with mystical meaning that is understood by all concerned. All ten colors of the Tree of Life, for instance. Most people are aware of the effect that colored clothing has upon humans and how it affects their moods or expresses them. All the psychology of this applies in particular to ceremonial clothing. It is meant to help both wearers and viewers achieve a correct working mood.

The Outer Robe of Concealment is not always a dark and hooded cloak of anonymity either. It can be an elaborately embroidered covering that signifies the nature of whatever ceremony is being performed, or the occasion for which it is being worn. There are two main types usually adopted, the first being a sort of scapular that is not unlike a heraldic tabard, often called a dalmatic because it seems to have originated in Dalmatia. The second is on the lines of a poncho, being almost circular with a hole in the middle just large enough for the wearer's head. Both types are said to have descended from Roman outer clothing, the dalmatic being a kind of working overall, and the other an overcoat, or *impervius*, which was a simple kind of waterproof garment for bad weather. Again, like the apron, a protective garment.

When worn for purely ceremonial purposes, both garments were meant to accent the ideology of service per se, to indicate that the wearers were *doing* something for or on behalf of Divinity. That is to say, they were *in action*. Nowadays that saying has a purely military meaning, but originally it signified those who *did* things that others had only thought about. Therefore these types of garments are usually reserved for the principals of any esoteric performance. The poncho, being circular, is symbolic of God and so is normally worn by the chief celebrant, whereas the dalmatic, having square corners, is symbolic of human beings and hence is worn by assistant servitors. If there is but one celebrant, however, that person could quite well wear a dalmatic to indicate his/ her office if it has appropriate ornamentation.

So the general rule for determining the type of clothing to be worn will depend entirely on the nature of the ceremony. The more solemn the action, the more elaborate and careful is the clothing that proclaims its purpose. For informal gatherings and workings, the more "token" becomes the attire until it might be only a lapel badge or some very minor sign of recognition. Yet it does not follow that the more important an action is, the more solemn and formal it must become. Importance and solemnity are two different factors and are not to be confused with each other. An action can be very important and intense without being solemn in the sense of hushed quietude at all, and an intensely important action may be done with a minimum of formal clothing. The word *solemn* derives its roots from a meaning of "whole, or entire," and is intended to convey that everything possible is being brought to bear on some particular enterprise, and has no connection at all with sadness or lack of enjoyment. Those factors could be involved but by no means necessarily.

Possibly the next item of importance with ceremonial clothing is the girdle, or Cord, which is a major symbol in its own right. When used as an item of attire it has specific significance. Firstly it marks the middle of its wearer, dividing the body into an upper and a lower portion. Thus it indicates our natural tendency to classify everything into higher and lower categories of consideration, or superior and inferior natures. Theoretically there has to be a dividing line somewhere between our superior spiritual faculties and our inferior animal natures concerned with purely bodily functions such as food, sex, and excretion. That line is symbolized by the girdle, which indicates the central control point of our esoteric extremities.

This is especially symbolized by the knot, which has to be of the reef type, or left over right, then right over left and tied. This forms a hexagram, or Solomon's Seal, which is the sign of Truth, and that is or should be our central pivot on which the whole of our equilibrium turns. A girdle is normally tied so that the knot is centrally in front of the waist, with both loose ends falling equally so that the tassels come to about half way down the shins. In such a position they represent the umbilical cord. This, as we know, is the lifeline connecting us with our mothers during our prenatal existence and here it signifies the connection between ourselves and the Great Mother of all Life, who supplies us with spiritual sustenance while we stay on this earth.

During an inaugural initiation, a blindfolded candidate is often led around a Lodge or Temple by his/her two sponsors, each holding one end of his/her girdle. This is to represent the candidate's early guidance on his/her way by others, and when the initiate "receives the Light," they drop the leading strings to show his/her freedom to find his/her own way for him- or herself in the future. Forever afterwards the initiate is advised to remember what the free ends of the girdle mean: severance from dependency on all except God for guidance, which means the candidate must assume full responsibility for leading him- or herself through life along spiritual lines. Sometimes the tasseled ends of his/her waist cord are pushed into his/her hands for a moment so as to emphasize that from thenceforth the control of his/her conduct lies in his/her own hands.

In olden days the sign of a porter awaiting hire in a public place was the cord or cords carried loosely on his person, often slung around his shoulders. That meant he was available for bearing burdens that other people were unable to carry for themselves. With his cords he would attach those to himself and take the load to its destination for payment. Similarly the candidate wearing a ceremonial girdle-cord indicates a willingness to bear at least a proportion of his/her brethren's spiritual burdens so as to lighten their life loads when they become insupportable for a single soul. Moreover, since the ends hang freely, that signifies that no demands for payment will be made and the obligation offered is purely an honorary one.

More seriously we have to remember that old-time sacred kings were bound to their sacrificial stones or trees with strong cords so that they would not instinctively struggle or flinch at the last moment and thus spoil the action. The girdle still symbolizes its wearer's willingness to sacrifice him- or herself for the sake of all he/she believes in and on behalf of his/her brethren who share those beliefs with him/her. The Cord is a special symbol of the blessed bond between them all. A bond that is stronger than death since it is a link of life among an entire family of a common faith. Since so many multiple meanings may be attributed to a girdle, it is quite amazing that such a simple symbol may mean so much.

One purely practical use of a girdle worn around the waist was partly for hitching a robe up to keep its edge clear of dust and mud and also for hanging personal valuables from. The girdle kept the robe in close contact with the body so that its upper part became a sort of bag that was convenient for carrying suitable objects in, such as spare clothing or light materials. Such usage specially called for a non-slip type of knot to avoid any loss of property. Before pockets were invented this was a very common way to carry odd possessions around, especially something that needed to be kept warm and dry. Bowstrings and tinder boxes in particular, or messages in writing. Anything intended for special safekeeping went into the bosom of its guardian's garment, and that was only possible if the girdle was secure. Hence the saying that a soul was safe in Abraham's bosom.

Translated into terms of spiritual significance, this meant that a girdle enabled its wearer to store his prized possessions in close contact with his body, where they would not be lost unless his "Truth tie" became undone. Therefore it was vital that he tied it properly before he started. First make sure of Truth before consigning valuables to the bosom. Safety first and storage afterwards. All part of the procedures a girdle is supposed to teach symbolically. The proper care and protection of intimate internal secrets and securities. Externally, other accretions may be attached to the girdle so that they cannot be removed without the wearer's knowledge. In old times inkhorns and penholders always hung from girdles. So did keys, scissors, and toilet articles. Modern girdles or belts should still mean the spiritual equivalents of such items and imply the skills needed to use them. Thus when trying a girdle, something like this should be thought, "I am girding myself with every attached ability so that I may be of the best service."

Something else to consider about a girdle is its color. This has a lot of significance, like the grade belts of wrestlers. With one system there were only three girdle colors: white, red, and black. The white represented the innocent inexperience of a neophyte; the red, someone who has symbolically shed blood for the common ideal served, and the black, the same blood aged by a long lifetime of experience and service. Other systems have different colors or combinations of colors to denote grades or offices. They may also signify the type of service being currently offered, or the particular principles by which the wearer feels bound or constrained to act at that particular moment. For instance, a blood red girdle could mean that someone felt bound by the Sangreal or Blessed Blood, while a bright blue one would be worn by someone working in a spirit of magnanimity and mercy.

The customary form of girdle ends is an ornamental tassel, but sometimes there is a tassel at one end and a loop on the other. This accentuates the bisexual significance of the symbol, because when the tassel is put through the loop there is a simulation of the sex act. The loop stands for the female genitals, and the tassel represents the male scattering seed therein. If this is carried to a conclusion, we are presented with a picture of the cord passing completely through its loop in an ever-diminishing circle until it entirely inverts itself and we come back to the beginning again, like a repetitive eternity emblem. One advantage of this type of girdle is that it can be used to trace a circle, with the loop pivoting on a central fulcrum while the tassel end is held with a marking implement by the hand tracing it around a perimeter.

Often the girdle is bicolored from the center, usually black at the female end and white at the male. This is purely to indicate the biology of life and the interaction of birth and death, which connect with each other to make the cycles of creation. The length of the girdle stands for the duration of a lifetime, and therefore represents the circle of time in the Three Rings of Cosmos. It is also important to remember the polarity of the girdle ends, which accord with the Tree of Life. Here we usually take the right-hand Pillar as masculine and the Left as feminine, but that is the mirror view of the Tree. If we regard ourselves as Trees in our own right, looking out at each other, the white masculine Pillar would be on our *left* sides. The black portion of the girdle-cord

Breastplates and Headgear

should thus hang on the *right* if we are male, and on the *left* if female.

This may sound confusing, especially when everything depends on which sex is being mediated, since a physical male may be making a spiritually female approach, in which case the black end of the cord would hang on the left of the body and of course vice versa, yet this should not be considered incongruous since metaphysically a properly balanced human soul consists of both polarities, each of which can be expressed in its own right or combined however necessary. As a rule the male and female side of an active being should be about level with each other, but sometimes there may be a call to emphasize one polarity as a dominant energy. The external evidence of this during a ceremony is the siting of the girdle to the right or left.

The stole is a somewhat strange piece of ceremonial clothing, being no more than a strip of embroidered material hung around the neck and falling down each side of the body. It is believed to have originated from a band of cloth or skin from which depended the priestly sacrificial knife, and indeed its related vesture of a shoulder sash was once a sword belt, or baldric. The word *stole* derives from a Greek word meaning "garments or robes," especially official ones.

In modern times a stole is purely ornamental, but it is full of symbolic significance mainly expressed by its color and attached or embroidered designs. It is normally indicative of office and usually hangs with weighted ends level with the knees or somewhat higher. There are two ways of wearing it: either hung straight down from the shoulders or crossed over the breast with the ends secured by the girdle. The former is the "king" arrangement, meaning rulership, and the latter is the "priest" position, signifying sacrifice. Where the stole is marked to indicate the outer Pillars of the Tree, it will obviously have to be available in two versions, or else be of a reversible nature so that black or white can be on either side to meet requirements.

With most of the fraternal orders the stole has been made in one piece to form a complete collar with the pectoral symbol hanging from the breast point. This does support a suspicion that the stole might connect with the practical purpose of a sweat rag usually hung loosely around the neck of a perspiring worker, frequently a cook. Since a priestly person is presumed to provide people with their spiritual food and drink and does factually offer them the sacramental elements, this idea does have a great deal of meaning. Especially if it is remembered that in very ancient times the literal flesh and blood of a sacrificed sacred king was literally cooked and served to an attendant congregation. In any case, the stole indicates a willingness to work until the spiritual equivalent of sweat is produced in the cause of whatever may be worked for.

Again the concept of exhausting service on behalf of others connected with ceremonial items of clothing. Sweat, like blood, was once considered a sacred fluid, and sometimes the word was a euphemism for male seed. Tears were thought holy too, and the stole is reminiscent of old-time neckerchiefs often used to wipe the eyes of weeping people. Thus it became symbolic of willingness to share sorrow with others in an attempt to lighten their grief. It is still considered a kindly act in some parts of the world, when anyone is stricken to tears with anguish, to sit down with them and cry a lot louder and more wetly in sympathy. So what a stole should proclaim is: "I am willing to work and weep with you for the sake of all we believe together. Because we are brethren I offer this service out of love."

When a stole represents the two Pillars of the Tree and is crossed over the breast in a priestly style, it signifies either Mercy controlling Might if the white is uppermost or Might predominating over Mercy should black be on top.

Both might be justified, depending on circumstances, and the appropriate position should be decided well in advance. It is always well to discover the reasons behind the trivial points of every ceremonial occasion. A great deal that is of interest might otherwise be missed entirely. For instance, since the stole represents the second or space ring of Cosmos, especially when kept in place by the girdle, its loose ends will signify limitlessness or freedom from fixity, which is an end in itself. Like the ends of the girdle, they signify divine guidance as if they were reins held in the holy hands of God. This thought should inspire stole wearers to offer the ends up with the uttered or unspoken prayer "Guide me, O God, wherever I may be led in life."

Another dual item to be worn is the shoes, sandals, or slippers. Strictly speaking, they should be kept on the Temple premises so that no dirt from elsewhere will be brought in. This is seldom enforced, however, and the usual practice is for members to keep their slippers in special bags and bring them to each attendance. These days they are normally ordinary household slippers, but officials may wear somewhat special footgear.

Shoes are one item of human clothing that has remained basically the same from the very beginning. A covering of leather bound around each foot to protect against excessive friction, which would otherwise wear out the skin beyond repair. We know there are primitive people who do not wear shoes, but these tend to remain primitive and are limited to the warmer parts of the world. Civilization in colder climates would not have been possible without protective footwear, and that is true on inner levels of life as well. We have the spiritual equivalents of feet, or the extremities that we advance to come in contact with good grounds for belief so that we shall be supported well enough to stand firmly thereon. Just as there are stones, thorns, and other discomforts to walk over on earth, so are the metaphysical counterparts to these equally difficult to traverse spiritually. Therefore we need to be properly shod in both dimensions.

Consider the various types of footgear specifically designed for all variety of experience. Think of climbing boots, skating boots, riding boots, and working boots, and then contrast these with dancing shoes, dress shoes, court shoes, and bedroom slippers. Compare that lot with waist-high wading boots, knee-high gumboots, and early aviators' fur-lined overboots. Lastly perhaps a fireman's asbestos boots. Each type made for some human specialist activity, and each suitable for that alone and nothing else. Why then should it seem odd if we postulate a comparatively varied range of symbolic spiritual footgear?

In mythology we hear of several types of idealistic shoes and boots. Notably the famed "seven league boots," which reduced distance to a triviality, and the winged sandals of Hermes, which took him anywhere with great rapidity. Otherwise a magical sort of transport that enabled large quantities of space to be covered in a small quantity of time. We have seen this come true in our days with air travel, which has enlarged human experience enormously. So what we should be looking for here is a valid method of designing ceremonial footwear to suit every kind of esoteric occasion without too many complications.

The simplest way out would seem to be a neutrally colored pair of slippers, say in mid-grey, with a set of detachable buckles to indicate intentions. After all, it is essentially the specific intention that constitutes the validity of the item in question, and that intent is expressed by the symbology and design of the artifact. Thus slippers with a winged design on the buckles obviously suggest a need for celerity, and those marked with a step or ladder symbol, climbing by one's own efforts. It would also be feasible to label one shoe with the point of departure and the other with the point of intended arrival. This might easily be conveyed by the signs of the ten Spheres, or even in plain English.

Another way of dealing with the shoe problem is to use a black-and-white pair, worn according to whichever polarity is being worked. If, for instance, the white one is on the right foot, let this be first extended while positive or projective energy is pushed forward as powerfully as possible. When the left foot with its black slipper follows, experience a swing through the central neutral position and then alter to a negative attitude as it comes to the front. Keep on walking and alternating in this fashion, maybe to suitable music, until it becomes completely familiar. It is best to begin this exercise by tramping around a conveniently sized circle.

When Astronaut Neil Armstrong walked on the surface of the Moon and said, "That's one small step for a man, one giant leap for mankind," his remark became famous for all time. Yet the most remarkable step we have ever taken was the first time a human being stood erect and then put one foot after the other as a regular means of progression. Step by step we have come a very long way since that moment, and we have an incalculable journey ahead of us still. Physically, mentally, or spiritually our progression along our paths has always been accomplished in that fashion, and the sign of a shoe or slipper signifies our journey through life from beginning to end on all levels.

Footsteps have always been considered something special since the days of primitive hunters. They had a custom of stabbing at animal spoors as a kind of mimetic magic to ensure eventual killing of the creature itself, and a human footprint was anciently regarded as being linked with the individual who made it, frequently considered as the sign of a human soul. Pythagoras in particular warned his followers not to damage anyone's footprints, for fear of injuring the individual even at a distance, though this does not seem to have influenced Roman soldiers, who often had the number of their legion done in iron studs on the soles of their sandals so that viewers would know who had passed that way. That practice throws interesting light on the accusation against the Templars: that they had the Christian cross stamped into their boot soles so that they might defile it in the dirt. They may have only been trying to show that a Christian army was in the vicinity. The Danes in particular honored footprints by sprinkling them with their blood on conclusion of a treaty, and kissing the imprint of a loved one's foot was thought to send kind feelings over a great distance to the person. Kissing the outstretched foot of an actual monarch of course was a public sign of complete loyalty in his/her service, and to kiss the foot of the Pope was once the pious hope of every pilgrim. Somehow or other the human foot has always held much meaning in spiritual terms and is literally clothed in ancient customs.

We also have hands with very special significance, and it is our fully opposable thumbs that are the unique mark of humankind, since they alone account for all our dexterity and possibly for the whole of our civilization. We could say quite justifiably that humanity has built itself with its own hands. Especially since not a thing constructed anywhere in the whole world would have been possible without hands. Certainly no Temple or artifact therein could ever have existed otherwise. The hands of Temple officers in particular are accentuated by two items of apparel: ornamental cuffs and the Ring. Cuffs are relatively recent and mostly in use with the fraternal orders. They were introduced mainly as utilities, since the wide sleeves of old-fashioned gowns often made trouble for their wearers, especially when their wearers were trying to manipulate smallish symbols on an altar. At first the cuffs were only plain bands, but they became increasingly ornamental until their present form as emblems of office was reached. Originally utilitarian, they became an almost cumbersome superfluity.

There could still be a practical use for cuffs if they are employed to emphasize the polarity of hand gestures, so frequently an important part of ceremonial work. If the cuffs are differently colored or just black and white, they will act as underliners for the intention being put in action. Supposing the right hand is taken as Might and the left as Mercy, this point becomes increasingly clear if the former appears from a red cuff and the latter from a blue one. Similarly in the case of a polarized positive and negative power if the cuffs are black and white like the Pillars of the Tree. Should both cuffs be the same color, that would indicate both hands were being put to the same purpose. On the whole, however, cuffs are becoming increasingly obsolete since sleeves are seldom of any great width today.

The Ring is entirely a different symbol and counts as regalia, or that which pertains to the kingly side of a human character. Ceremonial rings are usually worn on the index finger of the right hand, and symbolize the directive drive or True Will of whoever is working. The index finger is called such because it points at or indicates something intended by the person pointing. The Ring's design or engraving may be the personal signet of its owner, or the logo of whichever association he/she belongs to. It is supposed to show the special relationship between its wearer and the directing Divinity controlling his/her esoteric operations. Almost any design at all that clearly conveys the message "This is my will, which I believe derives from the Deity expressing itself through me."

Traditionally rings had subservient spirits attached to them, who obeyed the owners insofar as they were able, though they had only very limited abilities, often confined to one capability alone. This signifies our circumscribed personal powers as compared to the far greater ones we are invoking through ceremonials. In effect a ring means the concentration of Cosmic forces through oneself until they focus in the compass of a single finger. It is almost like a lens or laser, which intensifies the quality of light but reduces its area proportionately. Or an electrical transformer, which increases voltage at the cost of current. Anything that alters one factor at the expense of another for the sake of effecting a pointed purpose. One might certainly liken this to the art of putting a maximum of power behind the tip of a finger so that when properly applied to exactly the right place on an opponent's body, the results are devastating.

Not that such force is often needed. Consider the things we do nowadays with very slight pressure indeed. We can make elevators full of heavy humans ascend and descend. We can operate typewriters and computer keyboards. Drive vehicles of all kinds. With a little pressure on the right buttons we could even destroy our entire world. So much of what we do nowadays depends on finger pressures applied in a correct sequence. All we need is the knowledge of which and when to press in order to cause whatever change. That knowledge on spiritual levels is symbolized by the finger ring. Most of us are familiar with the old phrase "If only I could put my finger on it!"— meaning a need of knowing how to understand or control some particular problem. The ceremonial ring signifies precisely that ability in spiritual terms. It does not guarantee that such an ability will automatically be acquired as the ring is assumed, but it is an evident sign that the ability is at least being hoped and prayed for.

In former times children were constantly being told "It's rude to point at people," and in former beliefs, pointing a finger at anyone was part of a cursing process. This had to be done with the left hand only, however. Shaking an admonitory right forefinger only meant "I am pointing something out for your attention, so please listen care-fully." The gesture is in common use today, though few people regard it as anything of great significance now. Since pointers in place of a finger are still employed in Orthodox synagogues for reading the Scrolls of the Law, an almost automatic respect is often given to the "finger" that comes into such close contact with what is regarded as the direct Word of God.

In certain sections of the Christian church the fore-fingers and thumbs of priestly right hands are specially consecrated since they in particular hold the Sacred Host, which is believed to be the actual body of Jesus Christ after the words of consecration are spoken. For that reason alone, it was regarded as an honor to shake hands with a man who had held God between his fingers. They are the same digits that apply the holy annointing oils of extreme unction or the soul-saving waters of baptism. Although Christian priests seldom or never wear rings nowadays, a bishop still does as his seal of authority, while the Pope's is yet termed the Fisherman's Ring and is defaced at his death because it is purely personal to himself and no one else must ever wear it.

It is a custom, though rarely done now, to kiss a bishop's ring as evidence of submission to ecclesiastical authority, though this is more a survival of civil rather than religious convention. Old-time potentates regarded their rings as a sign of their powers and would entrust them to special envoys acting in their names at a distance. The presence of a royal ring meant that the monarch him- or herself was ceremonially present, and orders given in his/her name must be obeyed accordingly. Every written royal command was not considered authentic without a seal, and although the state seal ruled supreme, personal requirements would be sealed with the monarch's private signet ring. To touch this ring with one's lips was an admission of everything to be expected of a faithful subject. Eventually, hand kissing became a general custom mainly between men and the women they acknowledged or wished to honor as rulers of their passions—if only momentarily.

In palmistry, the double line that is sometimes found at the base of the right forefinger is termed a *Solomon's Ring* and is considered to be the mark of someone naturally devoted to the occult sciences for maybe more than one incarnation. This derives from the legend that King Solomon possessed a magical ring that gave him authority over many legions of spirits who obeyed the symbol impressed into it. That symbol was reputed to be the hexagram, or six-pointed star, which is now the emblem of Israel. It is also, as we have seen, the Truth tie of the girdle. The mystical meaning of this is that all intelligent life, whether embodied or not, must be subservient to the supreme principle of Truth in the end. Especially when pointed out with a finger bearing Its special symbol.

Thus the wearing of an appropriate ceremonial ring implies the intention, if not the actual ability, of ruling wisely according to what is believed in or followed as the truth. It should certainly be the seal of personal and individual sincerity. Bearing in mind that the word *sincerity* comes from the Latin *sine cire*—without wax—which implies that one's word alone was sufficient without a written bond bearing one's legal seal, we should see the importance a signet ring was held in formerly. If a modern counterpart can be held in equal significance today, it would be well worth wearing. Otherwise it will mean nothing more than personal adornment. A little-known advantage of a ceremonial ring is that it can be worn on its own to solemnize any occasion provided it is worn for such purposes alone, and never for pure display or decoration.

Sometimes classed with the ring as a piece of jewelry

is the Lamen, or breastplate, frequently called a pectoral since it hangs on the breast more or less over the heart. It signifies the active authority behind the ceremony being worked, or its essential directing consciousness. The heart of the matter so to speak. Thus with Christians it would probably be a crucifix; with Jews, a Star of David (or Solomon's Seal), and so on. With Wesoterics it would be the central symbol of whichever association they belonged to, or else some other symbolic item they had chosen to represent their relationship with whatever Power they believed would further their purpose best.

This Lamen, which is seldom more than medallion sized and often of precious metal, is the official seal set on its wearer as a mark of authority and authenticity. Symbolically it should explain, identify, and justify that individual in whatever work he/she is doing. A single glance at it should be sufficient to convey everything that needs knowing about the wearer and the ceremony he/she may be conducting. It is more than an identity card, being not only an authorization but a passport and certificate of competence as well. However, it can only be genuine if the wearer has the actual qualifications to back it up. Observers on inner levels of life are never deceived by false colors or lying Lamens since they see the soul directly. Therefore there is no real point in decorating oneself with unearned symbols of authority.

That is always a great temptation to free-lance esoterics with inadequacy problems. They tend to overdo their ornamentation in an attempt to enlarge their egos, if only in their own eyes. In a way they are not unlike certain historical characters who covered their uniformed chests with totally unearned medals. All that happened was that they made everyone laugh at their expense and were often ridiculed behind their backs or made money for clever cartoonists. In similar fashion do their esoteric equivalents afford amusement to those who are aware of spiritual authenticity. There could be a touch of pathos about such a spectacle also.

There is absolutely nothing against esoterics wearing symbols they have invented for themselves or symbols in general usage, such as the pentagram, hexagram, astrological signs, Tree of Life glyphs, or anything of that nature. It is only when they sport ensignia of some esoteric order they do not belong to, or something that advertises them to be of greater importance or ability than they really are that the trouble starts. That action would invalidate the rest of their habiliments, which could be quite genuine. Not unlike someone wearing full surgical clothing while carrying a certificate, hung around his/her neck, proclaiming he/she was a fully qualified member of the Plumbers Guild. One glance at that, and who would admit the individual into any hospital except a mental one?

It is therefore vitally important that the total symbology of a Lamen or a pectoral plate be completely understood not only by its wearer but also by those working with him/her. The esotericist must be entirely capable of completely supporting its meaning and implications. Otherwise it would be much safer to adopt a good general symbol such as the cosmic cross or something of like nature that any human of average abilities and intentions could claim quite legitimately. Should a need for something more unique be felt, why not a circular or maybe square medallion engraved with its wearer's name and spiritual specialties? Or maybe a miniature horoscope of that individual? Anything identifiable with him/her and no one else. That could be enclosed in a locket hung from the end of a neck chain and consequently invisible to all but inwardly authorized eyes.

Such a chain in itself is part of the regular regalia and represents the event circle of the Three Cosmic Rings. So when it is solemnly assumed, with or without its attached symbol, the petition "Guide me through *what*ever may happen during my life" should be made to the directing Deity. This completion of the cosmic circle around the spiritual supplicant should never be omitted. With the waist girdle being the *when*, the stole the *where*, and now the neck chain as the *whats* of life, existence has been covered from all angles. This only leaves the last significant item of ceremonial clothing to be considered, the headdress or crown of the whole lot.

The first crowns ever worn by mortals were probably floral, or consisted of some kind of foliage. Eventually these had definite meanings—such as laurel or palm for victory, olive for peace and prosperity, and cypress for grief and mourning. Sacred kings were always so garlanded with such crowns, which could have very complex symbology if specific vegetation appeared in prearranged patterns. The tops of altars were once crowned with garlands, and the floral decorations in modern churches are a memorial of that ancient custom.

A headdress is usually the last item of clothing assumed before making an official or public appearance, and so symbolizes the height of achievement attainable in any incarnation. The top of the tree so to speak, and on the Tree of Life, Kether the Crown is exactly that for humanity. What individuals wear on their heads represents their highest hopes and abilities. At the same time, headgear stands for needed protection against adverse influences affecting thought and intelligence. If it is a helmet it is meant to protect the head from damaging blows; if a headcloth, from sunstroke, and if a coronet or crown it is supposed to inspire respect from beholders so that they will treat the wearer with honor. For that matter a policeman's helmet is intended to make people respect the law for what it can do to them if they break it, while a soldier's helmet stands for the armed might of the state, which is only to be invoked in desperate need. The harmless headdress of a priest or esotericist is only intended to represent the spiritual power of whatever church or Temple he/she serves.

The ancient floral crowns of sacred kings were symbolic of the highest service asked of any human. Namely the offer of his own life at the hands of the people he loved. Nothing could be higher than that. In the case of Jesus his crown was one of thorns fixed on his head by Roman soldiers who would have known quite well the meaning of their act intended as a cruel joke. Possibly some of them may have heard the very ancient legend that at the beginning of Creation God had asked man what he wanted most in life, and man had answered, "Fame." Whereupon God put a garland of roses firmly on his head and replied, "There my son, your wish is granted. While others are admiring your splendid appearance all you will know is the pain of the thorns." In other words, the price of fame is private suffering.

It has often been said, "Uneasy lies the head that wears a crown," and this is meant to imply the weight of responsibility imposed on monarchs who take their office seriously. That is precisely what a priestly ceremonial headdress ought to symbolize. The tremendous spiritual burden that the officiant is seen to bear on behalf of others. In old times heavy burdens were usually carried on the head, and normally there was a sort of flat fibrous pad first placed on top of the head to help support and cushion the weight of the load. That is the sort of crown a priest/priestess is supposed to assume in the name of whatever God he/she believes to be the power behind his/her people.

Theoretically a ceremonial crown or headdress for the principal celebrant should be a heavy one to remind him/her constantly of the burden he/she has to bear on behalf of his/her brethren. It is seldom so in fact these days, but it could be a good idea to reintroduce the element of weight so as to affirm the original significance of this spiritual symbol. This could be done by having a heavy crown only worn momentarily at an appropriate part of the ceremony, or loading an ordinary headgear with sheet lead. Otherwise the sense of weight should be acknowledged symbolically when the headgear is assumed, even if it is feather light in actuality. The general rule is that the higher and more responsible the office, the heavier the crown is supposed to be.

This was one reason for jewels in former crowns. In old times coins were worth their weight in the metal they were made of, and jewels worth a lot of gold coins were considered to be the weight of that value. Thus a crown with many jewels of large value was considered to be a weight far too heavy for any ordinary mortal to sustain, and therefore a monarch was symbolically superhuman. Christian bishops and abbots formerly had special so-called precious mitres emblazoned with precious stones and they were only worn on very important occasions. These were very rarely personal possessions, but part of the wealth owned by the community those clerical officers served. Once they had been deconsecrated they could be sold or pledged to raise necessary funds.

The mitre was thought to represent the head of a fish with its allusion to Peter the Fisherman, who was the reputed first bishop of the Christian church, but in fact it was very much older than Christianity and followed on the lines of a Jewish high priest's headgear, which was roughly of a triangular shape. This more or less conical headcover was in effect the human triangle of a hexagram representing humankind pointing itself at the heavenly God. To some extent it is reminiscent of a space rocket's nose cone and suggests the ideology of human beings aiming themselves at the stars they are supposed to have arrived at this earth from. Magicians in art are often depicted wearing a high, pointed brimless hat, though this probably derives from early Persian headgear that was actually a lot shorter in the crown.

A triangular headpiece would be in the shape of a high priest's blessing on a congregation. This was made by placing both hands together just above face level, with fingers and thumbs touching at their tips while the palms were turned outward. The triangle was said to stand for the three essential letters of the Name—*IHV*. In the Scriptures this headgear is specifically termed a mitre of fine linen and is referred to at Exodus 29:6, "and thou shalt put the mitre upon his head and the holy crown upon the mitre." Later, in Leviticus 8:9, we have "and he put the mitre upon his head, also upon the mitre on his forefront did he put the golden plate the holy crown." The golden plate referred to had "HOLINESS TO THE LORD" engraved on it. The highest of human ideals inscribed at the physical focus of consciousness. The actual word *mitre* does not mean an exact shape, but simply means its function as a turban or headband.

The idea extended to the laity in the form of *tefillin*, or the small black leather boxes with scriptural texts in them that strict Orthodox Jewish men bind on their foreheads (for thinking) and their left arm (for feeling) before they commence morning prayers. Thus they signify that they are placing both brains and brawn in the service of the All-Highest. A ritual sacrificial gesture to show their voluntary bondage to beliefs and devotion to Deity. It should be remembered how ancient sacred kings were bound before being sacrificed, and this is a symbolic representation of that act. Later in history their place was taken by martyrs, or those who died for the sake of their religious faith, and their recognized reward was a special golden crown in heaven.

There is a rather lovely legend concerning the Merkaba, or chariot of God, which is a wheeled throne in which the Deity is said to traverse the whole of creation. During this progress, the archangel Sandalaphon reputedly goes down to earth, collects the prayers of all the faithful and presumably throws them up to his celestial colleague Metatron, who catches and weaves them into crowns that he then presents to the driving Deity, though we are not told what the Deity does with them. We cannot help being reminded here of old Roman triumphal processions in which the principal victor rode in a chariot, with a slave behind him holding a crown above his head while occasionally whispering the admonition "Remember man, thou art but mortal." This was supposed to be a timely reminder of his true condition in Cosmos and prevent him from developing hubris, or the sort of presumptuous pride that the Gods were liable to punish very promptly.

Any or all of the foregoing thinking should accompany the wearing of any ceremonial headdress. When someone has several official functions to fulfill, he/she may be asked, "Which hat were you wearing when you said that?" The query was being raised as to which capacity he/she was speaking in at that moment. In a similar way, a ceremonialist should know what spiritual function he/she is fulfilling when assuming the appropriate headgear. Is he/she officiating as a lector? Then let him/her assume the square black cap of law and learning. As a healer? The soft silken or linen nemyss with the Aesculapian serpent frontal. As a sacrificial priest? The crown-cap of the sacred king combined with priesthood. As a preacher or prayer leader? The plain skull cap of a suitable color. Merely meditating? An ordinary conventional hood. Nothing more than the hat to go with the job, like everyone else in a working human world.

Although the choice of correct ceremonial clothing does depend a lot upon the particular spiritual system being followed and the styles suitable to that system, we have covered here a good average of the clothing in common usage in contemporary practice among Wesoterics. The modern tendency is to simplify everything as far as practicable, mainly for the sake of economy and expediency. The most important ceremony *can* be carried out with a minimum of elaborate clothing and a maximum of substitute symbology, but that does not mean that it *should* be carried out that way if more adequate means are really available. Every class of ceremony should be conducted with the very best materials and with the highest standards of proficiency currently at hand. In other words, there is no excuse for deliberately offering inferior or carelessly done work.

Ceremony is both an art and a craft calling for care, exactitude, and skill in its practice so as to present it properly. Correct and adequate clothing is a part of this and should be treated accordingly. There is no rule stating that clothing must be expensive, but there are plenty requiring it to be symbolically correct, clean, and worn only by those who understand its full functions and implications. If worn by an initiated individual, a staff cut from a hedgerow and an apron of sackcloth secured with binder twine are more valuable esoterically than the most expensive pastoral staff and silken-bound lambskin that decorate an egotistic ignoramus. Yet there is no virtue in wearing the inferior substitute for its own sake if the better quality is equally available.

Therefore, in all questions concerning ceremonial garments, the determining factors should always be the spiritual significance of each item and its applicability to the work in hand. It is better to wear nothing at all rather than the wrong or inappropriate clothing. That would be comparable to the case of the European diplomat's wife who once asked a Chinese craftsman to make her a set of carved ivory buttons. A superb set was indeed made and paid for, but she could not understand why Chinese gentlemen tended to avert their eyes from her at official functions, and why others showed signs of unseemly mirth. Suspecting the buttons, she asked a cultured Chinese acquaintance of hers what might be wrong. He absolutely declined to translate their meaning, but did inform her it might be best not to wear them in public, since the carved characters cast the deadliest doubt on the integrity, morals, and habits of European women in general and her in particular.

It must never be forgotten that each item of ceremonial clothing is a symbol like the letters of an alphabet or anything with mathematical meaning. When a complete collection is assembled on a single individual, will it make sense or otherwise to the inner eyes that will read its message? The only way to ensure this is by comprehension of what everything means and of when and why to employ each item. Once that understanding is acquired, it will be possible to gain a spiritual dress sense that will guarantee a good appearance among those that appreciate such artistry.

Chapter 5

ATTITUDES

Here we come to the very important question of attitudes both outwardly on physical levels and inwardly on mental and spiritual ones. Each is taken to be a reflection or likeness of the other. That is to say, the outward and visible appearance of ourselves in bodily form during any esoteric ceremony is supposed to be a symbolic representation of our inner mental and spiritual condition as human creatures. The underlying idea is that a unification of all the self-aspects ensures a maximum of available energy. We might be reminded here of the text "Whatsoever thou hast to do, do it with all thy might." In other and more modern words, "Put all you've got into it."

Now it is obvious that civilized and cultured people do nothing of the sort when it comes to expressing emotional and internal feelings. We do not normally yell, howl, or scream when we are angry, wail when hurt, or roar when offended. Yet such reactions are quite normal for a baby or small child reacting to adverse stimuli, in addition to violent motions of the body. In circumstances of pleasure, the bodily movements slow down, vocalization reduces to giggles and gurgles, and facial expression to smiles or chuckles. Extreme fear, however, may produce silence and immobility, while exceptional degrees of shock can cause unconsciousness and even death.

As adults, we have been conditioned to suppress external evidence of our inner feelings, or at least reduce it to an absolute minimum especially when in company with other humans. This may be a convenient convention, but it does mean that we are living polite lies most of our lives. Eventually we become accustomed to presenting an externally urbane appearance while possibly undergoing internal upheavals and emotional stresses that may be wrenching mind and soul apart. Or possibly longing internally to laugh, sing, shout, and dance for sheer joy while permitting ourselves to do no more than smile politely and murmur a few stereotypical phrases. Many psychiatrists are convinced that such social inhibitions are causing most of our mental and behavioral problems if not also having a bad effect on our physical states of health. This presents an immediate difficulty to the ceremonialist who needs to gather up and focus all possible force into a concentrated field of consciousness. If the physical vehicle (the body) is resistant or at least nonresponsive to inner energies, how is it possible to maximize these energies through psychodramatic procedures? There seem to be only three answers. Invent new techniques, adapt or expand present ones until they serve such a purpose—or do both. We might also try reducing the levels of physical and mental resistance to inner stimuli, or making the response to inner stimuli more efficient.

In all forms of ceremony we have definite sets of bodily behavior, each with its own meaning and application. These were mainly arrived at through the experience of many people who, over a long period of time, found them satisfactory because they expressed or demonstrated the purposes of ceremonies quite adequately. For example, military ceremonies are meant to show both observers and partakers that disciplined bodies of troops are capable of exerting energies as directed by their commanders. Religious and esoteric ceremonies should likewise demonstrate a condition of contact between humans and their directing Deity or authorized agents thereof. In each case, attitudes that are expressive of inner awareness have to be adopted. Each individual soldier is placing his/her personal will at the disposal of the communal commander, whose legitimate orders will be promptly obeyed, while esotericists are placing theirs under the command of whichever Spirit they acknowledge as their Superior Being.

The main difference between these divergent types of command is that the soldiers hear their directions through their physical ears and respond immediately, while the esoterics get their instructions through inner senses alone and respond as impelled. Furthermore, the soldiers' response is a standard movement to which they have been conditioned by special training, whereas the esoterics' answer consists of attitude alteration determined by their own natures, which are conditioned by beliefs and customs. Moreover, the soldiers only alter attitude when commanded, and esoterics alter theirs on their own initiative. Otherwise there is a lot of similarity between the two bodies.

The soldiers have one advantage over the esoterics. They know in advance exactly what attitude to adopt on any given command and precisely why to adopt it. This is purely because they have practiced so often and know the procedures so well. Esoterics could do the same with their behavior patterns if they were prepared to put in the same amount of work, but remarkably few ever seem sufficiently dedicated, and there is no recognized program of procedures administered by initiated instructors. Programs themselves do exist, and so do initiated instructors, but these are so much at varience with each other that agreement between any seems highly unlikely, especially when all are claiming an authenticity they deny in everyone else. Hence the art of attitude adoption is insufficiently appreciated among Wesoterics, who mostly take for granted that a minimal one of a solemn face, folded hands, and limited movements ought to cover most contingencies.

It seldom seems to strike them that there is an entire "alphabet" of body language; each "letter" has its own meaning and when combined with others, they will spell out whole "words" expressing the theme-intention of the entire working. Correct arrangements of this amount to esoteric choreography. For example, when the body movements for any ballet are being plotted, its story or theme must be known, and every action allotted to each dancer should have its reason for being germane to the theme at that instant. It is the dancers' progression from one movement to another that is supposed to tell the whole story from beginning to end. Experienced balletomanes can follow this just as literate people read the same story from printed pages. Much the same should be the case with ceremonial workings. From a limited number of basic attitudes, each with its own meaning, an entire vocabulary may be built up that should make the intention and initiative behind any ceremony absolutely crystal clear to its sharers on all levels of life. This must be a lot more than merely a dumb show or meaningful mime because the minds and souls of those who make the movements have to coincide and concur with them completely.

In old-time practice every formalized God-aspect had its own distinct set of attitudes that were supposed to be copied by whoever wanted to invoke the Deity from any angle. These were either shown in pictures of the God or described in detail by mythographers. There were also oral instructions handed down to the initiated; but few of these directives have survived into our times yet they remain indelibly impressed into our ancestral memories. What is important is that we recall them in terms suitable to modern living and conducive to a greatly improved future. Such stylized God-attitudes are more common in the Oriental Inner Tradition than in our own, because Western culture does not encourage anthropomorphic deities. Nevertheless there are certain conventional attitudes imposed on those addressing themselves to Deity per se, but they are based on the type of God-quality needed—i.e., if Mercy is being appealed to, then one specific attitude is adopted; if Retribution is being sought, another and different attitude, and so on.

Most of these are very stilted and inadequate, being the remnants of formerly less restricted behavior. Among the revivalists and charismatic sectarians, however, there are far wider limits on bodily movements, limits that permit extravagant expression of emotions and feelings: extremists like the Holy Rollers can actually fling their bodies on the ground in contortions. The Society of Friends earned their title of Quakers solely on account of their early members' literally shaking from head to foot as they felt themselves being influenced by the "Holy Spirit" during their religious exercises. That is actually quite a common phenomenon among mystics of all persuasions.

It might be supposed that every type of attitude has been tried and tested by a wide variety of people, and that could be true, except that the different types have been generally uncoordinated and unrelated to any recognized scale of behavior unless in the very broadest sense. Only choreographers and old-time theatrical directors seem to have standardized any physical styles and attitudes as authentic expressions of inner feelings and emotions. Perhaps some relics of those persist with certain orders of priesthood, but only faintly so, and with modern esoteric ceremonialists it is becoming very much a lost art. The practice of assuming attitudes could very well be reassessed and related to some standards generally acceptable among Wesoterics. The question is where to begin.

The assignment of definite meanings to bodily attitudes has been brought to a fine art with the practice of semaphore, which relates various positions of flags held in one's out-flung hands to letters of the alphabet and to numerals. In that way intelligent messages may be transmitted over distances that can be covered by the eye but not the ear. What we need is a spiritual equivalent of this process whereby an intelligent human can communicate inner conditions of consciousness with agencies that share that consciousness on all life levels.

To a great extent we do this naturally anyway. If we are pleased and happy we smile; if sad, we weep or look downcast; if hurt or wounded, we might suck, rub, or protect the injury. Our feelings and bodily expressions do coincide. Why then, when we encounter inner energies esoterically, should we not have an appropriate body language for expressing this? Furthermore, an organized and comprehensible one that covers every reasonable range of contingencies and is easily understood. If possible, a communication code that can be reduced to a sort of shorthand by minimizing movement without losing meaning in the least.

Let us start by analyzing the meaning of some commonly accepted attitudes adopted in general ceremonial practice. Then let us see if and how these may fit in an extended scale of significance. The obvious place to start is with the seated and motionless position. The esotericist should be positioned on a relatively hard-seated chair of a height so that the thighs and shins are at a right angle to each other or possibly a trifle higher. Both feet are to be flat on the floor and parallel with each other, and legs or ankles never crossed. Both hands, with fingers extended, are to rest palms downward lightly on thighs, fingertips level with knees. The back is to be held as straight as possible, preferably unsupported by the chair back. If the eyes are closed the head may be slightly bent, but if open, then the head is to be upright and the gaze concentrated on some fixed point while features remain immobile. Breathing is reduced to a slow steady rate, and all body movements kept to an absolute minimum. If there have to be movements, say for blowing one's nose, this must be done with great control and expeditiously. No fumbling or attempts at furtiveness. For that reason handkerchiefs are best kept tucked up sleeves, where they can be plucked out, used, and replaced with neat and economical gestures.

This position is the basic attitude of attention through which the sitter signals that he/she is ready and waiting for whatever may eventuate on inner levels. From this position it is possible to rise into action quite easily or sink back into meditation at any moment. To do the latter, one need only alter the hand position, close the eyes, and incline the head slightly forward. The hand position will depend on where attention is being directed. If externally, the hands are simply turned over so that the palms are upward and the fingers together, loosely curled. If internally, then they will be clasped while held together in the lap. The deeper the attention is directed, the closer will be the clasp until in the end each wrist is being gripped by the opposite hand inside the sleeves of the gown. Alternatively, if attention needs to be directed toward a talk or lecture, the hands may be left loose on the knees and the back supported by the chair while the gaze is fixed on the speaker. Should an orison be called for, it will only be necessary to bring the hands together before the body in the prayer position, with palms and fingers together pointing upwards.

To arise into action from this primary position, it is sufficient to begin by bringing the fingertips together simultaneously with straightening the legs as the palms press together while the forearms come in contact with the chest and the hands are held at just above heart level. This says symbolically "I am holding all that is in my heart at the disposal of Divinity." If we think of the mirror image as reflected by the Tree of Life design, it should be evident that the right hand of Might is being brought in touch with the left hand of Mercy, and then placed in a Middle Pillar position between Harmonious Balance and Experience (*Tiphereth* and *Daath*). The hands are being used as indicators of intention just as those of a clock indicate the time. What the hands are doing shows what the head and heart are doing.

It follows that what the feet do has a significance of its own. Though this is mainly expressed through dance patterns and rhythmic movements, there are definite meanings behind static positions too. When the feet are side by side and flat on the floor, they mean "I am adopting a balanced attitude about this and am facing it squarely." If the right foot is advanced ahead of the left, it means "I shall approach this with favorable intentions." Should the left foot be advanced, that means the reverse. "I am approaching this with suspicion and distrust." Hence it is important, when commencing to move off, that the appropriate foot be advanced first.

Ceremonial rising or sitting should be a neat and economical movement. A straightforward approach to the chair, a turn that brings the backs of the legs in contact with the seat edge, and then a simple folding of the body into the sitting position and rearrangement of the hands with one movement. No unnecessary fumbling or groping around. Just movement, then stillness. Each motion precise and positive. This can be done with equal precision slowly or rapidly. In fact, ceremonial movements are very rarely rapid, but they are always definite and deliberate, never vague or hesitant. Even the slightest movement must be made with the greatest precision.

On reflection this will be found to be no more than the Western form of yoga. Its Oriental version consists of adopting specific bodily postures that are physical symbols of inner states of soul and mind. These postures are relatively few and are held for prolonged periods. In the West, exactly the same principles apply, though the physical postures are less pronounced and are varied a great deal more frequently. Otherwise, the purposes and aims are identical. Linking (or yoking) oneself with the Universal Spirit through whatever distinctive attitude may have been chosen. Harmonizing oneself with the Highest.

There are three categories of attitude in which we can do this.

1. Humbly. As an inferior being, conscious of its own condition while approaching a superior spiritual power from a lower position in life, yet with confidence in the rightness of such a relationship. Appropriate attitudes will therefore symbolize this as prostrations, kneeling with bent head, masking face with hands, and all such subservient gestures.

2. Hopefully. As an equivalent entity on its own scale of existence. We are reputed to be "in the image and likeness of God" in this world, and therefore the agents of the Almighty here. This means adopting an upright attitude that is nevertheless deferential toward Deity while maintaining a competent one toward others. A Middle Way position of mediation involving a balanced mixture of movement and stillness.

3. Honorably. As an authoritative agent of the Omnipotent, through which its will and work are accomplished in this world. All attitudes here should be commanding and confident, though never on any account with the least suspicion of arrogance or presumption. Simply a quietly positive assertion that whatever is intended by the Divine Will must be obeyed according to the instructions given.

Thus the approach to the Infinite may be made from these three different angles. First as a supplicant, second as a coadjutor, and third as a responsible representative. These cover the broad field of attitudes from one end to the other. From that point on, it becomes a question of fine tuning them, categorizing them until a distinctive range of meaning is reached.

Taking these three components as a basis, it should be relatively easy to reconstruct the appropriate attitudes in a Wesoteric way. There will obviously be few at the top end of the scale, most of them in the middle, and a fair proportion at the bottom. One might compare them with the three vital letters of the Name. First the Yod (י), whose smallish dot represents a creature crouching in a submissive position; then the Heh (ה), showing someone standing on two legs while moving about actively; and finally the Vau (ו), typifying an individual upright in a position of authority, waiting for things to come to him/her rather than going in search of them. Rather an appropriate symbology. Related with the entire Tree of Life, the attitudes could be considered as the top to bottom positions of the Spheres, while their characteristics might be attributed to the Positive (Right), Negative (Left), and Neutral (Middle) stations of the Spheres. Perhaps we can further classify our set of attitudes in the light of this last so that we may place them in some sort of categorical order that will have meaning for the majority of those who see the Tree as being the backbone of modern esoteric activities. If we are to take this as a workable standard of attitudinal orthodoxy, then, obviously, the place to start is at the top.

1. KETHER. The Crown or Summit. The complete prostration or self-effacement attitude in which the entire body is flat on the ground, with the legs and feet held together and arms outstretched forward. Since this is difficult to sustain for long, an acceptable substitute is achieved by kneeling on both knees and bending the whole body forward so that the forearms and hands are pressed to the ground and the forehead touches the backs of the hands. This could be described as "keeping a low profile," and it was formerly adopted by those of lowest social stature before a ruling potentate. The reason was that an individual in such an attitude would be unable to attempt any kind of attack without giving plenty of warning to the guards. It symbolized utter helplessness and total dependency on the authority being approached, and is actually the safest attitude to adopt in the event of being caught outside in a bad thunderstorm. In that position a human body is at its lowest electrical potential and is least likely to attract lightning. The eyes of course should be closed. Another substitute position is one in which the ceremonialist is seated, wrapped in a cloak with the hood up, head bent, and arms clutching the body very closely.

The mental and spiritual attitudes to match this have to be those of the humblest. Absolute self-surrender to the Supreme Spirit, with complete confidence in the authority of the Almighty. Total loving trust. Some might say this is more of an Ain Soph Aur attitude than a Kether one, but it has to be remembered that all the attitudes mentioned are those of a human when confronted by the ruling powers, or God-aspects, of each Sphere on the Tree. When facing the Lord of Life, there is only one reasonable thing to do—acknowledge that Power absolutely and even abjectly.

The shorthand version of this attitude is accomplished through bending the head briefly, closing the eyes, and rapidly touching both hands to the forehead while accompanying this with appropriate thinking.

2. *CHOCKMAH.* Wisdom. Here we have to link attitudes with enlightenment via the faculty of sapience. Therefore the esotericist will still be kneeling, because of awe, but with the body upright, head uplifted, arms and hands upraised beside the face, and facial expression rapturous, with slightly parted lips and wide-open eyes due to wonder and astonishment.

The inner attitude to go with this should be one of gratitude to God that such a high faculty as wisdom should be available to humankind. All animals have intelligence, sometimes to surprising degrees, but we alone have wisdom, which transcends this immeasurably. As acknowledgers of wisdom we should remain on both knees, but as those determined to arise and seek it actively, let the right knee be raised so that the foot is on the floor, ready to raise the body.

The shorthand version of this is raising the right hand to the forehead while eyes are open and face uplifted. Thoughts to match.

3. *BINAH.* Understanding. The esotericist is still kneeling, but with face in hands, eyes closed, and serious expression. Understanding is an altogether inner experience arrived at by intuition, and should be shown as such. The inner attitude should be one of alert attention while quietly awaiting enlightenment with an open and anticipatory awareness. Once it is felt that a degree of understanding is being reached, the left knee may be raised in acknowledgment. There is frequently a sad feeling at this station because so

much of life is somber and serious in import. Understanding the necessity for this is a necessity in itself that has to be met here with courage born of comprehension.

The shorthand version of this is raising the left hand to the forehead while the head is bent and the face unsmiling.

4. CHESED. Mercy. The ceremonialist is usually seated with the right foot forward, both hands held out open with a welcoming gesture, gaze directly forward, and a pleased smiling expression. This is the first station of the "hopeful" section at the positive side of the Tree, and all attitudes are supposed to be warm, gracious, and benign. The love and compassion of the Creator extended through oneself toward other humans. Although a set pattern of attitude is being given with each Sphere as an example, any others of a similar nature should be included in that category. In this case, any attitude of merciful kindness would be appropriate provided it was supported by sympathetic thinking. The inner attitude for Sphere Four should be one of concern and care coupled with as much love and fellowship as possible.

The shortened version is an outstretched right hand and a warm and kindly countenance.

5. GEBURAH. Might. Here we have the exact opposite. The physical attitude is one of alert wariness, conventionally expressed by holding the left hand before the body in a "warding off" position while the right hand is held close to the body as if grasping a weapon. Stance is upright, left foot advanced, countenance severe, and eyes keenly focused. The matching inner attitude is one of intense preparedness for an action against adversities from any direction. Here it is necessary to hold oneself in readiness for any emergency threatening spiritual stability anywhere.

The shortened version is rapidly raising the left hand palm outward in the gesture of rejection. Appropriate thinking of course.

6. TIPHERETH. Beauty or Harmony. This is a very difficult Sphere to symbolize with any single physical attitude since it embraces so many. The conventional way, while standing with feet level, is to bring the hands together in the usual prayer position just above the heart, showing that everything is being held together at the center of things. The countenance should be serenely smiling. Sometimes the hands may be extended sideways about level with the shoulders and palms outward while forearms are raised from the elbows. This is the common attitude of a praying priest. There is so much work done on this level that it forms more or less a "happy medium," or general attitude covering a very wide field of action. The inner intention has to be one of trying to balance everything between both extremes of life into a beautiful state of harmony.

The short way of showing this is by bringing the fingertips of both hands together in contact with the center of the body while thoughts of harmony are being held in mind.

7. NETZACH. Victory or Triumph. The traditional bodily attitude to adopt here is that required by driving a chariot in a triumphal parade. That is, the body is upright, head held back, elbows into sides with hands lightly clasped forward as if holding reins, right foot slightly forward and a pleasant expression on the face. Much like the driver of a modern car, with feet controlling the behavior of the engine and hands controlling the course of the vehicle. The symbology is that of someone in full control of his/her life course, which is the finest victory of all to gain. The inner attitude to adopt here is one of confidence and pleasure, yet with a feeling of responsibility because every victory imposes its obligations. It would be well to remember the whispered injunction to old-time victors. "Remember man, thou art but mortal." Victories are never had without cost to someone, and this is where to consider that price.

The short form of this is to grasp something firmly with the right hand, especially anything controlling a flow of force, such as a tap, valve, switch, or the like.

8. HOD. Glory or Honor. Both of these qualities lie in achievements, and in the case of God and humans alike, these achievements are their creations. The appropriate attitude therefore is one of a master craftsman. This posture could be one of many, but there are two that are mainly adopted. First the standing one of the Mason: the left foot is advanced, and the left hand held down before the body as if grasping a chisel while the right is raised as if holding a maul. With an expression of concentration, the eyes are fixed on imaginary work. The second attitude is that of the scribe: usually seated, left foot forward, with the right hand positioned as if holding a pen and the left as if keeping the paper or parchment in place. In each case the exercise of a craft is indicated, one practical and the other intellectual. The inner attitude to be adopted with either should be one of placing all personal skills at the service of the Life Spirit. There ought to be a feeling that one's capabilities will tend to the greater honor and glory of God.

The brief shorthand version of this is almost any movement of the hands that suggests the use of craft tools, and that is made before the left side of the body at waist level. Fingering a keyboard would be quite legitimate in our times.

9. YESOD. The Foundation or Basis. The appropriate attitude is one in which the ceremonialist is standing or sitting with both feet level, though somewhat apart. If seated, the hands are brought together in the lap, finger and thumb tips touching, with the backs of the hands resting on the thighs so that the hands form a downward-pointing triangle. When standing, fingers and thumbs are interlocked while arms are held straight and in close contact with the front of the body so that the hands form a sort of cup held at lowest bodily point. This stance may also be held in the military "at ease" position, with the arms behind the back. It symbolizes sexual energies held in control for whatever may be required. The inner attitude should be one of stabilizing all possible life energy so as to build a basis for the operative intention. The esoteric must realize that life is a biological phenomenon and that each sex has only half the key; and therefore the thought is: "Here is my share, which I offer freely. Complete it with its equal offered for the same intention by another human of the opposite polarity."

The shortened version of this is to press both hands to the lower abdomen to indicate the genitals while thinking appropriate thoughts.

10. MALKUTH. The Kingdom or This World. The conventional attitude here is that of a monarch commanding his/her kingdom in the most perfect possible way. That is to say, with all the qualities of the preceding Spheres applied in action. This means to say, *responsibly.* A true ruler must be prepared to carry the full responsibility before God for what happens in his/her especial kingdom. Being a monarch in the real sense of the word is the most onerous task in the world. Almost any gesture or attitude is permissible here provided it conveys an impression of royalty in the best sense. That means to say, carefully, thoughtfully, and gracefully, yet suggesting authority of an unquestionable nature. The inner attitude to go with this Sphere is necessarily one of extreme caution combined with full awareness of individual onus in all situations, yet without undue anxiety or apprehension. There has to be a sense of confidence that if Deity is indeed acting through oneself, it will do so to the best of the capabilities provided.

The short version of this is to press both hands to the top of the head so as to suggest a weighty crown.

If those ten categories of combined physical and mental attitudes can be taken as a sort of standard, they will be found very helpful in assessing other attitudes. For example, how should one classify a bow from the waist? This involves a forward motion of the torso from the hips, but its interpretation depends on how far forward the motion is made and where the hands are positioned. The overall significance is obviously one of recognition and acknowledgment, but the degree of such an admission is indicated by the depth of the bow itself. The deeper the bow, the greater the acknowledgment. If only the head is moved (*Kether*), then the gesture compliments an equal. If from the shoulders (*Chockmah* and *Binah*), then this means recognition from the intelligent level. A waist-level bow (*Tiphereth*) would mean great respect and admiration. Should the bow go deeper than that in the almost floor-touching style of previous centuries (*Netzach*, *Hod*, and *Yesod*), this could only indicate subservience to a point of voluntary slavery, which might lead to suspicions of exaggerated insincerity. Therefore a horizontal bow is considered adequate in normal Wesoteric practice.

The interpretation of a genuflection, or momentary bending of the knee, depends on which knee is bent and how far. Also the polarity of the sexes. Thus for a man to bend his right knee would mean that he was placing all his might at the service of whom or what he was genuflecting to, but if a woman does the same it would mean she was offering her mercy and compassion. Then the depth of the genuflection tells its own story. If the bended knee goes to the ground (*Malkuth*), that carries the implication that service is being offered at the level of this world, but if to a lesser extent, it signifies the service is limited to successively higher levels of life.

The genuflection is mainly of military origin, since if it is carried to the point of kneeling on the right knee, this puts the man in an alert position with his right hand free to launch a spear or draw a sword as he sprang into action impelled by the left foot. The partial genuflection is also the stance adopted by athletes at the start of races, and suggests the swastika, which is a symbol of pure power set in motion. Thus in effect it says "I am placing all my power at your service." Its feminine counterpart, the curtsey, or diminishment of height by bending both knees briefly, signifies a voluntary abandonment of stature in the presence of a social superior. All such gestures made in the direction of any symbol representing Deity are therefore token admissions of inferior spiritual status.

So the conventional prayer position of an average Westerner (on both knees with hands at face level) conveys the meaning of: "Both my honor and success in life are due to Deity. Therefore I place all my might and mercy at the disposal of Almighty God with all the wisdom and the understanding given me to rule my life." This is said with body language alone if that is classified according to the Tree. It makes sense, it is reasonable, and it only needs associative exercises in order to implement all body movements with intelligible meanings and sentient significance. After all, why should any bodily position be without meaning? For instance, when anyone seats him- or herself before a TV, does this not plainly say "I want to be entertained by what I hope to see on that screen"? Should a favorite pet adopt a certain stance with eyes fixed on its human friend, is it not saying quite clearly "I want to be fed and attended to"?

Words may convey intellectual meaning, and for that reason, should never be underestimated, but pure intention or True Will is unmistakably indicated best by the attitude of an individual.

Spoken words may not be true or may not even be intended to be true. They may describe wonders and beauties in remarkable terms yet never convey them to hearers because of their speaker's tone and style of delivery. Words can be meaningful or merely mechanical according to how they are spoken or presented. They are no more reliable than the intention of their producer and the abilities of both speaker and hearers combined. Visibly interpretive signals are far more reliable than uttered words. For example, if a dangerous-looking character across the street calls out: "Come over here a moment, will you? I only want a few words with you," while he appears to be getting out a gun, any hearer would be forgiven for shooting first if he/she could. When optical and aural evidence clash, the optical should be given preference until subsequently proved wrong.

In the end, the only sensible thing to do is to make a detailed study of all the ceremonial attitudes that can be connected with the Tree of Life, and to practice them until they produce a comprehensible language of their own that will clearly express every spiritual sentiment attainable by human beings. There is such a vast vocabulary to choose from by combining the Spheres and associating the Path so formed with a specific type of attitude identified by the alphabetical letter assigned to that particular Path. While there is no need to cover all the Paths (there are twenty-two) with detailed descriptions, it may serve to illustrate the principles of this process with an example or two.

Suppose we choose Path L, connecting Spheres Four and Five. This would involve standing in an alert and prob-ably aggressive position, then sitting in a relaxed and peaceful one. Finally, holding oneself poised ready to adopt either attitude as need be. The thinking could be matched with the movement by imagining oneself rising to encounter a possible enemy and then discovering that it was only a harmless and pathetic being in need of help that one sits to administer. This could be reversed into a situation where someone approaching with apparent innocence suddenly becomes hostile and one has to rise hastily to face the emergency. Lastly comes the realization that in this world one has to be ready for either contingency at any moment and so must cope with each accordingly.

If we choose Path B, which connects Spheres One and Two, the basic attitude would be first kneeling in a crouched position, with face covered by the hands, and then with both face and hands uplifted to the dawning light of wisdom. This might be enhanced if there was an actual flame to look at as supportive symbology. The thinking here of course is a dramatic alteration from the depths of devotional worship to the heights of realization that enlightenment by illumination from a spiritual source of sapience is possible for humans. Then the alternation of humans changed by wisdom asking for absorption into the Absolute and so adopting the appropriate attitude. Paths should always be worked in both directions. After that comes the combined awareness of being created especially to find our ultimate spiritual freedom through liberation into Light by attaining True Wisdom.

As should be seen from those examples, there is a wealth of experience to be gained from combining a few basic attitudes so as to provide a whole compendium of ceremonial procedures. The underlying principles are *make every move meaningful* and *never do anything that is not fully comprehended*. If there should be an impulse to adopt any attitude, it is essential to discover why, and if unsatisfied with the findings, call it an "attitude X," as one does with an unknown factor in algebra. The overall requirement is to find or form a complete system of attitudes that is rational as well as adaptable to all ceremonial circumstances. It would certainly seem difficult to improve on the straightforward Tree of Life system suggested here.

In the event of some physical impediment preventing the full adoption of any attitude, especially kneeling or prostration, it would be perfectly permissible to accept some convenient substitute provided the correct thinking went with it. For example, to sit down and then bend forward with the face hidden in hands would be adequate in place of the crouch at Sphere One. It should surely be obvious that in the case of physical disability the thing to do is substitute the next nearest attitude possible. Intention is the vital element of every esoteric operation. If it is present most things will fall into place somehow, but if absent they tend to drift aimlessly around.

It will possibly prove helpful, when practicing this type of attitudinal Pathworking, if suitable musical cues can be chosen for each Sphere and combined for the Paths. Since there are no recognized attributions of music for the ten Spheres, it will be for all esoterics to select their own favorites. Here, however, is a suggestion for ten distinct musical instruments to match the different Spheres, in descending order:

1. A gong, since it is a single-noted instrument and symbolic of the initial "big bang" reputed to have begun Creation.
2. A harp for distinctness and ethereal qualities.
3. A flute for penetration and clarity.
4. A violin for sympathetic and heart-stirring properties.
5. A trumpet for its martial connections.

6. An organ for magnificence and beauty.
7. The pipes for celebratory significance.
8. The bells for their glorious chiming.
9. The piano for versatility and interpretation.
10. The drum for its earthy emphasis and repetitive monotony.

Despite all the purely technical points involved, the overriding factor throughout attitudinization is the major importance of mental and spiritual simulations and the interchangeability of these with intentionally adopted physical attitudes. The end idea is that by deliberately altering bodily attitudes, the mental and spiritual ones will alter in keeping with them, and since it is easier to change a physical attitude than a spiritual one, the perfected practice of such a change should afford a relatively simple method of controlling the quality of life in this world as well as on other life levels.

In former theatrical times it was necessary for actors to communicate with large audiences by means of widely made bodily gestures that could be visibly comprehended at a distance. For instance, grief was illustrated by tearing at the hair, wringing of hands, mopping at eyes, and hiding the face in the hands. All accompanied with loud wailing or exclamations. Fear was expressed by shrinking of the body, cowering away, and making shielding motions with the hands. Aversion was indicated by turning the head away from the object, screening the face with one arm and extending the other hand palm outward in the direction of disgust. Supplication, by falling on the knees with hands clasped and upraised. Joy, by flinging the arms wide and then hugging the body briefly with rhythmic motions, or placing both hands to one side of the face. Denunciation, by extending an arm to point at the character, and so on. There was a standard movement for every feeling of the slightest dramatic interest that might be seen by an audience. The "goodies" had to be fair haired and dressed in light colors, while the "baddies" were always dark haired and clothed in black or somber shades. Moreover there was a convention that good characters had to enter from the right of the stage as viewed from the auditorium, and bad ones from the left. Hence the association with the word *sinister* (L. left), which persists to this day in regard to ill-motivated people.

The drama was not a sacred art for nothing, and its practice has enriched our lives enormously in far wider fields than those of entertainment. Skilled actors are supposed to be exponents of human experience and capable of imparting a similitude of this into other participants of the drama. A genuine audience, however large or small, should not be mere observers of a dramatic presentation but should be actual sharers of what is shown. Formerly this happened to a great extent with time-honored cheers for the hero, hisses for the villain, and every other demonstration of emotion. This lasted well into the days of silent movies, but in these TV times it has been reduced to either imbecilic laughter or stony silence. There may be noteworthy internal responses that show no surface evidence, but on the other hand, far wider audiences are being reached by far fewer actors. Whether or not this is a good thing may be a moot point.

Although the expression of emotions and feelings in our times tends to be increasingly conveyed by facial movements and nuances of vocal inflection, there is still a great need for expertise and practice in spiritual expression through bodily and mental attitudes. Just as the old-time actor's skills were only gained through knowledge of what represented which, and through constant practice with association and presentation, so are a modern ceremonialist's abilities achievable only by the same painstaking methods.

Feelings are classifiable into two broad categories:

those arising from physical reasons and those deriving from purely inner origins. There is an interrelationship between these two that is of great importance. Physical pain caused by disease or trauma interprets into anger, revulsion, frustration, and other related emotions on higher levels. Physical pleasure due to sexual or similar satisfactions translates into joy, gratitude, elation, and the like emotionally. Physical needs for food are equated with a hunger for knowledge to satisfy the mind, and every material fear or discontent has its emotional equivalent. As any psychologist knows, the reverse is equally true, and prolonged experience of specific emotions will eventually produce physical results. Worries, fears, and irritations on emotional levels are now well recognized as contributory causes of often needless physical diseases.

At very low levels of evolution, what we call the higher types of feeling (such as spiritual joys and sorrows) are either unknown or so very rudimentary as to be insignificant. For example, a worm cannot know remorse or grief. Even among humans, abilities of feeling spiritual sentiments vary enormously from one extremity to another, and the ability of arousing these so-called superior sentiments intentionally and controlling them consciously has become an instinctive art once cultivated and developed mostly by actors. In early Temples this was presumed to be for the purpose of making the right relationships with the higher types of entity known as *the Gods* or simply *God*. It is interesting to think that the furthest and highest part of the theater (usually with the cheapest seating) is still called *the Gods* in theatrical parlance.

Since such Divine Beings were assumed to be so much better than we were, the obvious thing to do was not only aspire to such a status but also imitate it to the best of our ability. In other words, *act* it as if we were really far more advanced or interesting creatures than we actually were, even though this might be only temporarily. Simulate the spiritual status we were aiming for and hope this might ultimately come true. The childhood game of "Let's pretend" raised to adult stature. The most sophisticated ceremonialism is only another form of that brought to a pitch of perfection.

This must *never* be either underestimated or relegated to any level of unimportance. To the contrary, childhood play pretences are of the utmost significance in the formation of character and self-determination. Strictly speaking, children do not play at all but *work* with their imagination and intention of developing and exploiting their genetic inheritance that will later become their individuality and conscious capabilities. Later still in life, adults transfer this activity into other fields, and their subsequent behavior becomes an enlarged reflection of their childhood characterizations. Their juvenile attitudes to life eventually turn into their adult alterations of these according to the influencing factors concerned.

Esoteric ceremonialism is exactly this same propensity cultivated into an adult art with the same childhood aim: expansion of self-entity and enlargement of experience. Enrichment and enhancement of individuality through psychodramatic means. A child might say "This makes me feel bigger and better, so I like doing it, "whereas an adult might say "I hope to improve myself through this practice," but both amount to the same sentiment. The motivation is not only justified but also admirable. Furthermore it is necessary for the evolution of our species. We only evolve to the extent that we intentionally alter ourselves from one generation to another, and the rate at which we do this is governed by the intensity and proportion of the humans consciously engaged in this occupation. Therefore whoever means to increase the rate of evolution had best maximize every effort as soon as he/she can.

As an example of the direct relationship between inner

emotions and bodily expressions we need look no further than the physical reactions to common sexual urges. Every male will be aware of what happens to his body when his mind dwells on erotic thoughts. Visual or tactile stimuli result in the same effect on the "virile member." Other types of thinking may have much less evident results after a considerably longer time, yet they do have definite effects all the same. If sexual feelings can be physically demonstrable as a consequence of thinking about them, so can other emotions have their effects also and otherwise. All they need is calling up into consciousness and applying accordingly.

Professional actors begin developing this ability by imagining or staging life situations that would normally induce specific emotions and feelings in themselves. They collect love imagery, hate imagery, anger imagery, and every other kind of circumstantial stimulant that may prove practical. Most actors have their own favorite collection. These are usually concepts, not physical objects, though it has been known for an actor to use a set of photographs of people he/she loved, hated, respected, etc., that he/she claimed "sparked off" the appropriate feelings he/she intended to portray. How many servicemen have imagined some hated superior's face in the center of their targets and got a good shooting score thereby?

Using the same mental mechanism as a man using the picture of a naked woman to stimulate his sex function, the esotericist may use literally any suitable object to stimulate any related feeling known to human beings. It is only a question of intention and practice. One might call it psychosuggestion. The Christian church once brought this to a very fine point with all their artwork and imagery. Each item was supposed to inspire or awaken typified religious sentiments in the beholder, and there is no reason to believe the Church failed entirely in such an objective. This practice stems right back to the earliest times, when the most powerful human feelings could be invoked by crude little fetish figures mostly suggesting fertility one way or another. All we have done over the millennia is refine this instinctive drive into a state of sophistication.

Arriving at attitudes by means of imagery was the purpose of idols in Temples, and it still is the custom in Christian churches with statues of reputedly saintly humans or idealistic inscriptions. All it needs is something suggesting a spiritual principle strongly enough for viewers to react with. Eventually the external article should prove unnecessary when the mind becomes capable of creating the inner image powerfully enough. Initially, however, it is useful to have a complete set of psycho-suggestive stimulators, which are not unlike the armature that a sculptor uses to model clay around when forming a figure, which then becomes the temporary image for the permanent one that he/she will make from stone or metal.

We all need these reliable "basic thoughts" for arranging in patterns around which we shall hang all our other thinking. That is why collections of them like the Tree of Life were invented. Every major religion or philosophy consists of just such a scheme, and so for that matter does any system of human thinking and feeling. As our physical bodies consist of solid bones around which the mobile and semi-liquid flesh is assembled, so do we have the mental and spiritual equivalents of "bone thoughts," which are the solids, and "flesh thoughts," which are the more mobile and adaptable, if less permanent, portion of our self-structures. We have to build these for ourselves out of the material made available by our mystical studies over the centuries, and of which there is a plentiful supply.

This simile of making "belief bodies" for ourselves with mental and spiritual materials that are comparable with the components of our earthly bodies is quite a valuable idea. Anyone with a working knowledge of physiology should easily be able to figure out a practical list of what type of thinking corresponds with which bodily basic, and then combine them so as to form at least the framework of a sound and presentable "persona" that will be the "clay model" for the finer and more permanent spiritual state of existence altogether. Suppose we start with the minimum requirements for constructing a human body and begin linking these with various types of thinking. Apart from actual organs, let us list bones, flesh, blood, muscles, nerves, brain, skin, hair, teeth, and nails. Just an arbitrary choice for the sake of an example.

1. *Bones.* Here we have to accept all the solid and basic principles of our firmest beliefs and rock-solid life faith together with relatively unalterable values. The "2 x 2 = 4" type of thought. These may be moral, religious, or any other kind that stiffen the structure and form of thinking with firmness and precision. These constitute what might be termed the bones of our spiritual skeletons.

2. *Flesh.* This is made from the bulk of our thinking and is more or less the mass from which we select whatever we will shape into specific organs. The raw material, so to speak, out of which we shall build our spiritual bodies.

3. *Blood.* This in particular is the most precious part of our spiritual circulation. It is made from our most intimate awareness of life, love, and all we hold dearest in existence. Consciousness and feeling for family, friends, and loved ones. A sense of self-sacrifice and whatever we believe would be worth shedding our physical blood to defend.

4. *Muscles.* These are formed from thoughts and inclinations that actually move us or impel actions and deeds on

any level. They do not motivate but simply supply energy to whatever must be moved in us. They could be described as applied intentions.

5. Nerves. Here are all thoughts of information, instruction, and communication between different parts of our psychic structures. Also the metaphysical mechanism of sheer sensations and responsive feelings. They are our means of knowing rather than knowledge itself.

6. Brain. Our center of consciousness and memory where thoughts are originated, calculated, and computed. Here is where we put ourselves together in order to make some sense and meaning out of life. All our thinking and learning faculties connect at this point.

7. Skin. This is built from our ideas of self-protection and external inner appearance. It develops from our concern about how we should look to others rather than our state of spiritual reality. It marks the boundaries of our differentiation from other souls by awareness of this fact.

8. Hair. This links partly with self-protection and partly with apprehension in sensing approaching adversities. Physical hair bristles at the approach of danger, and its psychic equivalent is our sense of warning in the presence of threats to spiritual security.

9. Teeth. Physically they are the means of mastication, and inwardly they are the efforts we make at reducing our mental intake into convenient sizes for consumption. What we cannot swallow whole without choking, we must slowly chew into fragments that may be easily assimilated.

10. Nails. These are our means of hanging on to what

we hold and getting a good grip on whatever our minds want to maneuver around. They enable us to climb the Tree of Life more easily and to pick up things with improved accuracy. They are also our built-in means of self-defense in close encounters of an unpleasant kind.

This list could be indefinitely extended to cover every single item of the body and the whole field of physiology, extending from there into mental-spiritual equivalents. Some consideration should be given to this by anyone seeking further enlightenment, for that is how we construct and create our inner bodies: by mentalizing their physical functions and then lifting them toward spiritual levels. Our hereditary genetics produce our physical bodies, but subsequently we have to develop their superphysical counterparts by ourselves with whatever aid may come our way. This again is the "Temple not made with hands" of esoteric legend, and the "work" that good Masons are supposed to accomplish with the help of all their symbology.

So the adoption of a correct or suitable attitude is probably the most important part of Temple procedure. It means to intentionally adjust the inner self-status according to the contingencies of the psychodrama being worked. This does *not* mean adopting an external physical attitude while the inner being remains aloof and uninvolved. That is no more than artificial acting, which is only too common with professional actors of commercial rather than artistic competence. When a genuine actor assumes anger, for instance, he *is* really angry, though his is under perfect control and can be altered at will into anything else. That is the ability to aim for with Temple workings, and the end result should be an ability of self-control far beyond average reach. It was once said that all magic is the art of change in conformity with will, and this is true with every esoteric operation. The first thing to change or alter, however, is oneself. Whoso cannot change his/her own attitudes in conformity with his/her intentions will never be able to alter anything else.

By far the major proportion of modern Temple practice is taken up with the recitation of verbal matter of varying styles and purposes, whether spoken or sung. Each section has its own intrinsic meaning and should have its own place in the structure of the entire presentation. Unless this is properly understood, even the simplest esoteric ceremony is likely to be a bewildering affair. So let us look at the function of verbalization and consider the whys and whats of its significance in terms of today.

Chapter 6

WORDS OF WILL

Early esoteric ceremonies had few if any words, being mostly in meaningful mime. They were mainly "dumb shows" to tell the Gods what their human actors wanted. For example, if success in warfare was the required objective, there might be a few males dressed as the "enemy," or with some symbol to indicate their identity (say a totem animal's skin), who would make threatening gestures and after a mock skirmish fall to the ground, pretending to be dead while the victorious ceremonialists danced around them, waving weapons and brandishing symbols of their tribal Gods. With all such action would be the sounds of conflict, groans of the wounded and dying plus shouts of battle triumph, blowing of conch shells, and appropriate sound effects possibly terminating with the winning side's cries of their God-names with hopes and confidence that what had been enacted would indeed eventuate because their Gods were more powerful than those of the other side. We still put on such shows except that we now call them spectator sports.

If good hunting was sought for, an agile man dressed in a skin and horns of the animal they were after would dance around and mimic its movements while mock hunters moved in and appeared to kill the prey and strip off its skin, which would then be laid before their God-image. Possibly in some cases the kill was for real. When farming and agriculture took the place of hunting for food supplies, the early rituals altered in character, though not in essentials. They danced, shouting and leaping to show how high they wanted the cereals to grow, urinated with gestures to demonstrate they needed rain, and ejected their seed into the ground to invoke the principles of fertility and production. Many made human sacrifices to the Gods of their beliefs. All the subsequent mysteries of psychodrama descended from such ancient and primitive practices now termed mimetic magic.

This was more or less the same principle behind the instinctive methods used by humans to explain wants or needs to others who did not understand their language. Hunger, for instance, was demonstrated by pointing to an open mouth, which then made chewing movements, after which the stomach was patted and belching noises uttered. Thirst was shown by cupping the hands and raising them to the mouth. Sleep, by closing the eyes and putting both hands to the side of the face. Pure sign language. This had a practical value among hunters, who did not want to alarm their prey, and soldiers, who did not intend to betray their position. Remnants of the ancient sign language are still with us, and American Indians brought it to a very fine art indeed. Before humans evolved their sonic abilities of speech to distinct degrees, the thing to do was demonstrate what was needed rather than try to say it with sounds. There could scarcely be any mistakes made with what people could see with their own eyes. The practice of indicating needs silently is still kept up by monastic communities at meal times, so the silent food mime exists yet.

All this arouses the interesting idea that human awareness of a Superpower behind the evident world began long before humanity had evolved any forms of sophisticated language. That is to say, humankind's awareness of God originated with instinct rather than intellect, and was appreciable by feeling greatly in advance of thinking. Thus the many divergent ways in which humanity has recognized Divinity all begin with the same fundamental roots in our deepest relationships with life itself. This is true today except that we are substituting socio-politics for religion and worshipping the spirit of a materialistic society in place of a once postulated set of personal Deities.

Exactly what those first human concepts of Deity were, we can never be certain, though they are still in our genes. The strongest possibilities are that these were vague apprehensions of invisible entities, who were nevertheless evident by the behavior of everything around them. The sum of such apprehensions was that a power or powers existed that might be approached on a person-to-person basis by placation and subservience. It would obviously pay to be in favor with a Being who could cause earthquakes in the twinkling of an eye or make volcanoes erupt, storms devastate whole areas, and strange illnesses wipe out entire tribes in days. Conversely, it could send herds of eatable animals, large harvests of fruits and nuts, and shoals of fish into the hands of those it was friendly with. So the best thing to do was cultivate a good relationship with this mysterious controller of creatures, who or whatever it might be.

All beings have their own peculiar recognition rituals for making relationships with each other, and these fall roughly into three classes: friendly, neutral, and hostile. Hostile behavior is easily recognized by a display of natural armaments like talons and teeth plus threatening movements. Neutral behavior is marked by simply ignoring each other's presence with obvious deliberation. Friendly intentions are shown by approaching very carefully, with non-threatening movements, while displaying bodily attractions likely to interest viewers and favorably dispose them toward the demonstrator. Each of these attitudes will be accompanied by appropriate emissions of sound. Hostility, by growling and hissing; friendly advances, by barking, purring, and chirruping; and neutral, by silence or normal noises unconnected with anything except occupational interests.

This would determine the class of behavior with matching sonics by which primitive humans most probably made approaches to their Deities. Since they wanted to curry favor, they would make friendly or obsequious advances in whichever direction they deemed Divinity to be most attentive while emitting obliging and soothing noises and displaying what they considered to be their most attractive attitudes and appearances. Is there any real difference between that and a modern churchgoer dressed in Sunday best and singing hymns? In the old days, since thunder, lightning, and rains fell from the skies, that seemed to be the general direction to be faced when addressing Divinity, and now the major symbol for that same Being is regarded as a focus on altars or walls of contemporary gathering places for would-be worshippers.

In those very early times, the primitive advances made by humans beings to God would probably be carried out by only a few humans at first on very tentative levels. Subsequently their types would become priests and prophets, and their far-off descendants turn into politicians. The chances are that they began by making placatory sounds and leaving offerings of food and drink in places where they felt the strange influence of the unseen Being most strongly. This could be at isolated stones of peculiar shape suggesting power or purpose. Phallic-shaped stones certainly, or those with deep clefts in them, suggestive of a vagina. Also mountaintops, springs of water, or special trees. Having selected their favorite locality for whatever reason, they would next decide what to do there and, later, when to do it. Eventually others in the tribe would come and watch from motives of sheer curiosity, and the first church congregations and theater audiences had collected. It would not be long before the priests began to capitalize on this situation.

The strongest likelihood is that these first "services" consisted of often-repeated calls and cries combined with other noises intended to attract the favorable attention of the invisible Entity. Then would follow a mime demonstration of requirements, culminating in some kind of sacrifice or offering. Lastly there would be assurances of fidelity and promises of future behavior in return for benefits received. Undoubtedly such early vocalizations were the original Barbarous Names of Evocation, which later writers insisted must never be altered by even a syllable, although nobody could ever remember what they were supposed to mean. Considering the depth of genetic association from which those sonics derived, that was very sound psychological advice. Their continued use was definitely the quickest way of making conscious contact with our inherited sense of spirituality. To this day humans make meaningless but satisfying noises when they are aroused emotionally in the mass, as at sports stadiums, revivalist meetings, and the like.

Eventually humankind began to evolve meaningful speech consisting of shaped sounds with definite meanings attached to each combination. This was a great step forward, especially when it became possible to formulate increasingly complex ideas and abstract concepts in verbal symbology. Words were factually sonic symbols representing an enormous expansion in thought and ideology as humans developed their potentials of conscious awareness and manipulation of mind energy. Not only could they communicate with each other to a far greater and more significant degree, but they were convinced they could make much clearer contact with their Gods, which had by then become synonymous with every relationship they made with natural energies and all their attempts at culture and civilization. Their Gods entered their lives at every point.

Eventually came the triumph of writing, or making recognized marks on suitable materials to represent specific sonics and combinations of them as words. Writing is thought to have had a commercial beginning through the use of single strokes for each item and then different marks for multiples in order to record amounts of trade goods. Pictorial art had long been possible, so it would soon occur to artists that if quantities might be indicated by markings, so could qualities be coded when a suitable system was invented. As with most human undertakings, once the initial idea was born it was only a question of time and effort before it became workable in physical terms. When at last writing became practical, there was a far wider field for the meeting of minds and advancement of ideology among mortals. This of course had its dramatic effect on religion and philosophy, though not for quite a long time.

The reason for this was that very few people could read, and the primitive practices of relationship with Deity had become more or less set by sheer repetition and established custom handed down from one generation to another. These did have regional variations and differences due to altered interpretations through the centuries, but the general trend showed the same fundamental elements continuing in different forms all along the line of descent. Supplication, singing, and sacrifice combined with dance, display, and drama to make religious ceremonialism a very important procedure of human behavior.

Once literacy became established and words could be recorded, human culture grew at a far greater rate. Esotericism per se began as a kind of counterculture that was exploring away from the main line of advance largely because of dissatisfaction with the orthodox priesthood and the established way of doing things with apparently spiritual aims, yet factually was productive of so much that brought power and profit into the hands of an astute administration that did nothing with it but benefit themselves. Not that esoterics were seeking any spiritual secrets from altruistic motives like sharing them with needy fellow mortals. Their main motivation was a sort of spiritual one-upmanship that made them a bit better than their common or garden brethren. Thus they began their independent investigation in very different directions from those approved by official religions and generally revealed teachings.

Not all esoterics practiced ceremonialism, but those that did naturally based their practices on previous religious customs and altered these in accordance with their findings and inclinations. In the end esoteric ceremonialism began to acquire its own characteristics, though it never developed the hereditary and authoritarian orders of priesthood with their established hierarchies of senior controllers like those it sought to circumvent. Its practitioners were frequently proscribed or persecuted by its religious rivals, although they presented no particular threat to such organizations. Far from trying to convert masses of humans to their ways of thinking and so depleting orthodox congregations, they made strenuous efforts to keep all their affairs entirely to themselves and to stay as private as they could. Some of their security methodology, such as special handgrips and recognition codes, remains with us to this day.

The broadest advances in both religious and esoteric fields, however, were in the fields of literature and verbal techniques. Nowadays we should say script writing. Poetry and prose were being formulated and structured into highly sophisticated compositions with both power and beauty in their manner of presentation. Words had always seemed magical things since sound and abstract meaning had been married in the distant past, and those who had knowledge of words with strange significance and an extensive vocabulary were considered very superior souls by the masses of human beings whose speech was very likely limited to those words that concerned daily life and their occupations. It is scarcely necessary to say that on average the widest vocabularies were found in urban areas, and the narrowest, in rural areas. We would therefore expect to find our oldest verbal religious roots in country districts.

So far as we can trace them this is true. Many of the general sounds still occasionally made by British country people were once old God-names. One of the commonest among West Country rustics, *Oo-Arr*, is a relic of *Hu Ah*, one of the very ancient High Gods. The druidic *Ahoon* is a reversal of it. Again the Hebrew syllable *Yah* is another old God-name coming down in Yiddish as *Oi Veh*, meaning "Oh God!" Even the modern *Hi-Ya* and *Yoo-Hoo* are instinctive legacies from our primitive past, and so are most of the otherwise meaningless exclamations stemming from surprise, stimulus, or just spontaneous sonics. Our oldest Gods and Goddesses remain with us in one form or another and are likely to remain so for a very long time yet.

Even our expletives and most obscene expressions had a very different meaning in former times. The word *bloody* derived from an Anglo-Saxon term meaning to bless by scattering blood from a sacrifice over the congregation. Our so-called worst word *fuck*, said to be derived from an Icelandic word for the sex act or from the name of the Norse goddess Freya (patroness of conjugal love), could equally come from the Greek *phucktos*, meaning to be shunned, escaped, or avoided. It could therefore be connected with a sense of the statement "God keep this away from us." Seafaring men bore many of the most ancient words around the world, and the Greeks were very widely travelled mariners in former days. Our well-known word *shit* has the closest connections with Satan and the Egyptian Deity Set or with the Hebrew-Arabic *Shaitan*. Even the slightly comical expression *balls* (for testicles) has links with Baal, the fertility god whose name simply meant overlord or ruler.

Ancient Gods become modern Devils, and the growing use of the name Jesus Christ as an expletive is probably part of that process, which normally takes many centuries. As for example, English schoolboys were forbidden to swear "by God" because that sounded blasphemous to their elders, but they might perfectly well say "by Jove" since that name meant a pagan deity that counted either as a demon or an unimportant fiction. Thus the mistake was made of assuming the word *God* to be a proper name, which it never was, meaning no more than whichever Deity was being worshipped. For a fairly large section of humanity the Supreme Deity must never be named at all because knowledge of God's personal name would be too presumptuous for any human to claim, and so the only references allowable were impersonal allusions such as *He, That, It,* the *Ancient One,* and so on. If a new name for God had to be found in our times it would probably be a mathematical formula like the famous Einstein equation, or possibly a computer program keyword.

So as might be expected, rural people preferred the simple and time-tested versions of religious practice, while the urbanites were prepared to accept the more polished liturgies and types of Temples. This followed into the fields of esotericism, where those that sought eclectic and unorthodox methodologies would either revert to primitive paganism or separate into small and very selective groupings with special ceremonial texts and possibly their own terminology and types of presentation. There could be a strong tendency to regard themselves as those who were selected by the Deity itself for some revelation that transcended all others and made them masters of superior secrets setting them above everyone else as regards divine favors and preferential treatment. This not uncommon attitude of exclusivity and secrecy gave rise to the generic title of the *Mysteries*, sometimes termed the *Holy Mysteries* to distinguish them from those purely concerned with craft, trade, or professional secrecy.

Within these Holy Mysteries was a very great variety of sects or schools, each claiming its own specialty of spiritual theory and practice that differentiated it from all the rest. In effect the descendants of those schools are with us now insofar as we have inherited their teachings in altered forms and changed customs. They were famed for applying very ingenious tests and ordeals to applicants for membership that revealed character peculiarities and made the individuals easy to classify. In fact, they probably originated the first scientific character-assessment methodology based on applied psychology in our whole world. Ordeals for testing courage and fortitude, etc., are of very ancient origin, but the skilled application of them to determine all the finer points of a person's character and also assess his/her potentials in all fields, including future possibilities, was something the Mysteries brought to a very fine art.

Another specialty of theirs was intelligence tests and "brain brighteners" by means of word puzzles, riddles, and crypto-communications that had to be worked out by minds capable of comprehending the inner meanings of the spiritual system being operated. Hence the strings of questions and answers that have now become mere formalities but were once direct challenges that had to be accepted and answered as they were applied. We have a relic of this in university viva voce examinations, but in olden times the mind and soul had to answer all applied stimuli with appropriate responses. Ever more complicated words were being used to stimulate increasingly intellectual reactions from their hearers.

In the course of time esoteric practice moved closer and closer to intellectualism and further from direct emotional appeal to Deity. Words were beginning to be more important than deeds in ceremonialism, and action was being increasingly translated into visual or verbal symbology. As the human mind developed, it was afforded ever-widening scope in terms of its own expression, which was mainly mathematical and verbal. Early mathematicians, who started with simple commercial trading values, later extended their art into more and more abstract fields dealing with time, space, and astronomical calculations. They also advanced their areas into theological and mystical speculations. The most noteworthy of these of course were the Qabbalists, who related numerical values with ideological concepts and tried to work out a satisfactory system of dealing with them. Astrologers were also attempting to relate temporal and spatial cosmic calculations with individual and collective human destinies. In other words, humans were trying to reach God with reason and intelligence rather than with pure instinct and hopeful guesswork.

The impact of all this fundamental alteration in human characteristics was a general division of humanity itself into two distinct categories, those that were soul-pointed and those that were mind-pointed. Early humans were mostly body and soul with the accent on body, while developing humans were body, mind, and soul with the accent on mind and body. Modern humans are in the process of uniting mind, body, and soul with Spirit, while all the accent is on mind and intellect. Hence modern esotericism is becoming more and more a matter of trying to unite mind directly with Spirit, while using the body as a convenience for the brain, the physical medium of the mind. Soul, the sentient component of human beings, is being steadily relegated to the back benches of our general government. This is a great pity, because the best ideal would be the balanced development of all our psychic qualities so that we might mature evenly at every angle of our beings.

In actual fact, very much of what used to be available only in esoteric Temples has nowadays become accessible under quite commonplace circumstances. The onetime dramas meant to stimulate minds to thought and souls to sympathy are now on every TV screen. The stringent tests for rapidity of reaction and accurate assessment of situation are applied all the time in driving a motorcar. The long lectures and obscure teachings are mostly available in paperbacks or from public libraries. The music and singing can be heard on tapes and records. Even the orgiastic dancing and psychedelic effects of the Orphic Mysteries are offered to a paying public in virtually every commercial center on earth. To press the point home to its hilt, what would any modern Temple have in it that would not be easier (and probably cheaper) to obtain outside it?

The only possible answer to this would be in one word. Atmosphere. Put another way—ambience, and pushed to an ultimate conclusion—presence. Certainly nothing audible or tangible. Discernible most definitely by anyone of an appreciative nature who is sensitive to psychic influences. A concentration of inner energy available for others to absorb because practicing members had accumulated it by their thoughts and actions in that particular place. Yet all that made that effect possible was a disciplined and devoted relationship with Deity by those who became truly able to be OF ONE MIND, IN ONE PLACE, AT ONE TIME. In other words, people concentrating their maximum energies into a single expenditure for a common purpose in the consciousness of all concerned.

Could this not apply to other places than esoteric Temples? It *could* do so, yet how often would that be likely? There are many places where people would be together at one time yet very far from being of one mind concerning a spiritual ideal. A church service whereat the whole congregation are all thinking their private thoughts the whole time does not fulfill the necessary conditions at all. The desideratum is that everyone should think the same thought at the same time and continue doing so with active harmony until the conclusion of the ceremony. That is to say, the thinking should be like a symphony played in the head so that every note coincides in everyone's head at the same instant of time, and the entire total of mentalization amounts to a complete production of effective artistry. This is possible with music because of the conductor and the score in front of each instrumentalist. With ceremonial workings the equivalent can only be possible because of the words and their readers' facilitating the following of a concerted thought train by all present.

This may sound simple, but it calls for consummate skill in directing consciousness, and only those capable of employing that to a practical degree should really take part in esoteric ceremonies of any marked importance. Nothing but communal practice sessions will bring the art to anywhere near a condition of proficiency. What everyone has to do, and do effectively, is coincide his/her thinking with the action and tempo of the ceremony until an inner state of complete mutual harmony prevails among all. This means that nothing else except the ceremony and its meaning must be thought of for its entire duration and that thinking has to match the rate of its progress. No faster and no slower. Once the mind is engaged on the work of that ceremony, it must be kept on the same course with the accuracy of a guided missile.

That would be not at all unlike the performance of a concert orchestra. Each instrumentalist must know exactly when and how to contribute the sounds of his/her share. Some, like the pianist and string players, usually have to keep going the whole time, while others, like the percussionists and wind players, may have only momentary work to do, yet if that went wrong it would ruin the whole presentation. All have to follow the entire piece in their minds at the pace of its playing so that they can time their entrance with split-second precision. Nothing but the most devoted discipline and attachment to music itself will ever make this possible, and until ceremonialists are able to equal that much in their own terms of reference, nothing but discordant and mediocre performances are likely to ensue.

The advantage of orchestral practice over ceremonial is that any false note will be instantly audible and can be as rapidly reproved. This is very seldom so in ceremonial practice, however, unless an outstandingly sensitive soul is present and becomes aware of who or what is responsible for the discordancy. What more usually happens is a vague sense of disquiet or feeling of failure after the conclusion of the ceremony, while no one is able to point with absolute certainty at the cause, no matter how strong suspicions may be. There is no mistaking, however, the sense of mutual satisfaction that follows a well-conducted and properly performed esoteric working. That is beyond all argument.

Synchronization of thinking starts by linking thoughts with audible or visual signals as they are received. Thus concepts are created in the mind as their suggestive stimuli are accepted by the body. Since in the case of esoteric or religious ceremonies these are normally words and symbolic actions, they have to be read, heard, done, or viewed at a convenient rate for the consciousness to respond adequately. That is a primal requirement. Next is the style of presentation. If the signals are audible in verbal form, they should be pronounced expressively in a manner indicating or accentuating their meaning. This could quite well be done in a chant or intonational fashion provided the hearers are accustomed to such a method of reception. Visual signals must be made in a clear and appropriate way unless they are supposed to be clandestine.

The whole idea is for both reader and hearers to actually involve themselves and their feelings with both words and acts as they occur. Therefore the pace must be most carefully calculated for the average capabilities of the congregation and then set very slightly on the slow side of that. Getting the tempo right is of the highest importance. If it is too slow the interest of the more responsive esoterics will be lost, and if too fast the effective attention of the less responsive cannot be gained. It is best to err on the side of generosity toward the slowest members of any gathering.

Even if there is only a single ceremonialist working alone, the same principle applies, although the individual will naturally proceed at his/her own pace since there are no others to worry about. All the words and actions still have to be accompanied by their correct thinking and in the right order and style, whether they are spoken aloud or silently. Here, mere repetition of the words alone is totally useless and a waste of effort. It is far better to think the meaning of the ceremony through without a single word uttered aloud than to give a technically splendid performance without a single appropriate thought. Strictly speaking, audibly uttered ceremonies are for the benefit of many esoterics seeking to synchronize their consciousness. If there is only one person present in bodily form, there is really no need to verbalize the ceremony, though most celebrants like to work it that way for the sake of practice.

We have become so accustomed to regulating and

shaping all our thinking with words that we tend to forget what words are in themselves. Essentially they are symbols that are visually and audibly interchangeable as containers of consciousness. Only familiarity with them and their use makes them meaningful to us. Otherwise, they are nothing but noise and marks on paper. To make the best use of them we should know all the meaning that can be compressed into each one and which to combine in correct order so as to convey whatever we want to express. Conversely, we should be able to take any collection of words and translate it into terms of pure awareness so as to experience its meaning consciously. For example, reading the phrase "It was an extremely hot day" should produce an actual feeling of heat and sunshine once those words have been applied to one-self. The opposite would be true if the wording ran "It was dull, wet, and very chilly." Firstly, however, there must be an understanding that "this is all happening to me, and I am going to experience it for myself."

Therefore the procedure for following a modern type of esoteric ceremony that consists mainly of words is to take them in carefully, react with them immediately, and then stay with them closely, by following their flow of meaning like a stream altering its ripples and wavelets according to the nature of its bed at all points. Here there may be whirlpools and there a drop making a miniature waterfall, or there could a broadening out with a smooth bottom making a calm featureless flow. There will be equivalents of these in ceremonial terms. Eventually there might be a damming of the stream to produce power for working a water wheel, the resistance of which can be felt as its blades are pushed around by the sheer weight and force of the flow. That is the equivalent of a climax in the ceremony, the instant when the accumulated power of all preceding mental and spiritual energy is directly applied to whatever point is considered likely to produce the result required. There may be many

such climaxes in minor ways, or one major effort somewhere near the end, or a combination of both. It all depends
on the nature of the ceremony.

The question always arises concerning who or what
hears all the invocations and prayers uttered except the
humans present. There is often an assumption that Deity or
lesser types of entities are invisibly manifest in various
symbolic forms of a physical nature held within the Temple
for such a purpose—as, say, the sacred Host and holy oils
kept in the tabernacle of a Christian church, or the Scrolls of
the Law stored in the ark of a synagogue. Therefore those
are regarded as centers of worship, according to custom.
There could be an element of truth in such suppositions,
but the underlying fact is that it is the Divine Principle
within themselves that "hears" their prayers through their
own ears, and the extent to which it hears them depends
entirely on the individual and collective connections with
the Life Spirit itself.

If indeed each human amounts to a single cell within
the "great body of God," or life considered as a conscious
entity throughout the whole of creation, then how would
such a cell attract the attention of such an entity toward
itself? In much the same way as an equivalent does the same
in an ordinary human body—by unusual, abnormal, or different behavior. Suppose a small group of cells alter their
behavior for any reason until a nerve is affected. Let us
assume a very minor but painful lesion in the small toe.
Totally trivial by most medical standards, yet quite enough
to send the sufferer in search of remedial treatment for the
sake of abating the annoyance and possibly preventing anything worse from developing. Yet if no contact with the
nervous system could be made, the originally mild infec-
tion could spread and increase until the entire limb was
endangered. It is for that very reason that we feel pain from
such small things.

In the same way, if there were sensations of pleasure aroused by the stimulation of nerves through originative cell activity (which could be tactile), there has to be unusual or attention-alerting behavior among the cells concerned before the mind will notice what the body is doing. Then it will acknowledge receipt of the message in whatever way it deems appropriate. Glands may function and pour their products into the system rewardingly. Dangerous by-products may be drained away by the opening of ducts. There are many ways of enriching cell life in a human body that is gratified by their behavior. Although this may not be an exact parallel with humano-Divine relationships, it makes a reasonable comparison and does suggest how a spiritual Being would "hear" prayers put up on earth. It would comprehend these through the minds and souls of the humans themselves because of the intentional intensity at which they originate.

This is why a desperate appeal seems particularly favored. It is purely because of the intensity and veracity with which it is aimed at what we may as well call the Containing Consciousness. Thus there is a priority of importance attached to it that gets it past the "blocks" that absorb irrelevant or insignificant messages, which comprise the bulk of human attempts at communication. Also there is another factor. It is uncommon or rare. On the face of all available evidence, it appears that unusual or uncharacteristic behavior has the best chance of being noticed by any intelligent entity beyond our levels of living.

That does not guarantee a response, but it does support a general rule of life: that it is always the odd one out that attracts attention. A single small black pebble on a shore of big white ones would automatically draw all eyes to itself. One sunflower in a field of a million daisies would do the same. So would a small single fish swimming in an opposite direction to a shoal of its fellows. The implication here is that humans seeking the attention of superior spiritual beings should demonstrate their difference or distinction from the mass of humanity in some way that is calculated to encourage the most favorable recognition.

Such is the primal purpose of ceremonialism employed in an esoteric way. To offer a means of unusual or even unique human behavior that is possibly more than likely to attract the attention of an observant omniscient or controlling Consciousness. Humans thinking and behaving in specific patterns that spell out quite clearly in "inner language" an intention of communicating with the Powers that be for some particular purpose. This would be true of any ordinary church service, which indicates by its very nature that humans are congregating in hopes of making contact with Deity, but an esoteric ceremonial is something else, and indicates that there is an especially significant or important communication to impart. Something that calls for priority of attention because of its character. This is similar to the practice of coloring or marking envelopes in some way that ensures their being opened as soon as possible by an attentive authority.

Abuse of such a system would naturally render it invalid and devalued in a very short time, or else retard the process of response considerably. Therefore it is essential in esoteric ceremonialism that, apart from training and practice sessions, nothing should be done without serious and genuine spiritual motivations. Certainly none that are trivial, frivolous, or reachable on the lowest levels ought to be offered on the highest human altars, which does not mean that ceremonials have to be joyless or gloomy in the least. Sheer joyous love and laughter are among the highest of human offerings, partly because they are so rare and genuine. It is the authenticity of any ceremony that gives it value in spiritual terms, which means that the smallest field flower offered by a child with sincere love and trust has a lot larger value than the largest lump of gold ever brought to any Temple in hopes of buying a favorable response to a request for heavenly assistance with some very shady enterprise on earth.

Because their unusual thoughts and actions seem most likely to receive special attention from spiritual sources, esoteric associations have often sought to keep their ceremonies secret and confidential. Each system is quite convinced that it is somehow superior to others and so must be jealously guarded against exploitation and all unauthorized intruders kept out. Most religious systems seem equally sure of their superiority except that they usually think everyone else ought to be converted to their way of doing things and would like to gain an absolute maximum of membership. So between esoterics trying to exclude other humans and exoterics attempting to include as many as they can convert, the spiritual situation in this world is a very confused and puzzling one.

So what might be particularly special and unique about any type of ceremonial esotericism that would single it out for preferential treatment or unusual attention from any supramundane intelligence? Why would a minority of humans working a clandestine psychodrama have any advantage over a group many times their number operating in a crowded cathedral with full orchestral accompaniment and a highly paid choir? Or for that matter, the Temple or meeting place of any organized religion in this world? Why should a socially insignificant or relatively unimportant group of people with probably inferior artifacts have any better chance of attracting the notice of superior spiritual beings than large gatherings of humans led by professional priests?

In the first place, from a purely spiritual viewpoint, no amount of pure quantity can ever equal, let alone surpass, the principle of *quality*. To illustrate this point, consider which alternative would be preferable to a connoisseur of music? To hear a favorite composition murdered by a million discordant and inept instrumentalists, or perfectly rendered by a single expert pianist? To extend the analogy a little, which makes the most sense: ten thousand people watching a ball game played by twenty odd men from famous teams, or those men watching twenty thousand assorted others of mixed sexes, sizes, and ages, propelling balls of every size and type without any rules except those of self-preservation? Effective presentation by the few is always preferable to a mediocre or muddled one by many.

The principal points of difference between esoteric ceremonialism and ordinary church services are firstly the basic beliefs, secondly the manner of setting these out symbolically, and then the choice of style and verbalistic expression. Most significant of all is the synchronicity and orchestration of thought and feeling among the few specialists assembled. They are all celebrators of whatever rite they may be working. There are no observers or outsiders at a genuine esoteric gathering. Everyone present is or should be practically partaking in the action going on. There may be a leader in the sense of someone formally uttering the words aloud, but those present are all priests/priestesses in the sense of sharing the intention and meaning of the Mystery they are making together.

In early days great reliance was placed on special keywords that were supposed to operate automatically by their own innate qualities. Sometimes these were God-names, or the sonic identity coding of esoteric entities, who, the utterers firmly believed, were bound to answer such a summons if it was properly pronounced. They sincerely supposed that this ability would give them control over those supernaturals and compel them to work the will of humans on this earth. Knowledge of anyone's "secret name" would always grant the knower power over that person, and for that reason the initiatory name of an individual must never be spoken aloud anywhere. That belief persists among esoterics of all persuasions even to this day.

It seldom if ever seemed to dawn on folk that any supposed God who would automatically obey the whims of a human being or come when called, like a faithful dog or curious cat, could not possibly be of a very high or advanced order. Keywords are certainly of value in shaping specific thoughts aimed at higher than human levels of life, but they can scarcely *compel* any superior Being to do anything we demand. It is a question of the well-known quote "I can call spirits from the vasty deep" and its indisputable answer "Why so can I or so can any man, but will they come when you do call for them?"

Strange to say, it has taken us until the present time to produce computers that will provide information about anyone whose identity particulars are fed into them, and this will indeed give the knower an advantage over the known individual, which could be very influential. Most of his/her once private secrets such as credit rating, social status, religious persuasion, educational qualifications, and even intimate details like sexual proclivities, with names and addresses of those involved, and a host of other information are available to anyone with access to the right keyboard and knowledge of the correct code to punch in. Yet the basic idea behind this was born thousands of years ago when humans started believing in Names of Power that would make men Godlike, or in the "magic of mathematics," which would do likewise in a different way.

That is really a hidden value of practical esotericism. Its practice sets human minds into patterns that pay off perhaps centuries or maybe millennia later. Sometimes sooner. Space travel first became possible when early humans gathered around to worship the Moon and wondered how to reach it. Computer science commenced when humans began playing around with words and figures, when they converted one to the other and made magic squares with them. Maybe medicine started when people began wondering what herbs would cure which diseases. Probably psychotherapy commenced with early exorcisms of evil spirits, and surgery, when they tried cutting out physical lumps, which they supposed were devils embedded in the flesh. It is esotericism of one kind or another that brings humanity in contact with seed ideas that later flower and fruit to our advantage or discredit. In recent generations we have seen an incredible number of very ancient ideas materialize in solid shape, and many others are hovering on the edge of discovery. Let us hope and pray they will eventuate in happiness for us all.

Any word will mean whatever its human users intend, because in the end it is only sonics or equivalent symbolism geared to pure ideology and intention. Nothing but agreement and acceptance makes any collection of words into a definite language, and only time and evolution sophisticate a language by constant improvements and expansions of communicable intelligence. The more meaning and significance can be packed into any word, the greater value it will have for esoteric purposes. Hence the somewhat special words and phrases that have become part and parcel of esoteric practice over the centuries, although their current value depends entirely on how truly the minds and comprehension of those employing them can condense and maximize their meanings into symbolic presentations.

That is to say, the mind must be trained and practiced in the art of associating more and more meaning to every single word used. What is mostly needed is the right methodology, because once that is acquired it will subsequently become an almost automatic habit. It is best to begin with quite simple words until the sense of the idea itself is clearly seen and appreciated. Then, when the habit is formed, we can progress to the more arcane ranges of our vocabulary. Suppose, for the sake of example, we start with the apparently easy first phrase of the familiar Lord's Prayer. This needs to be taken apart and dealt with word by word; each should be meditated on, experienced, and lastly a realization formed of the extent to which it can reach plus the significance of such extensions.

Our. A collective description in general, but of whom? Many or few? This word could apply to millions or only two people, since it is plural. It could be only one individual if that person were a king or someone representing many people and speaking in their names. Which do we mean? A few special people or everyone on earth? Maybe just those we have the right to represent. As individuals we do not have the right to speak for any except those we class in our own category. If that is so, then we limit the Being we intend to address into the definition we place on *our*. Is that definition inclusive of other categories of Creation, such as minerals, plants, and animals, and if not, why not? So what exactly are we going to mean by *our*? If the whole of humanity, then think of them race by race all over the world. Would they *want* us to include them? If only a few intimates, then think of those and wonder why the others should be left out. The word *our* covers so many categories of creatures, but first it must include oneself otherwise the correct word would have been *their*. *Our* must always mean "me and . . . ," so it signifies a classification of species among which the speaker or writer is including him- or herself. If spoken with an emphasis on the word, that implies a special awareness of limitation, but if unaccented it becomes more general. Sometimes actual possession or ownership of a definite article, or in a more abstract sense combining for some particular purpose. To be more specific, further words are needed.

Father. A male progenitor. Whose? Why and When? A

father cannot exist without a wife-mother to make him so with offspring. The term is meaningless otherwise. So how are we to understand the word *father*? As mate of our Mother? Some strange male Spirit who produced us out of himself, having no feminine counterpart to copulate with? If there were no Feminine Principle there would be no women in this world, and biological life could not exist. So we must admit the implications of this, even if we call it Mother Nature, or the term *father* makes no sense at all. Our fathers are senior figures who are partners in our production, since we develop from their seed fertilizing the eggs in our mothers' wombs. We inherit only half our ancestry from them. Biologically they are responsible for our gender but if we are using the word *father* in a spiritual sense, then a father signifies a strongly protective figure who defends his children from enemies, provides the wherewithal to keep the family together, and loves his children mainly because they bear his blood and are extensions of himself until the end of existence. So any paternal solicitude on his children's behalf is not entirely selfless if he continues himself through his children's consciousness. (This should start up a long meditation concerning all the implications of fatherhood.)

Which. Indication of whom or what. This is really a reiteration of the first two words, summing up both under one heading. "Our Father" as a single point of reference in order to link the concept with something else. It is a carry-over sort of word that we need for following ideas from one point to another. So let us take this for granted and continue exploring.

Art. An old-fashioned way of saying *are* or *is*. A word implying a condition of being without precision or definition. It simply affirms the existence of Our Father as such, and so far we have got "Our Father which art," or the ancient title of I AM seen from the observer's viewpoint. The eternal AHIH, which is the highest God-name on the Tree of Life. We might here consider that the word *art* is only used when the terms *thee* or *thine* apply. The usage of those words implies the closest personal connections of relationship to an intimate degree, otherwise it would be the formal *you* and *yours*. *Thee* and *thine* were very familiar terms and it is evident that the Deity was meant to be seen in that light when the Prayer was first translated in English. Considering the initial fatherhood concept, this seems entirely appropriate.

In. Contained by or surrounded with. Again limitations are implied. One can be *in* anything right up to its edges, but after that one begins to be *out*side it. So why *in*? There is an old axiom that it was only by self-limitation God made manifestation possible. Before that, Deity was Ain, the Unmanifest, or Nothing. Put another way, Nil contained All. Once Deity began internalizing itself, Creation began. It turned its consciousness *inward*, and so must we if we are to create ideas of any value. Up to here we have the statement "Our Father which art in." Otherwise a description of a deity that contains everything *within* its own consciousness. "All things exist *in* me, not I in them." This could be considered as a sexual implication of a father who has to enter or penetrate the *in*terior of a mother in order to produce life. We might also be reminded of a deity that is said to be with*in* ourselves as Inner Light. Again, it might be borne in mind that *esoteric* applies only to that which is *within*; so that concept supplies an idea of Divinity as an Inner Power, but exactly where or in what?

Heaven. This signifies a state of consciousness in a condition of eternal bliss, and also a location embracing the skies in general. As the latter it suggests the ancient idea of the Sky Father who lay above the Earth Mother and generated life out of her. Possibly one of the oldest concepts of Deity. Also a hint of human arrival on earth from elsewhere. In other words, if the Father of humanity was a heavenly or skyborne being, then the possibility has to arise that the origin of our species came from some other planetary source altogether. Many are the esoteric legends concerning our extraterrestrial origins, and this is another endorsement of them. Humans instinctively look skywards when heaven is mentioned, or turn their thoughts in that direction. Heaven considered as a condition of happiness could well be genetically inherited instincts of a former state of life in other worlds before we reached this one, wherein we lived harmoniously together in much better conditions than we have ever known here. It also implies that maybe we shall find our way back to those wonderful spheres again one day, and enjoy life to the full once more. Our efforts at space travel would certainly seem to support this. Heaven is always a hoped-for condition of consciousness, and this Prayer will later on suggest our best chance of regaining it. Everyone has his/her own idea of heaven, but all would agree that however it might work out in practice, it is definitely an ideal spiritual state to aim at. So now we have the phrase "Our Father which art in heaven" presenting a picture of humanity's origin from some very superior state, and thus so far a reminder of the noblest nature we can bear within us.

Those first six words of the Lord's Prayer alone are a complete ceremony by themselves if they are considered in the style suggested. The rest of the exercise consists of taking every single subsequent word and following it through into a similar or improved expansion. If this is done conscientiously, it not only will supply a totally new outlook on the Prayer itself but also should produce a fresh respect for

the possibilities of language in relation to conscious experience of life. Additionally it should show why modern esoteric
ceremonials have such a large proportion of verbalism in
them. Each single word of a well-constructed ceremony
ought to be chosen with an awareness of all its connected
implications, which have to be tacitly acknowledged while
the word is being uttered aloud. Thus every word must be a
condensation or compression of consciousness that will be
packed with all the power and precision available to the
mind that contains it.

Anyone intending to work modern esoteric ceremonies
should try this method of taking every word in sequence
and consciously connecting with it as much associated
intelligence as possible. This need only be done once while
findings are being written out in full for later reference. It is
indeed exhausting work but is worth the trouble for the
sake of the mental expansion it brings. When subsequently
engaged in the actual ceremony itself, the memory of all
previous thinking should result in the realization of how
important each word is and the consequence of their combinations. Especial care has to be devoted to the keywords,
or God-names.

These are mainly traditional titles for God-aspects,
which are usually descriptions of function on specific life
levels. They will be found in their Hebrew forms with the
Spheres on the Tree of Life. Choice of language is not so
important as complete comprehension of meaning. In fact,
words that are not understood by the utterer are best not
used at all. We have seen how to pack words with meaning
by dwelling on them with thought, and that much should
definitely be done with those of foreign derivation. Otherwise there can be some terrible muddles and mix-ups.
There is only one advantge in using foreign words or phrases
in ceremonial practice.

This is on account of their unfamiliarity and the need to

concentrate very carefully when they are employed. We tend to devalue our everyday language by sheer overuse and habit. By constant repetition we do lessen the importance of words for ourselves. That is a natural propensity among all humans, and we develop the ability of saying or writing one commonplace word after another while we might be thinking about something totally different. We tend to regard prolific talkers as "gasbags," or people with little but hot air in them, rather than "solid" speakers. That is to say, we consider their words to have no *weight* or *substance,* as if they had those normally physical properties. There is usually some truth in this. On the other hand, a relatively slow, succinct, and deliberate speaker is frequently listened to if not actually understood. His/her manner alone invites the attention that his/her words may not deserve on their own merit.

It is principally for this reason that most esoteric ceremonies are scripted in other than ordinary phraseology with a few difficult key phrases at culminating points. The language has to be in a different style than that used in everyday existence, yet not so difficult that it becomes incomprehensible. Here and there, there have to be challenging items that evoke unusual efforts from people seeking their import. Interest and curiosity must be maintained throughout while an effective amount of enlightenment is brought to bear on the theme of the whole production.

This raises the ever-controversial point of whether ceremonialists should learn their words by heart, thus avoiding the inconvenience of relying on a hand-held script, or whether they ought not to memorize the text so that it reaches them with fresh impact every time they celebrate the same ceremony. There are points in favor of either view and it is really optional which is adopted. Undoubtedly a frequently worked ceremony tends to be fixed in the mind eventually, yet if not irrevocably fastened beyond alteration, it will undoubtedly remain open to expansion indefinitely. If this open attitude can be maintained, it is surprising how a word or phrase that has been taken for granted over prolonged periods will suddenly trigger off fresh revelations from the subconscious mind. In that way a lot may be learned that would otherwise have remained hidden.

Very often an awkward crossword puzzle clue will solve itself if tucked away in the depths of the subconsciousness and left to simmer until the solution seems to boil out quite suddenly. Very often the worrying word comes to consciousness quite unbidden at an inconvenient time perhaps days later. This demonstrates that the processes of awareness do continue deeply down inside ourselves and eventually come to conclusions after the original problem has been commenced on conscious levels and then consigned to cold storage, so to speak, with instructions to surface when a satisfactory solution has been worked out. Esoteric ceremonial does exactly that on spiritual levels with its intellectually shaped verbal components having spiritual significance. What is more, since it is shareable on group-mind levels, anything inserted by one mind may be retrievable by others working the same connective system. That is another reason why esoterics tried to keep their ceremonies secret. They did not care for their intimate ideology to become available to other humans who happened to be communicating through the same code as themselves for entirely different motivations.

The basic facts are that individually or collectively an esoteric ceremony consisting of concentrated intelligent ideology is not unlike a beamed transmission of electronic telecommunication. Anyone with a compatible type of receiver in the right place can pick it up and make what use he/she likes of it. This is fundamentally true of all human thinking, but the vast bulk of it subsides into the background "mush" of unconnected consciousness. Specially shaped and esoterically energized awareness with pointed spiritual purposes is apt to persist and have a lot more effect than average thinking, and it seems to be beyond the reach of average minds as well, but is certainly within the range of experts who might want to intercept such a transmission for their own reasons.

We may have come a long way from early esotericism, with its primitive plaints and supplicatory sounds culminating in cryptic calls and other wordless wails that would make no sense to contemporary ears, yet would still be recognized by simple souls seeking contacts with Deity. Therefore there is some value in such practices today for those who are unable to appreciate the splendors of our literary and poetical heritage. Even our most advanced and sophisticated ceremonies would seem very crude in comparison with those on higher levels of intelligent life. Indeed it is doubtful if we would recognize such applications of consciousness as ceremonies at all. Our appreciation of spiritual circumstances only extends so far, and beyond those limits we cannot see sense in anything.

So it would be quite pointless for anyone who does not comprehend the beauty and benefits of a rich and rare vocabulary to try working such a cerebral sort of ceremony, but fortunately there are classifications of ceremony to suit all sorts of souls, none of which need disparage or undervalue other souls' ways of serving the same Spirit of Life with duty and devotion. The three Paths of Progression should be well recognized by now among Wesoterics who know that the Hermetic Path is best for intellectuals; the Orphic Path, for emotionals; and the middle Mystic Path, for those relatively rare souls who reach for Deity directly by sheer spiritual strength guided by love and devotion alone. Before committing oneself to any particular Path, it is essential to discover precisely which evokes the best response from one's own soul and mind. Once that seems certain, the Path may be entered and progressed along until a change-over may be indicated. Sometimes a soul may be suited best by the Orphic Path when young; by the Hermetic, for the most part of life; and by the Mystic, at the very end. That is a fairly frequent pattern.

The verbal content of ceremony is by no means always spoken, uttered, or chanted, but quite frequently is sung in rhythmical and often rhymed fashion. The normal purpose of this exercise is to ensure unison of intention among a congregation. If they are all singing the same words at the same pace with a regulated rhythm having emphasis on particular keywords, plus exerting a maximum of expressed energy, this must produce an effective flow of force for application to intentional ends. Such is the purpose of the usual sonic *amen* at the end of each hymn. It provides a natural resonance through which the preceding power can be connected to the purpose of the ceremony with final force, and this should be thought of with especial clarity while the *amen* is being sung into silence. Though the word has many meanings in itself, its ceremonial value is mainly as a methodology for linking verbalized passages with ensuing pauses that are supposed to be pregnant with meaning in themselves.

Silences in fact are just as vital a part of any ceremony as the words, and should never be neglected. They are principally for realignment of thinking and coordination of consciousness. During any ceremony there is always a tendency to drift out of phase with its major momentum, and silences are ideal opportunities for correcting this. They should certainly never be wasted with idle thoughts or speculations. They are like the spaces between letters and words, without which neither writing nor speech would make any sense at all. It is really silence that makes sound significant, and it should always be given its full place of importance in esotericism. In itself silence is the symbol of the Unmanifest, out of which anything can be expected, and it deserves honor as such.

Silences are given emphasis and value by their position and duration in esoteric ceremonialism. Position is normally decided by some vital point being made or the conclusion of an active incident. Duration is far more difficult to estimate and usually comes under the jurisdiction of whoever has to commence the next sonic section. As a general rule, the more significant a silence, the longer it lasts, but this is not a hard and fast direction. No silence should ever continue past the power of those keeping it to hold their attention on whatever point is being made. Some concerns make their master/mistress of ceremonies responsible for terminating silent periods by either a visual signal or a very low-key sound, such as a soft tap with a slippered foot or a fingertip. The duration of silences is mostly a matter of human judgment alone, which will depend on who is present. A few seconds is normally sufficient for minor periods, and maybe minutes for major ones.

Occasionally this duration procedure may be reversed: the sonics few and brief while the silences are prolonged. This calls for really dedicated types of ceremonialists well accustomed to this type of working, which is far from easy and seldom practiced. In such an instance it is the sonics that count as the separative interventions and the silences that contain the sense of the ceremony. The sonic is considered as belonging to the material level of life while the silence holds the entire inner action. In this style of working, one might imagine the entire Lord's Prayer being intoned one word at a time, with several minutes of silence in between each. That should illustrate the principle of this procedure.

While considering the verbal characteristics of Temple

ceremonials, it would be appropriate to think about the supportive sonics requiring instruments to produce. Apart from recorded musical and organ accompaniments, these are usually derived from a gavel, a bell or bells, a horn, and a gong. These correspond to the four elements of life, or Earth, Water, Air, and Fire, in that order. They are normally employed for these specific purposes.

1. THE GAVEL. This is used for calling attention to some particular point or signalling it by a numeral code. Knocks should always be counted if they occur in sequence. The Spheres of the Tree, for instance, are indicated by combinations of triple and single knocks. There are also variations of significance: a sharp rap on a hard surface with the pointed end of a gavel means "Think quickly," and a dull thump on a soft surface with the broad face of its head signifies "Keep this in mind."

2. THE BELL OR BELLS. They are usually of the ringing type, with clappers inside them so that they produce their effect when shaken by hand. They are for giving warning that something calling for serious attention is about to happen, and hearers had better collect any wandering wits and follow very carefully. Bells are associated with the herd leader, who keeps the flock more or less together and is supposed to set them an example. Hence the appeal of bells to the ears should also attract the notice of the eyes in their direction. Varying signals can be given by numerical peals or styles of ringing.

3. THE HORN. This is definitely a "summoner," though it has other meanings. It is a means of communication among all engaged in a hunt or quest, in this case for a spiritual objective. There is a whole code of signals connected with the style in which it is blown, the number of blasts, or alteration of tone. Also, since a horn may be put to the ear instead of to the lips, it can signify a need to listen most intently for any communications that may arrive at anyone's inner awareness. Symbolically it means that a summons is being sent to superior spiritual sources.

4. THE GONG. A sonorous and reverberant signal that virtually compels attention to any action. The best gongs are of heavy metal and are deep-noted. Each stroke should be followed and responded with throughout its sonation right down into the ensuing silence. Gongs are made to mark the climax of a ceremony. Sometimes there is more than one gong: a high-noted one for minor moments, and a lower-pitched one for the major moment of the entire affair. There are seldom many strokes made. The symbolic significance of a gong is that when struck it responds immediately, and that is something we should do when we are struck by an internal Holy Hand attempting to elicit a response from us. Something on these lines is what a resounding gong should suggest to human hearers when they say "A thought has just *struck* me."

The entire sonics of any ceremony, vocal or instrumental, should be a very carefully planned and coordinated sound scheme involving each individual contributor whether he/she produces any physically audible sounds or not. Hearing a sound correctly is just as important as making it, and if it is possible to make any sound wrongly or badly, it is equally possible to hear a sound improperly or inadequately due to faulty attitudes on the part of its hearers. This has nothing to do with physical impairment of hearing, but concerns misinterpretation by the mind connected to the ears in question, which may be accidental or deliberately intentional if it is not due to inadequate training or sheer inattention.

If there is an obligation on officiants to present the audible content of a ceremony in a clear and competent fashion, there is an equal and complementary obligation on those who hear this content to receive and react with it in a correspondingly efficient way. Listening is as much an art as speaking or singing. The only difference is that one is internal and the other external. A cycle of communication is only completed when what is inside one soul comes out of his/her mouth, or onto paper, and subsequently goes into another soul via that soul's ears and eyes. In a way this is not unlike a spiritual version of a sex act, with the utterer in the male role and the recipient in the female one. The factual happening is that one human (or more) is injecting meaningful material into the psyches of other humans, where this material may be retained and gestated or developed until it emerges in an altered form as an issue on its own. What is taken in passively will eventually come forth actively via the minds and souls of its acceptors.

Although this is true in principle with all human intercommunication, in the case of esoterics taking part in Temple ceremonials it is specifically a question of communicating with other than human intelligence. The responsible task of the apparently passive auditors is to act as relays or active agents of the spiritual Entity(ies) being addressed so that it (they) will become aware of what is transpiring and of the nature of the communication being sent. In very simple language, human hearers are there to be the ears of God. If only a single individual is conducting a ceremony, what is uttered aloud with the lips has to be received through the ears of that same human so that it reaches the God-connected part of him- or herself and so completes the circuit of consciousness.

Therefore the degree to which any ceremony is able to reach, impress, or influence an intelligent spiritual Entity will depend almost entirely on the ability of humans to set it up and administer it outwardly to others who are able to take it in and convert it into terms of awareness comprehensible or absorbable by superior classes of consciousness. So now let us turn our attention to the topic of how to hear and interpret the intentions of human ceremonials for the attention of Whom or Whatever may be listening on higher levels of life than ours.

Chapter 7

LEARNING TO LISTEN

"They also serve who only stand and wait" is an out-of-context Miltonian quote that must have annoyed millions of people on account of its seeming smugness and "putting-down" implications, yet there was no original intention of any such thing. It was written solely for the purpose of pointing out that those who held themselves available for service whenever required by a deserving deity were affording a service in itself with that availability alone. Waiting did not imply idle inactivity and a boring lack of interest in life. It meant keeping oneself in a state of fit readiness to answer whatever call might come at any moment. This could apply to any public service employee such as fire-fighters, police, or the armed services, but we shall apply it here to esoterics participating in ceremonials that require a maximum of attendance but a minimum of externalized activities. In other words, what amounts to the congregation in public religious practice.

There is sometimes a tendency among such people to consider the duties of a congregation as somewhat less or inferior to those of the active and evident "officers" who behave as actors by presenting the externals of the psychodrama they all should be working together. Such a misconception is without any real foundation and is due either to a lack of adequate instruction or to a failure to appreciate the realities of spiritual situations. The first thing they should do is get it into their heads that being part of a congregation *is* an "office" in itself, and unless they play their allotted parts in the psychodrama properly, it might just as well never have taken place.

Comprehending the purpose and office of a congregation and how they should fulfill it is not exactly an easy matter, and performing it satisfactorily is even more difficult. If the service of any ceremony is termed the *word*, then the active officiants are its *bearers*, the congregation its *hearers*, and together they are its *sharers*. Let us suppose that instead of an esoteric ceremony in a Temple, the gathering was an ordinary live theater with performers and audience. The actors would literally purvey the action of the drama to the audience, who would purchase it from them by following it with intellectual interest and emotional involvement so that it became an experience they could think and talk about for as long as they might remember it. Whether or not this made a good return for their entrance money would be for them to decide later.

Apart from any money, the audience members repay the actors by their reactions. They laugh at the funny parts, sit very quiet and still during the serious and tense ones, and at one time would have wept or groaned at the sad or pathetic incidents. There is a sort of empathy developed between actors and audience that is a kind of instinctive rapport that any theatergoer will recognize quite well. Few experiences are worse for a professional actor than playing to an unsympathetic or inattentive audience. They fidget, cough, look away from the stage, and in extreme situations make audible noises of disapproval, such as hissing and booing. At least though, that shows some kind of feeling, but when there is absolute stony silence at the end of a performance, that is the ultimate in audience rejection. Conversely, there can scarcely be a more rewarding experience than acting before a thoroughly appreciative audience reacting enthusiastically to everything presented.

Although there is not an exact parallel between a theater audience and a Temple congregation, there are sufficient points of similarity to warrant consideration. Both are located where they are in order to experience performances of meaningful words and acts in a prearranged sequence presented to them by trained people. Both groups have to react to these performances in some way before they can be said to have achieved satisfactory results. Most importantly, this interaction between the groups and the principals must be mutually beneficial. Each party must be fully aware of its responsibility to the other and to the outside interests concerned. The theatrical actors to the theater's backers, the audience to their friends and acquaintances, while the Temple officials and their congregations alike should see their obligations to the Tradition they serve and the Deity they honor within it.

The specific work of a Temple congregation as hearers of the Word is to accept the spiritual sense and meaning of what they see and hear, convert this into pure consciousness, and then re-present it to the Indwelling Intelligence of the Life Spirit inherent in themselves. It could be that the presentation they witness with their physical senses is far from perfect, in which case it is their responsibility to improve it internally so that it appears as well as possible before the Inner Beholder. This can be done once the process is practiced sufficiently. It is just a question of whether it is best to work on one's own or to cooperate as part of a congregation until ready to accept active office. Usually it is wisest to commence by oneself, continue as one of a congregation, and then accept responsibility for working as a Temple officer. After that it will be an enjoyable relief to take part in congregational work again with greatly improved proficiency.

In order to commence practice for becoming an effective hearer of the Word, it is necessary to acquire a sense of differentiation between one's ordinary self and the Divinity Within. This is done by meditating on this topic until it becomes intuitive, and that could take some time before the sense even begins to dawn. It could be best to begin by making a direct verbal appeal something along these lines:

> I, (name), am making a direct approach to the closest aspect of Almighty God, which is in actual contact with the senses of this body. Look through my eyes, hear with my ears, feel with my fingers. I place my senses at your service. Use me as your agent in this world. Take the thoughts that I transmit to you. Make of them *what you will*. Be conscious with my consciousness. In order not to trouble you with trivialities, I will agree to use a calling code to tell you there is something special to communicate. Let that code be _____ and blessed be this bond between us evermore, in the name, etc.

The whole idea here is to condition the psyche to adjust itself with a specific attitude by one particular keyword. This is the reason that official religious faiths have definite phrases to commence their God communications, such as the Christian sign of the cross, or the Moslem "In the Name of God, the Compassionate and the Merciful," etc. In esotericism, however, there is no equivalent official formula because each individual is supposed to find his/her own, which is frequently his/her particular inner name that comes with initiation. That is not obligatory, and any well chosen name will do provided it is kept for the sole purpose of prefacing communications intended for Deity alone. It should be treated in exactly the same way as one treats an emergency telephone number that will summon police, fire services, or an ambulance. That is to say, with proper respect and consideration.

There is nothing to stop anyone from adopting several code calls for various reasons. Say, one for communicating as part of a congregation, another for general informative purposes, and a final very special one to be used in desperate emergency. Just some kind of classification. It is surprising how quickly one can get used to this scheme once it is clearly set up in the consciousness. A few sessions ought to fix it quite firmly. How to determine each type of code phrase is a matter for self-decision, but it could be a good idea for each distinct esoteric group or organization to arrange its own by mutual consent. It might also be helpful if a separate code meant "Practice only" so that this might prefix practice sessions. It is only a matter of deciding which code goes with what type of communication and then sticking to that afterwards. Code phrases could equally well be numbers or a combination of figures and words.

Once this becomes clear in the mind and enough practice sessions have been held to establish workability, the rest is only a matter of application and experience. By and large it is a question of identifying one's inner polarity. That is to say, the active, outgoing, and projective part of oneself, which could be termed the "male" side, and the passive, receptive "female" aspect of one's individuality. Regardless of physical sex, every human being is so constructed. Everything depends on which polarity is being presented to whom. What we are taking in and where it may be given out or otherwise disposed of. In the present instance we are thinking about congregational behavior in Temple practice.

It is most probably for the preceding reason of bipolarity in the human psyche that the idea of a masculine, paternal deity arose. Previously the human concept of Deity was mainly feminine, via the Mother-image, but as human sophistication advanced it became clear that if that Deity were to be truly self-perpetuating, there would have to be a masculine element in it somewhere, and if that were true, humans should relate themselves with it according to their own sexual polarities—i.e., males with the Mother-aspect, and females with the Father-aspect. Later it began to dawn on humans that if they also had a spiritual nature, then it must also be bipolar, so that they could approach either aspect of Deity with whichever side of themselves might be most appropriate, or even both at once.

Eventually it occurred to speculative philosophers that if Deity were a perfect species of being and had created humans in its own image and likeness, the probability was that human beings were eventually intended to become a self-perpetuating species of life, each human creature being bisexual and auto-reproductive. Since we were not yet so constituted, it was assumed that this would be a future development as an ultimate state of perfection. Meanwhile we should be content to work toward that end, and this began by accepting Deity as a masculine being and offering ourselves from a feminine angle. Early relationships with Deity were quite frankly sexual, and people saw nothing peculiar or strange about this, although they realized quite well that it could scarcely be on a physical basis. Therefore they translated the sex act into spiritual terms.

In the case of a single esotericist working a ceremony in solitary fashion, it would be a relationship of the individual's outgoing male polarity seeking contact with the intaking female part, which should be mediating the meaning of the ceremony toward whichever aspect of Deity is being addressed. This may sound a little complicated, but it is theoretically true. Can we, so to speak, split off bits of ourselves for specific services? Why not. It is purely a question of definition and dedication. Is this not what any musician does when playing pieces composed by others? Suppose some expert plays a Chopin recital. The skills are his/hers, the hands are his/hers, and possibly the piano also, but to whom or what does he/she dedicate all these? Obviously the spirit of Chopin, unless it is the audience for whom he/she is interpreting it. So, what if there is no audience except him- or herself? He/She plays to that in him- or herself which loves or appreciates Chopin. So does the esoteric ceremonialist pray and practice to that in him- or herself which appreciates God and therefore will be in at least some kind of communication with that entity.

When it comes to active ceremonialists officiating at a ceremony with the cooperation of externally inactive participators, the actives have the male-outgoing role to play, and the passives have the female-intaking one. It should be remembered that they are only passive externally. Inside themselves they should be a mass of mental and psychic activity because the male polarity should be busy superintending the process of passing along the presentation they are receiving to the Inner Power, for whom it is intended. That is to say, they are *mediating* their experience toward the Blessed Ones. It was once called *witnessing*.

By analogy, this is comparatively what a TV does. A TV screen consists of a very large number of very small particles, each of which reacts with the oncoming program so that it becomes luminous in the color and to the intensity which is being signalled in sequence. Thus they produce an entire picture together provided everything is in harmony and that complete synchronicity is constantly maintained.

A properly receptive human being is not unlike one of those particles, and in combination with myriads of other mortals, he/she will present a "God's eye view" of the entire human picture. On a much lesser scale this is more or less what happens in a well-conducted ceremony.

In case someone may be thinking "Does this mean that such ceremonies are no more than TV shows for the entertainment of an observing entity?" it might be well to remind such a one that all our present Temple services derive from the precursors of dramatic art and that the primary purpose was not to amuse the Almighty Deity but to demonstrate—by music, mime, speech, and all other available means of communication with that Being—what our position in this world was and what we would like it to be. We were "showing God" by signalling our needs in as clear a way as we could, and this still applies in very altered form today. We probably imagined in olden times that the Invisible Entity was peering at us from every bush, and now we have grown to realize that the agency of human senses makes the closest convenience for Divine Consciousness to meet humankind through. It is only a matter of effective mediation, and a congregation of people who have this faculty to a highly trained degree is a very valuable asset of any esoteric Temple.

One of the best ways to synchronize oneself and one's thoughts with any ceremony is with a regular rhythm. That is why so many ceremonies are poetical or set to metrical recitation. There is a sort of swing to the wording of most effective rites, which is a great help to regular participants. Hence the reason for the chant style, which sometimes came first and had wording fitted to it later. So long as the meter is suitable for the script, there is no real reason why the lines should rhyme. Probably fewer chants are more effective for Westerners than the Gregorian, although the Mozarabic is a very close contender. The only problem is that the mind tends to settle down into the mechanical beat of the rhythm and thus becomes liable to lose the actual meaning of the words. Even so, that is better than being bored witless by a badly uttered text or inept activities.

When identifying one's bipolarity, a point to watch very carefully is that an idea of two separate selves is not created in the mind. This could lead to a split personality, which inevitably causes a lot of trouble. It must remain absolutely clear that there is only one self in command per individual, even if this is part of the Great Self comprising the whole of Creation. The self-structure may be bipolar in nature, but it must always remain unified in purpose and intention. Therefore it would be well to think of one's duality as a *complementary characteristic*, not as an opposition. A good analogy of this is an electrical current, which has a positive and a negative polarity, yet it is their combination that produces the actual power. So the relationship between one's own complements of character must never be allowed to become divisive, but should always be regarded as a power partnership beyond any breaking (like any other associated with the body, such as the two eyes, two hands, or pairs of anything).

Just as one's hands may be employed in different fashions to do the same physical job, so may the complementary ends of oneself be applied to the same spiritual work. So the application of the receptive female polarities of all the ceremonialists comprising the congregation of an esoteric Temple is no more than a natural and normal presentation of an appropriate agency to a circumstantial demand. This may be factually easier for human females, but males must be prepared to alter their attitudes accordingly and fulfill their receptive functions by mediating, together with the women, whatever may enter their souls during the service. This is no more difficult than for women to employ their male characteristics for processing what they receive as they direct it toward its divine destination. Thus the sexes in a congregation are doing the same thing at the same time in a concerted manner, instead of confusing their combined consciousness with discord and inharmoniousness.

This is probably the reason why official religions usually had a male priesthood in earlier times. It was easier for a dominantly sexed human being to follow the polarity of his physical body without the often-confusing complications of esoteric practice and the switch to whichever polarity might be required. Earlier religions that had priestesses usually trained them to fulfill the male role as a dominant side of their characters. There is no real reason apart from custom and usage why females should not function in priestly parts provided they can present that side of their natures adequately. In any case, whoever is presenting the active elements of a ceremony is necessarily behaving in a projective masculine manner; therefore it might be theoretically true to say that the priesthood belonged to males in particular, but who dares to say that a female human being cannot mediate a male polarity if called upon to do so?

The real obligation of specially consecrated women in old-time Temples was to become vehicles for returning sacred kings if they were selected for that office. Today this function is spiritual instead of physical, and both sexes share this in common. A gestating embryo is *within* its mother, and we are continually being told that Deity is *within* us. We speak of God-concepts in the sense that we "conceive" Deity to be this or that. To conceive means to take in with the aid of another, and that is what a female does with male human seed. For a male to conceive means that he has to do the equivalent of a sex act in metaphysical terms. Therefore a man who is willing to admit that he is capable of conceiving any idea at all is tacitly admitting the feminine polarity of his own nature.

It is an old aphorism that a man is really a woman turned inside out, and though this may not be accurate anatomically, it is not altogether a bad way of putting things. The main point of course is sexual and implies that male generative organs project externally, whereas female ones internalize to accommodate them. Therefore if a male is prepared to adopt a female role for ceremonial purposes, it makes a useful start if he imagines his sex organs inverting. The same process in the reverse direction would be true for a female trying to project the masculine side of her psyche.

The exact process is for males to visualize their sex organs reversing so that they point internally. Then let them imagine that the psychic energy of the ceremony is entering their bodies at that point and manifesting its meaning through the senses. Simultaneously they should be conscious as male priests, somewhere between head and heart level, offering all their share of that energy to the Deity, which communicates with the center point of their skulls at the top of their heads. Using physical body references, this is about as close as we can set the situation. God on top, man in the middle, and woman as the basis. This is very roughly the theoretical arrangement of this imaginary relationship.

It will be seen that if this happens as it should, the entire congregation, whether physically male or female, are doing the same thing inside themselves, and this is what creates a perceptible picture that becomes clear to the Creative Consciousness. That is to say, it makes an esoteric type of ceremony comprehensible to an Intelligence that interests itself in the behavior of humankind. The disciplined and constructive activities of human creatures who not only seem to know what they are doing but why they are doing it as well. Which makes a welcome change from the often-disjointed gatherings of humans who treat their Deities like a good fairy godmother or a cajolable cretin.

Suppose, however, there is no congregation, but only a single celebrant working in a purely private Temple, as is frequently the case in Wesotericism. The general rule then is to "speak with the lips, listen with the ears, mediate with the mind, and seek with the soul." In other words, fulfill all functions with faith and hope that the inherent contact of the Temple itself will work as it should. Every properly consecrated Temple eventually makes its own linkage with Inner Dimensions of existence, and will constitute an almost automatic contact therewith when an initiated human intelligence activates the symbolism inside it. This may sound like an alarm system alerting attention on higher than human levels, and to some degree would be a fair comparison.

Such an automatic action of a Temple, however, should never be taken for granted purely because it has once been ceremonially consecrated. That is no more than a formal dedication. The real consecration of a Temple depends on the extent to which it is used and the quality of the service provided in it. That is a *proper* consecration, which could take years to achieve by the hardworking efforts of all concerned. Eventually this will build up an atmosphere that will last for a long time or may stay dormant for centuries. Most of the old sacred sites have this "feeling" hanging around them to the present day. That is the reason why so many Christian churches were built over them, because the location itself had been a trysting place between Gods and humankind for so very long a time. Being consecrated by centuries of service to Deity under any name is of greater value than a single official opening by the holiest bishop or saint in the calendar.

Nevertheless a Temple has to start *somewhere*, and continue until its human congregational members become capable of carrying it around with them in their hearts and souls. It is they who give it continuity and duration as a spiritual reality, without which animation a Temple will slow down to a dormancy that may take much reawakening. Apart from the materials of its earthly construction, which constitutes its body, a Temple has a soul, which is only kept alive by its human congregation, who should hand this over from one generation to the next. Priests and prayer leaders may be prominent in promoting and organizing the activities, but it is always their congregations that keep Temples going by their presence and prayers while they listen to the words uttered within the structure and try to learn whatever spiritual lessons may be made available.

Here we come to the question of teaching through the Temple. At one time the God (or at least a superior spiritual being) was supposed to speak directly to the people through the mind and mouth of a mediative priest or priestess. Very often this came out as sheer gibberish that was credited with mystical meaning beyond the power of mortal minds to follow, but should be listened to very carefully and committed to the subconsciousness, which would work on it patiently and later on come up with some surprising results. This faculty is still inherent in some humans under the name of xenoglossy (stranger-speak). It worked on the same principle as a Zen koan, being words that worry their hearers' minds into seeking solutions that do not really exist. This takes all the inventiveness of individuals to create one out of their imaginations, and that was the object of the exercise in the first place.

In a way, this is a verbal form of Rorschach blots where hearers are supposed to make sense out of randomly presented sonics as one makes definite shapes from their visual equivalents. Sometimes quite extraordinary enlightenment can be obtained by this method provided the original "message" is correctly given and properly "received" by hearers who have learned how to listen. The problem is that humans have come to assume that they gain information

and experience of life only through words they can understand and appreciate intellectually, whereas this is not so at
all in reality. We are affected in some way by every sound
we hear, and it contributes toward our awareness of existence and interactions therewith.

What about music? Mechanical noises? Animal sounds
of all descriptions? These certainly do not appeal to our
intellects, yet they have a considerable effect on human
intelligence by affording information as to their sources.
Whether they please, annoy, worry, or just interest us,
every single sound entering our physical ears tells us something concerning the affairs of this earth. Something that
our brains take in, interpret, store, and eventually classify
for future reference. So why should there not be sonic
equivalents that connect our consciousness with an Inner
State of existence? In fact, music does this already, and the
human voice is a musical instrument in the strict sense of
the word, which does not mean that it only makes good or
pleasant music. With every type of sound a human voice
can produce, however, it always *communicates*.

Therefore it is theoretically possible for a human voice
to utter sounds that have no intellectual meaning at all, yet
communicate a spiritual content that only the deep subconsciousness can translate after possibly a considerably
long time has elapsed. This was once called the "gift of
tongues," which Pentecostalists claim in our times, but is
not uncommon among other faiths and sects all around the
world, especially within esoteric groupings. The trouble is
that it became so unreliable in old times that it was eventually discredited altogether in favor of a comprehensible
form of communication based on accepted ideology or
what passed for honest opinions hopefully inspired by contact with Inner Consciousness.

The reasons for this were purely human. Charismatic
speaking was so very easy to falsify and present as the real

thing by those wishing to appear important in the eyes of their companions. Then again there was little or nothing to guarantee the bona fides of such pseudo-speech. If it could come from a good source of inspiration, it could equally well arrive from a mischievous one and cause a lot of confusion or ill-effects among misguided mortals. On the whole, the gift of tongues seemed best confined to those who knew how to employ it and what to make of it most sensibly, which meant relatively small and responsible congregations of esoterics.

This meant those individuals who could take it in and then deliberately set their subconsciousness to work on sifting, analyzing, and assessing all their inner impressions so that anything worthwhile or valuable would be retained, and whatever might be dangerous and detrimental would be eventually rejected. In other words, people who were capable of discrimination and good judgment, or who knew the difference between good and evil and preferred to work for good. People who knew better than to accept everything that was pushed into their minds without query simply because it seemed to come from supernatural sources.

Therefore such souls had to learn the arts of listening and of filtering the good from the bad, which are the spiritual equivalents of our physical digestion and excretion. The human body, however, has acquired its automatic capabilities after millions of years of evolution, whereas our minds and souls are still in a much slower rate of development that needs a lot of conscious attention during this stage of spiritual unfoldment, which will take a great deal longer than physical evolution. The human psyche has reached a fair degree of autonomy already, but there are yet very large areas to be covered, especially where judgment of values and estimates of moral issues are concerned. So we have to control our consciousness very carefully where these factors are involved.

So when encountering anything of a spiritual nature for inclusion in your metaphysical or mental make-up, it would be well to phrase a self-instruction something in this way: "I must listen very carefully to this, because it might be beneficial, but I must not accept any of it until I have weighed everything with wisdom and examined every item as well as I possibly can. If I make any mistakes, then let me learn from them and profit from that learning. What I want is the actual truth of anything I see or hear, whether I like it or not. I realize that I can only learn this truth as it appears to me at the present time, but let me see that with an honest heart and an absolute sincerity of soul. So let my guiding motto be 'Keep in Good, and throw out Bad.' " If that kind of thinking can be concentrated into the acronym KIGATOB, that or its equivalent is all that needs to be said or thought before receiving any psychic messages. Anything that will arouse an awareness of alert responsibility for whatever may come.

What really matters is that an open and cautionary attitude of mind be automatically adopted before any communications are accepted as authentic pronouncements from higher sources of inspiration. Try to classify the contact and estimate its content accordingly, as for example, inspiration. Opinion, official dogma, political, trivia. It would serve equally well if classifications were allotted numbers in order of importance according to estimated grades so that no. 1 would be of greatest significance to the hearer and the rest in descending order of importance. This can only be done, however, where the subject matter is completely comprehensible and the ideological content entirely understood by the listener.

So far as the ritual script of a ceremony is concerned, hearers should just let it pour through themselves like refreshing or stimulating water while they direct it toward Divinity. Their consciousness should be like a conduit for connecting the flow with its intended destination. They should not let themselves interfere with this by allowing their thoughts to wander away along private paths, nor should they interject personal petitions until an available occasion offers itself. Every well-designed ceremony should have proper periods for this purpose, even if the subject for such supplications is made mandatory, i.e., "Let us pray privately for _____ ." So long as all minds and souls present are centered on the same subject, that is the main requirement.

Ceremonials of an esoteric nature, even of the most primitive kind, are intentional arrangements of psychic energy, and Life itself *is* a psychic energy, however closely it may be involved with its material media. Therefore the better we are able to deal with such finer forces of our existence, the better we should be able to live and evolve into what we ought to be as human beings. Strictly speaking, we are only acting as children do when they play at being grown up. Play practice is a major factor in advancing toward adulthood in any species of life, and it is of the greatest importance in human development. Although any human being may reach physical adulthood successfully enough, how many ever reach real spiritual maturity in this world? Frighteningly few indeed.

Our activities in esoteric Temples afford us the most valuable opportunities for "play practice" at becoming spiritual adults in terms of a much larger life than we encounter on earth. By merely attending such ceremonies we are automatically admitting that there must be something more to Creative Consciousness than physical confinement to one body for the short duration of a single incarnation. It is our efforts at making actual contact with that Consciousness that are of primary importance in themselves. We might think that humans worship very different Gods today than our ancestors did, but a moment's reflection should show that this is untrue. Whatever the Gods are, those energies are essentially the same now as they have always been. It is our ideas and concepts of that Condition of Consciousness that alter and evolve through the centuries and build up different pictures and impressions to correspond with our current state of ideology. Human concepts of Deity are usually those of ourselves as we would like to be if and when we ever reach the end of our evolution.

That is why esoteric ceremonials that clearly and distinctly deal with those facts of inner or spiritual life are the most valuable ones to attend for the sake of finding ourselves. This may seem like playing at being God, yet that is exactly what we must do before we shall be fit to *work* at such a lofty life level. Children take their play seriously, and so they should if they ever expect to become responsible citizens in our society. Their games might be called sociodramas because they help develop the social side of a child's character, whereas an esoteric psychodrama helps develop the spiritual side of a physically adult human being, especially if it is specifically designed with that aim in view.

Technically of course it is possible to do the exact opposite and design ceremonies that have a very bad effect on humans by lowering their ethical standards considerably while increasing their intelligence and capabilities much above normal levels. This was once called black magic, which really signifies applying esoteric energies for purposes regarded as evil by most of humankind. For example, cruelty to creatures and exploitation of helpless or foolish humans. By and large, encouraging the nastiest side of human nature at the cost of our best instincts for the sake of material or advantageous profit in this world. Plain greed and brutality with the assistance and encouragement of non-human entities once called devils.

The nature and efficacy of such supernatural beings is

not the subject of the present text, yet the efficacy of evil itself as a motivating force impelling humanity toward its own destruction can scarcely be doubted as an actuality on this earth. How far such evil extra-mundane entities have contributed to our present condition is purely a matter for speculation or inspired guesswork. It is true that Temples for the especial worship of evil as a principle do exist, but these cannot be in any significant numbers, since really dedicated doers of evil are not particularly inclined to esoteric practices per se. They usually find that they can work all the evil they want to without any kind of help from special ceremonials other than ordinary social, political, or commercial customs, which serve their purposes quite well enough.

Therefore the great majority of esoteric Temples are more than likely to be meeting places for souls who are seeking spiritual improvement in their own especial ways, and as such are hoping to share each other's innermost experiences through psychodramatic activities in common. Since these are usually held in private among very small groups of people, it is most improbable that there will ever be a large, or any, congregation in the real sense of the word. Nevertheless the function of hearing and sharing the ideology of esoteric ceremonials is very important since it is a main means of making conscious contact with the higher powers behind the scenes of our outer actions.

Even amongst terrorist groups the political indoctrination sessions, which amount to their type of esoteric ceremonies at which "social sermons" are politically preached, are considered indispensable and obligatory for all their membership, and they could not function efficiently without these sectarian stimulants. That is regarded by them as a normal principle of their practice, which is perfectly correct procedure in the formation and coherency of any human grouping in existence. How much more vital then should be the conscious coherency of humans who are sincerely trying to attain a spiritual status that will bring benefits not only to themselves but to our entire species.

So in the end the chief characteristic of an esoteric congregation is the members' expertise at coordinating consciousness and translating words into wills directed toward Deity; and an esotericist should not even contemplate being a part of a congregation until he/she has his/her own individual practice well in hand. When one is able to do that with consistent attention and intention by oneself, then one will be fit for companionship among the congregation of the Faithful, who stand and wait to serve the Supreme Spirit animating all of us alike.

Chapter 8

TYPING A TEMPLE

There are so many different kinds of esoteric ceremonialism in our Western Inner Tradition that it is only possible to generalize concerning Temple procedures. The comparison would be much like an uncommitted Christian's attending all the sectarian churches and chapels to see which style of worship he/she found most suitable for him- or herself. The concept of a Christ figure might be about all they had in common, and the methodologies of communal relationship with it could bewilder anyone who was unprepared for such extreme variation.

Perhaps a distinction might be perceived between the social strata applying to people and the type of church or chapel they find most comfortable for worship. That could coincide with political leanings as well. On the whole, conservative right-wing people tend to associate with establishment churches, left-wing socialist types with chapels or fundamentalist concerns, and liberal middle-of-the-roaders with nonconformist churches. That is about the broadest and loosest kind of classification so far as orthodox religion is concerned, but the basic social principles extend into the esoteric field also.

In esotericism though, class consciousness takes on a rather different aspect. Here it is mainly a matter of aesthetic taste. Birth, money, and education only come into it insofar as they result in appreciation of cultural and associated values. Roughly the division comes between heart and head. Romance or reason? Mind or mysticism? The cerebral types will mostly move toward the intellectual philosophies and speculative side of esotericism, while the romantics are likely to become involved with the more emotional side of ceremonialism and magical movements. The average middle grouping usually pick bits from both extremes to suit themselves. Even so, there is still a tendency for esoteric concerns of all kinds to become private clubs for those with a common social background.

The fact is that humans as a whole usually feel uncomfortable if they are compelled for any reason to associate with others whose social background, cultural standards, and possibly educational and financial standing differ very widely from their own. The concept of class or caste is an inbred instinct that is not yet dead, no matter how much it may be abrogated in our times. Left to themselves, classes or "grades" of human beings would prefer to stay within familiar circles of social status where they feel natural and happy. Being well aware of this, most official religions cater to it by building "upper," "middle," and "lower" types of meeting places in all larger localities. Thus one can belong to a definite religious faith and still find a suitable edifice catering to one's own social status.

In the Episcopalian church there is a maximum of ceremonialism at the "high" end of it, a minimum at the "low," and a blend of both at the "middle." Esotericism has the same equivalent categories catering to different cultural classes. Even the "lowest" tastes should find something to satisfy them in the extremely broad and versatile field of occult outlooks. Standards of behavior usually alter as well when we descend the ceremonial scale. This means that the esotericists become far less disciplined or controlled by codes of conduct, not that they become more ill-mannered or uncouth. Obligations are not taken so seriously, nor are responsibilities regarded with the respect they normally command in more conventional circles. Again this can only be taken as a generalization in either direction, but it does indicate a relationship between human social groupings and specific esoteric activities.

Behavior that would be deemed acceptable or even desirable in one type of group would be entirely rejected in others. For example, deliberate humiliation or exposure to ridicule and horseplay as part of an initiation test might still be considered permissible by some of the less cultured but quite authentic groups in our Tradition, while others would say they had "grown out of that sort of thing." Because something was done a few centuries ago does not mean that it should be continued in exactly the same way now, or even continued at all. Age alone does not authorize. Evolution does. While character tests are always advisable, they can be applied in much more modern ways, such as a polygraph or by any system known to psychological selection operatives. In fact, any esoteric concern that is willing to accept members without any kind of compatibility screening ought to be suspected of inadequacy to say the least, yet its conduct throughout should be entirely in keeping with the codes of what we call normal and civilized behavior. Anything outside those codes needs very careful querying indeed.

Therefore the behavior patterns adopted by most Wesoteric Temples are likely to be those of the social class from which the members are drawn, plus a few customs just sufficiently apart from those to make them interesting, a trifle unique, or even daring. It is, after all, the unusual things we say or do during a Temple ceremonial that give it importance and value as a combined contribution to our lives and our spiritual significance. If we did nothing in Temples except commonplace and everyday actions, they would be no more than workshops or houses, and there would be no point in constructing or consecrating them. The entire reason for having Temples at all is so that absolutely nothing except thoughts, words, and deeds connected with spiritual intentions in the style of the particular system should be carried on in them.

By many standards, human behavior in Temples could be considered abnormal since it differs so distinctly from that of our usual lives. We do not normally

1. assemble for esoteric purposes;
2. wear special clothing and adornments;
3. address invisible entities;
4. adopt strange attitudes while making extravagant gestures;
5. offer incense or scatter lustral water;
6. consume specially consecrated food and drink;
7. surround ourselves with mystical symbology;
8. solemnly dedicate ourselves to any Deity or supernatural being;
9. bless inanimate objects or natural phenomena such as air and fire;
10. listen to or read long passages of sacred or ritual script. Although each separate item of this list might be practiced outside Temples on certain occasions, a combination of them all in proper proportions would constitute a ceremonial Temple working of a fairly normal nature. That is to

say, these behaviors would only be considered abnormal outside of their collective environment—which *is* a Temple.

This means to say that concentrated and regularly applied demands for spiritual services in a Temple over and above those of normal living are imposing a special sort of stress on human beings that literally commands the deeper and usually dormant side of our natures to manifest in appreciable form. In "calling up the Gods" we cannot avoid calling up the God-side of ourselves to some degree, and that is the best part of a human character, which is rarely shown to others. Such a practice, if persisted with, will definitely develop and consolidate our finest inherited attributes, just as physical exercises will do the same for our bodies *if* they are properly administered.

Again that "if" of administration. Wrongly applied callisthenics can spoil the efficiency of a human body, and their equivalent on a spiritual scale can do the same to a soul. It should not be difficult to think of people so spoiled by religious or esoteric practices of an undesirable nature. The most frequent cause of this appears to be the "We-are-right-and-all-others-wrong" syndrome. In other words, exclusivity at the expense of everyone else. A sort of spiritual one-upmanship that always seems to bring out the worst in human nature, probably because it originates from that source. There is nothing wrong with exclusivity in the sense of creating a purely private atmosphere as all people are entitled to do in their own homes among their family and friends, but when it comes to denying the same right in the case of all other humans, then a basic wrong has most certainly happened.

It may be a hackneyed truism that one person's meat is another's poison, but there are few instances where this applies more than in Wesoteric Temples. Herein individualism has been carried to the point where most active practitioners are aiming for purely private Temples on their own premises. This is getting to be almost like huge corporate concerns where the mark of distinction is to have the use of more exclusive lavatories until the apex of the pinnacle is reached by the top director of all who has one entirely to himself (which he shares with no one except the cleaners of course). Though there has never been a census to show exactly how many private Temples exist, there must be several thousand of them at least. Most of them will be converted rooms in private houses, outbuildings in secluded gardens, or even screened-off corners in bedrooms, but these still count as Temples of our esoteric Tradition. Practicing Pagans, however, usually prefer open-air locations for their ceremonies and dislike indoor Temples, which they will only use in very adverse climatic conditions.

Here a distinction is being made between the "indoor" and "outdoor" types of Wesoterics, which is really academic, though there are specific differences that depend on temperament rather than social class. The "indoor Temple" kind of people are generally more conservative and conventional, perhaps the word *restrained* is a better description. "Outdoor" types are generally more exuberant and uninhibited, allowing greater degrees of latitude among their membership. The term *Pagan* is somewhat of a misnomer, permissible only by modern usage. Strictly speaking, it applied only to the old Roman rural populace inhabiting the pagi, which were fortified areas around the city. In the end the term was used descriptively for any sort of countryperson wherever. Perhaps the best option would be to distinguish these two types of esoterics by terming them *urban* or *rural* regardless of their domiciles.

There can be no question of best or worst in esoteric systems. What brings out the best in one soul may bring out the worst in another. It is all a matter of matching souls and systems. Many an individual has gone from one organized affair to another many times before settling down into a suitable slot. Many have never found such a thing and have remained in apparent solitude for life, although spiritually bound into brotherhood with the rest of us simply by being born into the same Tradition. These esotericists would probably find their invisible brethren quite incompatible if encountered as incarnate beings. Personality clashes seem to be the most frequent reason for the breakup of so many Wesoteric groups, which, sad to say, is scarcely surprising due to the intensely individualistic nature of Wesotericism as a whole. Few seem to have learned how to value the differences between each other instead of the similarities. They are usually more interested in finding themselves in others rather than looking for others in themselves.

Possibly the worst thing that can happen with any esoteric grouping is if it falls into the wrong hands and is misused for political or antisocial reasons. Should that be supported by Inner influences that have no wish to see the mass of humanity evolve into spiritual beings with corresponding capabilities, then the case is that much worse; and we can find instances of what might truly be termed a "Black Brotherhood" in the sense of evil esotericism. Such societies are almost never open to an average or ordinary human. They confine their membership to a very exclusive class of person who keeps well out of contact with those outside his/her circle, and they extend their influence through indirect agencies wherever it is likely to have the maximum effect on unresisting or unsuspecting humans.

While it would be quite wrong to credit such undesirables with unlimited supernatural powers that they do not in fact have, it would be equally wrong to underestimate the total effect they can produce on a worldwide scale. Although most of this is only possible because they are allowed to get away with it by the vast majority of permissive humans, this does not lessen the damage that mis-applied esotericism can do. The Thule Society of Nazi Germany is a typical example, and there are others like them that are dedicated to undermining and breaking up human society purely for the sake of their own expected profits. Conversely, there are plenty of the opposite type whose objective is the liberation of the human soul and spirit from bondage to bodily existence and the other ills that afflict our society. So in the end it all boils down to a straightforward goodies versus baddies affair, while the great bulk of humanity awaits the issue with a hopeful eye on the ground for possible pickings.

In case anyone may be wondering whether any particular esoteric associations might be controlled by such baddies, and if so how to avoid joining them by mistake, let it be said that such an occurrence would be virtually impossible for the following reasons. Such affairs only recruit their members through several complete weeding-out stages, each guaranteeing sufficient security to protect the next step of processing. For instance, if a likely prospect joins a relatively easy esoteric order to enter, perhaps as much as a year later someone might suggest a much more interesting and exclusive group to enter that "might just have a vacancy." That someone, of course, is a talent scout who will know nothing further except that he/she is being paid quite well for the introduction. From that point on, this could happen several times more before an ultimate group was reached. Even so, a candidate would have to possess a real aptitude for evil and an absolute devotion to what we might term *the Devil* as a concept of anti-Divinity. Furthermore whether for good or ill, the further one progresses along its path, every step calls for stricter discipline and demands severer penalties for failure in either direction.

So although it could be harmless enough if offers are made to join another esoteric group, this would warrant at least an eyebrow being raised and a few questions asked. However, top-class baddies prefer to do their direct recruiting from their own intimate families and small circles of operatives, though they are not averse to gaining strength from suitable people who are qualified to serve their purposes best. If they were advertising openly, it would be a case of "No one without experience and first-rate references need apply." They would certainly never try to compel unwilling workers since that would be a self-defeating idea. So there is little risk of black magicians in average esoteric circles.

Moreover, that kind of maneuver can only be carried out in largish concerns with a sizeable membership. Very small circles wherein everyone is known intimately by the others are the most difficult to infiltrate. They may not have the material resources of larger organizations, but they are probably freer from inimical influences unless they are formed specifically for ill-doing. Any reputable group will gladly agree to a probationary period during which a new member can get to know all the others, and if he/she is dissatisfied at the end of the term, he/she will be perfectly free to quit, with no ill-feelings on either side provided he/she respects any confidences he/she may have been entrusted with.

No Temple is a guardian of vital "occult secrets" that would wreck the world or do anything very extraordinary by themselves. That is pure fiction. Any Temple does have its confidential "family secrets" that should be guarded in just the same way as those of friends, relatives, or even employers. Things like membership identities, code names, recognition signals and handgrips, private symbology, and personal experiences. Nor should the private affairs of other members be discussed, though it is quite legitimate to mention personal opinions of the group or conduct of its members provided it is made absolutely clear that such remarks are purely personal opinions and not necessarily facts in themselves. The best policy though is undoubtedly silence.

A frequent question asked by would-be joiners of Wesoteric Temples is, "How am I to know which are genuine and which are not?" Not an easy query to answer with a positive or definite reply. What does *genuine* mean for anyone? How does one define *authenticity* as a value in itself? How, for that matter, is anyone to distinguish between a Temple or group that is in contact with Inner authorities who are helpful and beneficial toward the human membership, and that which is nothing more than an ego enhancement for some false prophet or, much more commonly, a money-making mechanism for the few that run it for their own personal profit. What exactly constitutes authenticity?

In terms of dictionary definitions, this means whether or not anything is precisely what it is believed or reputed to be, but *truth* and *falsehood* are relative terms. One can have such a thing as a true falsehood, or a genuine lie, because being known as such is indeed authentic. A reproduction of a Rembrandt painting would be unauthentic if described as an original, yet quite genuine if described as a reproduction. Authenticity is thus the difference between fact and fiction of hoped-for values, but need have nothing to do with the nature or capability of the thing in question. There can be an authentic piece of rubbish or a genuine load of garbage. So both terms are meaningless in relation to Temples.

Even if a Temple was run primarily for a profit by the biggest crooks in the business, it might still be used by well-intentioned Inner entities to bless and benefit a sincere membership of suckers who brought the highest hopes with them. If it taught them nothing more than the arrangement and management of Temple buildings, that would be something of value, and if it further gave them the opportunity of meeting and talking to each other, that could lead somewhere worthwhile in the end. Whether or not this was worth the money they paid for such a privilege would be entirely for those concerned to decide for themselves.

If it should be purely historical authenticity that is in question, that again is a moot point. It is incorrect to assume that any organization must be authentic merely because it can trace a line of descent several hundred years long; the organization's ancestry proves only that it is authentically old, *not* that it is authentically good or necessarily of great spiritual value. There may be a strong probability that something is worth preserving in its structure, otherwise it would scarcely have survived, but again all this does is demonstrate its durability and persistence, nothing else. A five-hundred-year-old house that has never been modernized might be a very interesting museum exhibit, but who in his/her right mind in our times would care to live in it permanently? Simply because an esoteric concern is old in name or ideology is no guarantee of its goodness or continuing spiritual significance. As a human institution it cannot be older than its most senior member, since it is an inheritance that passes from one generation to the next, and however much they may claim continuity, the people mediating its meaning in modern times are not the same as those who formed and framed it in earlier epochs. We always experience what is presented to us by our contemporaries, and it depends on how well or otherwise they are able to convert former spiritual systems into terms of present-day thought.

For example, although Christianity has a two-thousand-year-old worldly history, it also has a social history of altered outlooks, doctrines, and administrational alterations for the same period. It would not have survived otherwise. Even the Jewish faith has had to adapt to changing conditions of consciousness. Esotericism, with its amazingly wide range of spiritual exploration through all possible areas of ideology, can do no more than offer its adherents opportunities for advancing their thinking along whatever new lines or angles may be opening up for further development.

In the end it is a question of the proof of the pudding being in the eating: Temples being best known by their fruits, or how they help the spiritual development of their members. It is certain that any Temple can contribute something to someone, but the problem is fitting people into their most suitable frames. One day this may be done with computers, but at present, good judgment, guidance, and inspired guesswork must manage to fill requirements as closely as they can. The obvious need here is a kind of "Spiritual Selection Board" that would accurately assess the characteristics of aspiring candidates and direct them almost infallibly toward whichever system suited their needs best.

Their *needs* be it noted, not their *wants*. There is a very distinct difference between those two requirements. Needs are usually character deficiencies that are correctible by persisting with the appropriate exercises and procedures, plus of course the Inner influences invoked to assist the process. Wants, on the other hand, may be anything arising from whims or inclinations that are likely to do little or no good for anyone. A good example would be a small boy who wants an ice-cream but actually needs a laxative. If only we wanted what we needed how much better we should be!

Fitting human beings into suitable spiritual frames is a matter of matching their plus-minus characteristics with the minus-plus propensities of the type of Temple they need to compensate for their deficiencies and curtail their superfluities. They might not *like* the arrangement at all, yet if it balanced their instabilities and brought them into a wholesome state of harmony, what more could they reasonably ask for? Different types of Temple workings are compatible with matching types of mortals, and getting the two together seems to be more of a hit-or-miss affair than it needs to be. Still, the Holy Mysteries struggled along for many centuries before modern psychology with its selection techniques came into being, and doubtless they will survive a few more decades yet before being compelled to catch up with what passes for progress in our times.

However remarkable or impressive any Temple may be, its highest value will always be as a solid symbol acting as a ground plan for spiritual self-construction, and that is the way it should be seen by Temple users of all persuasions. For example, the basic thinking of rural types of Wesoterics was that all people should model themselves on Nature itself. So humans met in friendly circles around a central fire—symbolizing the Sun Spirit—which would warm them and cook their food, which the same Spirit thoughtfully provided for them. The pattern of life was all around them. If their bones might be as firm as rocks yet as moveable as water, while their limbs were as strong as trees, that would be wonderful! Then they looked at the animals to be emulated. Slow and steady like a tortoise, or lithe as a leopard. Every creature had its special lesson to teach. Humankind's job was to watch and learn. Supposing anybody could have the courage of a lion, the endurance of an elephant, the cunning of a fox, and the fabled wisdom of an owl or serpent? Every single creature had its own special quality for humans to observe and either copy or cancel in their characteristics. If humans could live by the "Book of Nature," that should be sufficient scripture for their salvation.

Urban Wesoterics had other ideas. Nature might be wonderful, but we were in this world to improve on it with the artifacts we made from its resources. Building a Temple was like building a body for the invisible Beings who would dwell therein as deities, like humans inhabited their mortal bodies as souls seeking shelter and accommodation. Inside the Temple, its symbolic artifacts stood for all the spiritual qualities that humans were supposed to develop by dealing with them in that Temple. The altar of sacrifice meant our bodily hearts and willingness to offer ourselves in service to the Spirit honored by the ceremonies. The colors of everything were the various states of mind and soul. Everything within range of the senses in the Temple had some special significance for the initiated that not only had to be known but also experienced at its appropriate moment. There was really little difference between the two spiritual systems except that one relied on Nature in the raw so to speak, while the other preferred it clothed and adorned by human ingenuity.

In the end analysis it might fairly be asked, What good have Temples of any type done us through the many centuries they have been in operation, and What especial advantage might esoteric ones provide with their minute membership and unorthodox ways of working? If they had no effect outside their confining circles, the influence of Temples, esoteric or otherwise, could be considered as relatively valueless so far as the rest of the world is concerned. However, they *do* have an effect and its sum total has shaped our history to a far greater extent than some might care to admit. They have done this by altering human characteristics; and by a process that may be likened to spiritual osmosis, this has spread around our whole world. Our present state of civilization has resulted from our past thinking, which was formed very greatly by Temple teachings and practices.

However much people tried to confine their beliefs and practices to the privacy of their Temples, thoughts cannot be confined at all, and they literally spread. Their exact details may stay concealed for long periods, but eventually their fundamental nature and essence will reach the pool of common consciousness in which all our secrets swim. Jung termed this the "collective unconscious," but it is only unconscious in the sense of being a totally different dimension to that of our so-called normal awareness, which is focused at the front of our minds and stored in our bodily brain cells. Most esotericists have been aware of this collective unconscious for a very long time, under different names like the "akasic records," which are supposed to contain every thought that every human ever had. Recording angels are a very old belief indeed.

This interchange of consciousness between ourselves and the collective unconscious is a two-way process. If a human mind can impress its thinking into the ocean of awareness around it, a superior spiritual intelligence using the same medium can certainly impress its thoughts into a human mind, and so can we humans eventually affect each other in the same way. This is really no more remarkable than thoughts expressed through the radio or TV influencing humans who receive them through their physical senses at a great distance. That is a much more rapid process than obtaining the same thoughts by absorbing them through psychic means such as meditation.

Meditation and active ceremonialism are part of the same psychic process, and together form complementary sections of a complete spiritual cycle. Since we can both transmit and receive our thinking on these deep levels of intelligence, the effect of this ability on our characters, genetics, and consequently our whole history has been incalculable. We are what we are purely through past developments, and we should be making our future better by our present performance. The closer we come to perfecting this process, the more advantageous it will be for us, and the only way we shall learn how to do this is by contact with more advanced intelligences than ourselves. Hence we need to explore and use all possible means of making conscious contact with "Them," whatever we might suppose Them to be.

Of course sacred ceremonialism is no longer our only means of making contact. A mathematician or scientist trying to think out principles or methods of managing natural forces is factually practicing meditation, whatever else he/she might call it. So is anyone attempting extension of awareness into unknown areas of inner space and transcendental time. The ability to concentrate and maneuver consciousness in that way, however, derives from inherent genetic qualities inherited from remote ancestors who implanted such a characteristic into their lines of descent by efforts made in their equivalents of Temples. We very often describe some individual as being "gifted" when we really mean that he was born with unusual genetic potentials. Development of these is the responsibility of the soul possessing them, and that is usually done during the early part of an incarnation with the aid of training and encouragement supplied by other humans.

Development of latent spiritual potentials may be done at any time of life however late, and at one time many Mystery schools would not accept candidates for training until they were in their thirties or even forties. By then a fairly developed degree of character should have appeared and the individual have become reliable and at least reasonably educated, while not being too old for accepting or adapting with altered outlooks. Though this scarcely applies today, the principle is sound enough in theory, and certainly no one should be allowed to participate in serious ceremonial working who might be spiritually unstable or otherwise unbalanced in any direction.

At this point we may as well raise the old vexed question of whether or not to allow pregnant women to be present at or participate in solemn ceremonials. All the old rulings said *no* very definitely. They also banned menstruating females, but that was because of the belief that the blood of sterility carried a curse with it that was likely to blight or abort all esoteric workings of a productive nature. Though we might discount this ban in modern times, the ancient prohibition applying to pregnancy should still hold good for a quite valid reason.

The major reason is the unwarranted exposure of the unborn soul to direct spiritual influences that may be unsuitable for it. An unborn child *is* influenced by environmentals that affect his/her mother and cause significant changes in her consciousness. Though we cannot be definite about the depth or extent of such prenatal influences, there seems no need to run quite unnecessary risks that could so easily be avoided by absence. It is certain that no modern mother would deliberately expose her child to x-rays, dangerous drugs, or possibly to microwave ovens, which are known to constitute hazards, and there are plenty more in our so-called civilization, such as loud sonics, cigarette smoking, drinking, and short-wave therapy.

All those are things of the body. Those of the mind and soul hold hazards for the unborn as well, even though they may not be anything of a menace in themselves. An expectant mother's condition of consciousness has a direct bearing on embryonic life, and no one has the right to put that at unnecessary risk by exposing the mother to influences she may not be able to handle. A great deal depends on the precise nature of the ceremony. In the case of straightforward prayer sessions, meditations, special blessings, or ordinary offices, there should not be any serious objection to her taking part in those, but when it comes to sacrificial rites, exorcisms especially, comminations, healings, and the like, no antenatals should be present because of the potent influences involved. It is the responsibility of the Temple Master to issue warnings in regard to such possibilities, but the ultimate onus must fall on the mother-to-be herself. If she is wise she will not take her child into an esoteric Temple until it is out of her body.

Although it is a physical presence we are questioning here, it is the mental presence and spiritual presence at Temple gatherings that are of primal importance. Should anyone be bodily present for the whole of a Temple ceremony yet thinking of something else all the time, any esoterically minded soul would agree that such a person had not been really present at all. Conversely, someone who was bodily absent yet whose mind and soul were engaged with the same working at the same time elsewhere could be counted as one of the congregation. Full allowance for this should always be made at every ceremony. Members must be encouraged to make imaginary visits to their Temples, going through all the admission procedures in their minds as if they were bodily present, and then concluding with the departure formula at the end of the exercise.

This a very valuable little practice to perform. It used to be called "constructing the Temple on the Astral Plane," i.e., making it in one's own mind. If enough people thought about the same place, and preferably at the same time and in the same way, then that place would really exist for them as if it was built with real bricks. This can be done with any-thing of course, but the preferential place is one's own Temple, which is supposed to be a symbolic substitute for a heavenly habitation, and a model for spiritual self-con-struction. An example of this is the "New Jerusalem" de-scribed in detail by St. John in his Apocalypse.

It would be rather unreasonable of esoterics to expect an invisible Entity to remain permanently on duty in their physical Temples if they are not prepared to visit these invisibly themselves. Therefore they should learn to do this as soon as possible after initiation, and as clearly as they possibly can. Every detail of one's Temple should be called to mind as if it were solid, and all the sensations and emotions experienced in it reproduced as clearly and sharply as if they were happening in reality. A routine for this might be arranged by whoever is responsible for running a Temple. Special services for absent members could be held. At some convenient time known to all, an available officer would celebrate a simple service in the Temple while members elsewhere visualized themselves present and participating in it.

The same could be done for those who work in rural conditions, except that they should remember to change the set scene to suit the climatic conditions of the prevailing season. Those people could in fact work from a picture or idealistic setting far closer to what they want rather than what is actually available to them. Many of the Sabbats in previous days were factually spent only in imagination by people lying in drugged stupors while visualizing all the things believed to be happening all around them. Although there are probably quite a few today who would not be averse to continuing this custom, it is not recommended for those intending to make serious spiritual progress. Drug-induced visions are very unreliable, and contribute no more, if as much, than watching a very trivial TV show.

For that reason, it is most important, when making mental visits to a Temple, to imagine oneself actually engaged in doing something rather than watching others work. In that way one avoids the bad habit of idle day-dreaming, which accomplishes almost nothing of solid spiritual value. Even if one visualizes nothing except activities of ordinary maintenance such as arranging flowers or polishing brass, that would be better than thinking of nothing but passive enjoyments witnessed with pleasure. This does not mean that one should *never* enjoy some spiritual spectacle during visionary visits; enjoyment of a spectacle is acceptable provided an active contribution of consciousness has been made to it initially.

That is what helps keep the "charge" of a Temple going. Such a charge or atmosphere is more difficult to explain than to experience. Any sensitive individual can feel it the instant he/she enters a Temple. It feels (or should feel) entirely different from the outside. A "presence" as it were of Someone or Something that seems to be invisibly observing the entrant. Old Pagans knew this feeling of being watched as a strange apprehension that got increasingly stronger as though something alarming were about to happen. They supposed this was caused by the god Pan, who might suddenly appear in a frightening form, which seemed to be his idea of a joke. Hence the word *panic*, which still describes terror. Pious Jews knew the same experience as "the fear of the Lord" that was the beginning of wisdom. They associated it with the "presence" they saw in the strange glow they could sometimes see hovering over the ark. This glow was actually a concentration of atmospheric electricity, which is not uncommon around metallic masses in desert atmospheres. Nevertheless, this was effective in evoking the required spiritual reactions among them, which contributed very greatly to the efficacy of their traveling Temple.

Such a charge might be compared to the patina that is so valued with authentic antiques. That is only acquired by attention over the ages, and its equivalent in a Temple is only accomplished by a sufficiency of spiritual thinking and acting in, or associated with, its location. As might be expected, the charge appears strongest in Temples where regular and repeated workings are carried out, and weakest where working is only occasional and more of an ethical or social nature rather than deeply devotional and sincerely religious. This is caused by consciousness, especially of a strongly emotional nature. The feelings and spiritual sensations of all present or consciously connected with a Temple actually remain as a field of force when the esoterics have finished a working; and this force persists for quite a while afterwards. It acts as a kind of residual magnetism from which future workings may rapidly be brought to maximum output.

Like all other energies this needs constant topping up if it is to stay in a state of efficiency. That is greatly augmented from two main sources. One is a steady stream of people using the place for their private devotions, and the other is a current of consciousness coming from those who are thinking about it at a physical distance. It will be found that where Temples are kept locked up between ceremonies and when no one thinks about them during the intervening period, they seem singularly lifeless and empty. That is why members should be encouraged to send their thoughts at regular intervals toward their Temples, and to imagine themselves actually doing something there, even if it is no more than sounding a gong or lighting a lamp.

This is where it helps if a Temple has some definite name or number as an identity mark of location in the spiritual world. As the mention of the name of a place will instantly call up a mental impression of it in the mind of anyone knowing anything about it, so will the name of a Temple help one to establish contact with its esoteric identity. Just as many a Christian church is usually identified by its tutelary saint's name plus the town or village it stands in, so is an esoteric Temple normally nominated by a code phrase indicating its type of activity plus maybe a number to signify its relationship therewith. This is really no more than its spiritual postal code, but it can be very useful indeed when it comes to establishing conscious links with any Temple in question.

A main difficulty here might seem to be the total lack of some generally agreed-on organized system of coding among esotericists on earth, but the likelihood of confusion is so slight as to be virtually negligible. Temple names are often suggested by imaginative members and formally adopted by a committee of members after consideration and discussion. Otherwise, it may be decided by lot so that Fate has a hand in it. A name may be picked from a list of those thought suitable, and written on slips placed in a chalice or other suitable vessel. There should definitely be a clear connection between the name and the specific work of the Temple itself or its type of membership, which can be done by combining words or using acronyms. For example, a Temple called "Hermes-Sophia 3" would indicate to anyone with the least esoteric knowledge that it was dedicated to Hermetic wisdom of a fairly wide range, and most probably of a very intellectual nature. Only actual members, however, might guess that the "Clecab 1" Temple stood for "*Cle*veland *Cab*balists Only," or that the "ERU 10" Temple meant "Earth Religions United" from ten different systems.

Once a Temple is definitely named, that name must never be altered without the most serious reasons, such as a total change of purpose or an inclusion of ideology greatly at variance with the original intentions of its founders. Even then, some trace of the old name should remain, maybe just enough for former members to feel in touch with. The proper use of a Temple's name means that all members, past and present, can be collectively called to mind very conveniently if one does not want to identify them individually by their initiatory names. From another angle, if telepathic communication with any member in particular is sought, it makes a useful contact point to call the member by his/her private name first, then the initiatory, and finally the Temple's. Just as sailors are collectively called by their ship's name. This of course should apply only to communications directly concerned with the Temple. On no account should casual social affairs or trivial topics be dealt with on Temple precincts, whether telepathically or otherwise.

In some modern Temples it is becoming a practice to use the same space for more than one purpose. Sometimes by just screening off the sanctuary the floor space is made available for lectures, discussions, or musical recitals. This is totally wrong in principle and should never be allowed by any responsible authority. It is most definitely desecration and especially so if money is made by the action. Strictly speaking, it is sacrilegious if sermons or addresses with political, financial, social, or similar motivations are made in the actual Temple. In adjoining rooms it may be permissible, even if possibly in poor taste. Sacred and secular subjects are best kept as far apart as possible.

The hallmark of any Temple is the standard of discipline observed by members and officers alike. Here should be noted very carefully the difference between strictness and severity. Even though a discipline needs to be strict, it should never be in the least severe. For a discipline to be severe means that it is imposed on people whether they agree with it or not. To be strict means that it has a high standard that all welcome and have agreed to abide by for the sake of effective performance. This really amounts to no more than what any reasonable person would expect to observe if something has to be done as well as possible. In other words, self-discipline, which is the best type of all.

Every rule of conduct should be explained to neophytes very clearly, and the exact reasons for everything made absolutely plain. Except of course when intelligence levels are being evaluated and they are supposed to work out the reasons for themselves with the aid of given data, which must be sufficient. In which case they must be fairly warned of the test being applied and never allowed to continue under a misapprehension. It is well to remember the famous phrase "A thing is not just because God wills it, but God wills it because it is just." That is to say, no rule is right because Brother Thing says it is, but he says so because he honestly believes it *is* so. His belief or opinion could always be called into question, but if it is, the querist should have all his/her reasons ready as well as improved alternatives and the reasons for them.

There is plenty of room in our modern world for esoteric Temples that are able to teach the values of spiritual disciplines to those who are willing to follow them faithfully. Even if all the ideology connected is totally inaccurate in substance, it is positively true in essence; and there is much to be gained from Temple practice that can be put to good use in most circles of human society. Courteous and correct behavior toward each other is a main asset. So are disciplined thinking, accuracy of attitude, self-control, and a pleasingly presented personality. Granted, all these qualities may be inherent in humans anyway and brought to the surface by many different means other than Temple practice, but that still remains a maximally efficient method of concerting and developing the latent characteristics of human beings if it is properly carried out.

This is done by combining the disciplines of dramatic art with the ideology and altruism held by the best type of human beings, and then applying this to the trainees and doing everything possible to carry it out faithfully. If a Temple is reputable and responsible, it will arrange a spiritual training program that is both practical and productive of greatly improved individuals. Such would be in effect a "character course" that instilled and encouraged a sense of ethics and moral responsibility in the membership, plus a certain amount of scholarship and artistic appreciation. (Similar programs were once administered by churches.) Esoteric Temples should be capable of doing this without the intolerance and impaired judgment so often imparted by church authorities and administrators.

Most of all, esoteric Temples should be able to sponsor, support, and enable every active member to follow successfully their ancient aim (so needful in all ages) of *knowing thyself*. If self-discovery is a major motive in life, where else is it best encouraged than in esoteric Temples dedicated to that especial idea? They should exist not to impose odd and possibly alien dogmas and doctrines on unquestioning and puzzled people but to search out the secret spiritual aims and abilities held in human hearts for so many centuries, and then to lead these out into the light of today for the illumination of free minds and souls.

On those grounds alone esoteric Temples are justified. They were and are designed not for the mass of humankind but for a minority of special souls capable of consciousness beyond the range of average awareness. These souls are outstanding not necessarily in intellect and intelligence but rather in an ability to sense the supernormal and appreciate life on its paraphysical levels. More importantly, souls with an aptitude for self-development on the spiritual side of life, who refuse to remain mediocre materialists and aim themselves at the very highest points of human perception, which are far above ordinary hopes and fears.

It is for such souls in particular that esoteric Temples exist. Souls with advanced outlooks and independent spirits and who are likely to be leaders of thought in this world because their own thinking has been led into other dimensions of existence elsewhere. Those needing facilities for condensing, correlating, and concentrating their uncommon type of consciousness into terms comprehensible by fellow mortals looking for enlightenment on their own spiritual problems. So long as there are souls of this type continuing to incarnate on this earth, there will either be esoteric Temples waiting to welcome them, or they themselves will become Temples waiting to welcome those who are able to share the same spiritual secrets.

Humans are, and will become, whatever is in their genetics. These either improve or deteriorate in the course of time due to breeding and environmental experience, which includes education and cultural qualities. Esoterics believe that they also improve or depreciate with the interaction of invisible and imponderable energies, which they do not claim to comprehend as yet but nevertheless have identified by convenient nomenclatures for the sake of making conscious relationships with them. They further believe that as a result of such encounters made chiefly through Temple ceremonials and procedures over many millennia of experience, human beings as a whole have developed finer characteristics and cultures. But, no one can claim that we have reached anywhere near our peak point of evolution.

This means to say that there is plenty of potential left in us yet to develop along the same spiritual lines. It may be that we shall have to alter our techniques or discover new ones. It could also be that there is very much in old methods that has not yet been brought to light or developed to its maximum possibilities. There is no reason to abandon a mine before it is exhausted, and the heaps of spoil accumulated from many old gold mines are now being reprocessed because, with improved techniques nowadays, about fifteen percent of the gold can be recovered from them. Who can guess the percentage recoverable from the residue of past spiritual probings? When early humans were hurling rocks at each other, they could not have suspected the secrets of silicon chips, which have revolutionized our civilization millions of years later. How do we know we are not behaving in the same way now with apparently valueless spiritual material? In which case, who is to keep it going and act as its custodian until its incalculable value becomes provable to all people everywhere on earth? One way or another, the answer has to be connected with esoteric establishments and all the types of Temples with which they are bringing thoughts into being through conscious contact with higher orders of intelligence.

From the first tentative touches of our earliest esoterics to the end of all our otherworldly endeavors and explorations, we continue to be "directed missiles" destined for divinity or destruction. Salvation and damnation are the ultimate alternatives of our existence as a spiritual species. Is there an escape route anywhere that leads away from both and toward a Truth transcending everything? If there is, only the few will find its starting point within the Temple of themselves, where they have learned to look for liberation into the Light from whence there need be no return.

Laus Deo Semper

STAY IN TOUCH

On the following pages you will find listed, with their current prices, some of the books and tapes now available on related subjects. Your book dealer stocks most of these, and will stock new titles in the Llewellyn series as they become available. We urge your patronage.

However, to obtain our full catalog, to keep informed of new titles as they are released and to benefit from informative articles and helpful news, you are invited to write for our bi-monthly news magazine/catalog. A sample copy is free, and it will continue coming to you at no cost as long as you are an active mail customer. Or you may keep it coming for a full year with a donation of just $2.00 in U.S.A. ($7.00 for Canada & Mexico, $20.00 overseas, first class mail). Many bookstores also have *The Llewellyn New Times* available to their customers. Ask for it.

Stay in touch! In *The Llewellyn New Times'* pages you will find news and reviews of new books, tapes and services, announcements of meetings and seminars, articles helpful to our readers, news of authors, advertising of products and services, special money-making opportunities, and much more.

The Llewellyn New Times
P.O. Box 64383-Dept. 274, St. Paul, MN 55164-0383, U.S.A.

•   •   •

TO ORDER BOOKS AND TAPES

If your book dealer does not have the books and tapes described on the following pages readily available, you may order them direct from the publisher by sending full price in U.S. funds, plus $1.00 for handling and 50¢ each book or item for postage within the United States; outside USA surface mail add $1.50 per item postage and $1.00 per order for handling. Outside USA air mail add $7.00 per item postage and $1.00 per order for handling. MN residents add 6% sales tax.

FOR GROUP STUDY AND PURCHASE

Because there is a great deal of interest in group discussion and study of the subject matter of this book, we feel that we should encourage the adoption and use of this particular book by such groups by offering a special "quantity" price to group leaders or "agents".

Our Special Quantity Price for a minimum order of five copies of TEMPLE MAGIC is $23.85 Cash-With-Order. This price includes postage and handling within the United States. Minnesota residents must add 6% sales tax. For additional quantities, please order in multiples of five. For Canadian and foreign orders, add postage and handling charges as above. Credit Card (VISA, MasterCard, American Express, Diners' Club) Orders are accepted. Charge Card Orders only may be phoned free ($15.00 minimum order) within the U.S.A. by dialing 1-800-THE MOON (in Canada call: 1-800-FOR-SELF). Customer Service calls dial 1-612-291-1970. Mail Orders to:

LLEWELLYN PUBLICATIONS
P.O. Box 64383-Dept. 274 / St. Paul, MN 55164-0383, U.S.A.

MODERN MAGICK
by Donald Kraig

Modern Magick is the most comprehensive, step-by-step introduction to the art of ceremonial magic ever offered. It will guide you from the easiest of rituals and the construction of your magickal tools through the highest forms of magick: designing your own rituals and doing pathworking. Along the way you will learn the secrets of the Kabalah in a clear and easy-to-understand manner. You will also discover the true secrets of invocation and evocation, channeling, and the missing information that will finally make the ancient *grimoires*, such as the **Keys of Solomon**, not only comprehensible, but usable. *Modern Magick* is designed so anyone can use it, and is the perfect guidebook for students and classes. It will also help to round out the knowledge of long-time practitioners of the magickal arts.

0-87542-324-8, 608 pages, 6 x 9, illus.   **$14.95**

THE NEW MAGUS
by Donald Tyson

This is perhaps the first book to give a rational philosophical explanation of how and why magic works, and shows why magic is not subject to the scientific method! Rather, it is an alternative, and this book gives the reader a practical framework on which to base his own personal system. It is virtually an encyclopedia of universal symbols (or principles) and a text of magical practices to make them live within. Even though magic may be seen as an alternative to traditional science and traditional religion, it also can be seen as the foundation upon which both are raised, and hence as the unifying principle to restore meaning and wholeness to modern life.

0-87542-825-8, 352 pages, 6 x 9, illus.   **$12.95**

THE SWORD AND THE SERPENT
The Magical Philosophy, Vol 2

Revising and expanding Books III and IV of the first edition, this is the comprehensive guide to the Magical Qabalah with extensive correspondences, as well as the techniques for activating the centers, use of images and the psychology of attainment.

0-87542-197-0, 500 pgs., 6 x 9, illus., softcover.   **$15.00**

MYSTERIA MAGICA
The Magical Philosophy, Vol 3

Revising and expanding Book V of the first edition, this book can now stand alone as a complete course in magick by itself. It is a comprehensive guide to the rituals and practices of ceremonial magick, including those of Initiation, Banishing and Invoking, Forming the Circle, Identifying with God-forces, Rising on the Planes, Working in the Astral, Scrying, Magical Dance, Sigils, Enochian Magick, Consecration and Use of Magical Weapons, Sphere-Working, Evocation to Visible Appearance, Talismanic Magick, Elementals, etc.

0-87542-196-2, 540 pgs., 6 x 9, illus., softcover.   **$15.00**

THE GOLDEN DAWN
by Israel Regardie

The Original Account of the Teachings, Rites and Ceremonies of the Hermetic Order of the Golden Dawn as revealed by Israel Regardie, with further revision, expansion, and additional notes by Israel Regardie, Cris Monnastre, and others.

Originally published in four bulky volumes of some 1200 pages, this 5th Revised and Enlarged Edition has been entirely reset in modern, less space-consuming type, in half the pages (while retaining the original pagination in marginal notation for reference) for greater ease and use.

Corrections of typographical errors perpetuated in the original and subsequent editions have been made, with further revision and additional text and notes by actual practitioners of the Golden Dawn system of Magick, with an Introduction by the only student ever accepted for personal training by Regardie.

Also included are Initiation Ceremonies, important rituals for consecration and invocation, methods of meditation and magical working based on the Enochian Tablets, studies in the Tarot, and the system of Qabalistic Correspondences that unite the World's religions and magical traditions into a comprehensive and practical whole.

This volume is designed as a study and practice curriculum suited to both group and private practice. Meditation upon, and following with the Active Imagination, the Initiation Ceremonies is fully experiential without need of participation in group or lodge.

0-87542-663-8, 744 pages, 6 x 9, illus.   **$19.95**

A GARDEN OF POMEGRANATES
by Israel Regardie

What is the Tree of Life? It's the ground plan of the Qabalistic system—a set of symbols used since ancient times to study the Universe. The Tree of Life is a geometrical arrangement of ten sephiroth, or spheres, each of which is associated with a different archetypal idea, and 22 paths which connect the spheres.

This system of primal correspondences has been found the most efficient plan ever devised to classify and organize the characteristics of the self. Israel Regardie has written one of the best and most lucid introductions to the Qabalah.

A Garden of Pomegranates combines Regardie's own studies with his notes on the works of Aleister Crowley, A.E. Waite, Eliphas Levi and D.H. Lawrence. No longer is the wisdom of the Qabalah to be held *secret!* The needs of today place the burden of growth upon each and every person—each has to undertake the Path as his or her own responsibility, but every help is given in the most ancient and yet most modern teaching here known to humankind.

0-87542-690-5, 176 pages, softcover.   **$6.95**

THE MIDDLE PILLAR
by Israel Regardie

Between the two outer pillars of the Qabalistic Tree of Life, the extremes of Mercy and Severity, stands THE MIDDLE PILLAR, signifying one who has achieved equilibrium in his or her own self.

Integration of the human personality is vital to the continuance of creative life. Without it, man lives as an outsider to his own true self. By combining Magic and Psychology in the Middle Pillar Ritual/Exercise (a magical meditation technique), we bring into balance the opposing elements of the psyche while yet holding within their essence and allowing full expression of man's entire being.

In this book, and with this practice, you will learn to: understand the psyche through its correspondences on the Tree of Life; expand self-awareness, thereby intensifying the inner growth process; activate creative and intuitive potentials; understand the individual thought patterns which control every facet of personal behavior; regain the sense of balance and peace of mind—the equilibrium that everyone needs for physical and psychic health.

0-87542-658-1, 176 pages, softcover.   **$6.95**

ENOCHIAN MAGIC—A Practical Manual
by Gerald J. Schueler

The powerful system of magic introduced in the sixteenth century by Dr. John Dee, Astrologer Royal to Queen Elizabeth I, and as practiced by Aleister Crowley and the Hermetic Order of the Golden Dawn, is here presented for the first time in a complete, step-by-step form. *There has never before been a book that has made Enochian Magic this easy!*

In this book you are led carefully along the path from "A brief history of the Enochian Magical System," through "How to speak Enochian," "How to Invoke," "The Calls," "Egyptian Deities" and "Chief Hazards" to "How to visit the Aethyrs in Spirit Vision (Astral Projection)." Not a step is missed; not a necessary instruction forgotten.

0-87542-710-3, 270 pages, 5¼ x 8, illus., softcover.   **$12.95**

ENOCHIAN MAGICK: A MAGICIAN'S MANUAL
by Gerald Schueler

This is a sequel to the Practical Manual. In this book Schueler provides everything for the serious practitioner of the Enochian system—a system that is complete in itself, and yet easily related to other systems of Qabalistic or Shamanistic magick. All students of the Golden Dawn, Aurum Solis and other mainstream systems of Western practice will find this work a practical 'working manual' combining theory with exercises, complete rituals and outlines for multi-level magical operations. New students will find the Enochian system particularly modern, reflective of the new physics; others will be attracted to the feeling of working at the frontiers of the New Age.

0-87542-710-3, 271 pages, 5¼ × 8, illus., softcover.   **$12.95**